GERMAN CARS

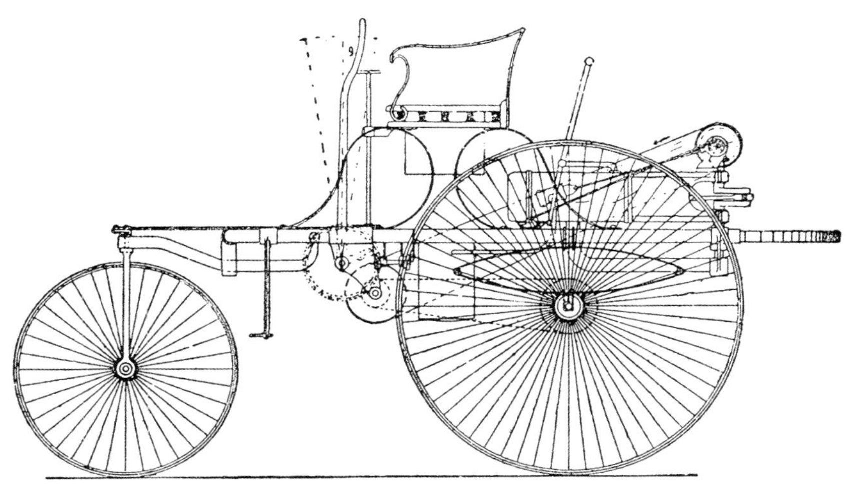

whitestar

Carrera GT

MERCEDES
BENZ

McLaren

GRAPHIC DESIGN
Maria Cucchi

CONTENTS

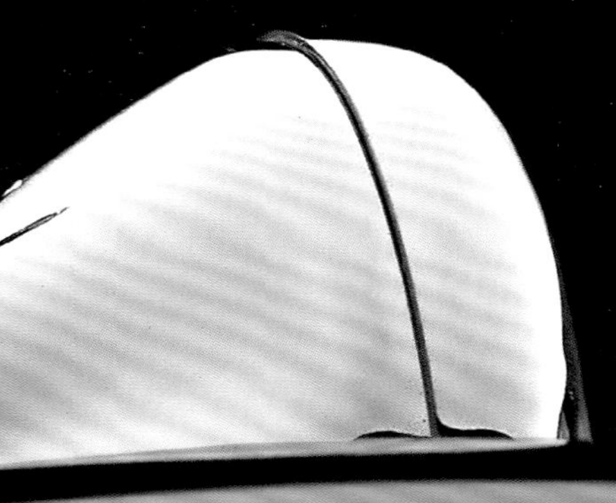

INTRODUCTION

Even though different players are currently battling it out for the title of world's best car manufacturer, top honors go to German automotive brands: they make up the majority of leading car manufacturers in terms of technical feasibility, quality, and image. Despite some of them having been acquired by large European groups (such as Opel, which is now part of Stellantis), Mercedes-Benz is still the most renowned name in the automobile sector and BMW is synonymous with sportiness around the world. Porsche is the most-profitable car manufacturer, and Volkswagen Group products have the best performance in their respective segments.

German engineers were the ones who taught cars to walk. Otto and Diesel invented the most important motor concepts; Benz and Daimler built the first cars; figures like Horch, Maybach, and Porsche (the latter is Austrian mixed) defined the first decade of automobiles. The greatest model of all times is probably the VW Beetle, which obviously comes from Germany; the most famous sports scar of all is definitely the Porsche 911, which is also a quality German product, much like the all-time best off-road vehicle, the G class from Mercedes. Immortal legends like the Mercedes 300 SL with its gull-wing doors, the BMW 507, and the VW Golf were (and are still) "made in Germany," and today German cars are a point of reference in virtually every segment. Despite the fact that competition (including from China) has become increasingly fierce, they will most likely stay that way for a long time because German companies are famous for the impressive effort they dedicate to research and development. That includes Formula 1, where Mercedes is consistently on the podium.

It is often said that German auto manufacturers lack charm, and their products transmit very few emotions. Yet the Germans have always preferred to leave these qualities to the Italians and the French, relying rather on exceptional technical solutions and the refinement of quality. Their success has confirmed their strategy, and today the German auto industry continues to shine, even if it must continue to look over its shoulder at the Chinese, Korean, and indestructible Japanese manufacturers hot on its heels.

A simple book cannot do justice to the entire history of German automobiles. What this book offers instead is a completely subjective (and sometimes judgmental) selection of cars. Because, even in Germany, not all that glitters is gold. The challenge of today is anticipating what will happen tomorrow, starting with the transition to clean energy. Indeed, the European Union has set 2035 as the goalpost for an end to combustion engines (though admittedly that date isn't set in stone), and investments in electric cars by a few groups (VW first and foremost) have been massive. However, it remains to be seen to what degree consumers will embrace battery-powered cars, a challenge that will involve all global players and one in which Germany will certainly have its say. No other nation has done so much for cars as Germany, and this fame is also a promise for the future.

1 A draft of the first automobile, the 1886 Benz Patent-Motorwagen number 1.

2-3 Race cars: Porsche Carrera GT, 2003-2006.

4-5 Audi takes off: studio Audi Quattro Le Mans, 2003.

6-7 Already legends: BMW M3, from 2007.

8-9 Revelation: Mercedes-Benz SLR McLaren Roadster, from 2007.

10-11 The great Mercedes from the 20s and 30s were fancy status symbols and even the prominent star on the radiator cap expressed their incomparable position.

13 On 3 July 1886 in Mannheim, the first public test drive with a Benz Patent-Motorwagen took number one place.

14-15 How it all began: Porsche 356, 1948.

16-17 Immortal: Mercedes 300 SL 'gull-wing', 1954-1957.

18-19 Authentic beauty: BMW 328 'Mille Miglia', 1939/40.

20-21 Awesome: VW Beetle, 1938-2003.

PORSCHE

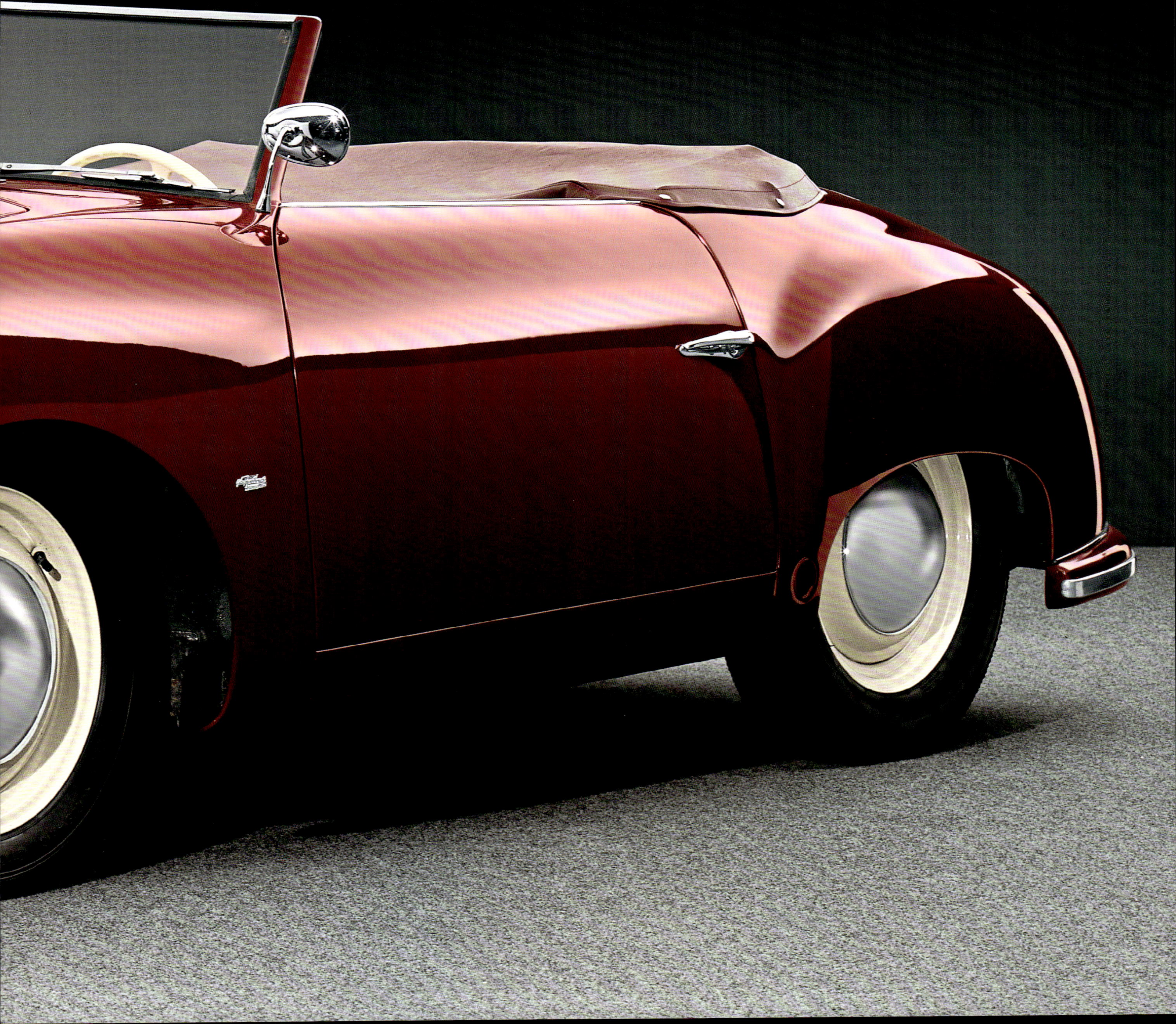

MERCEDES BENZ

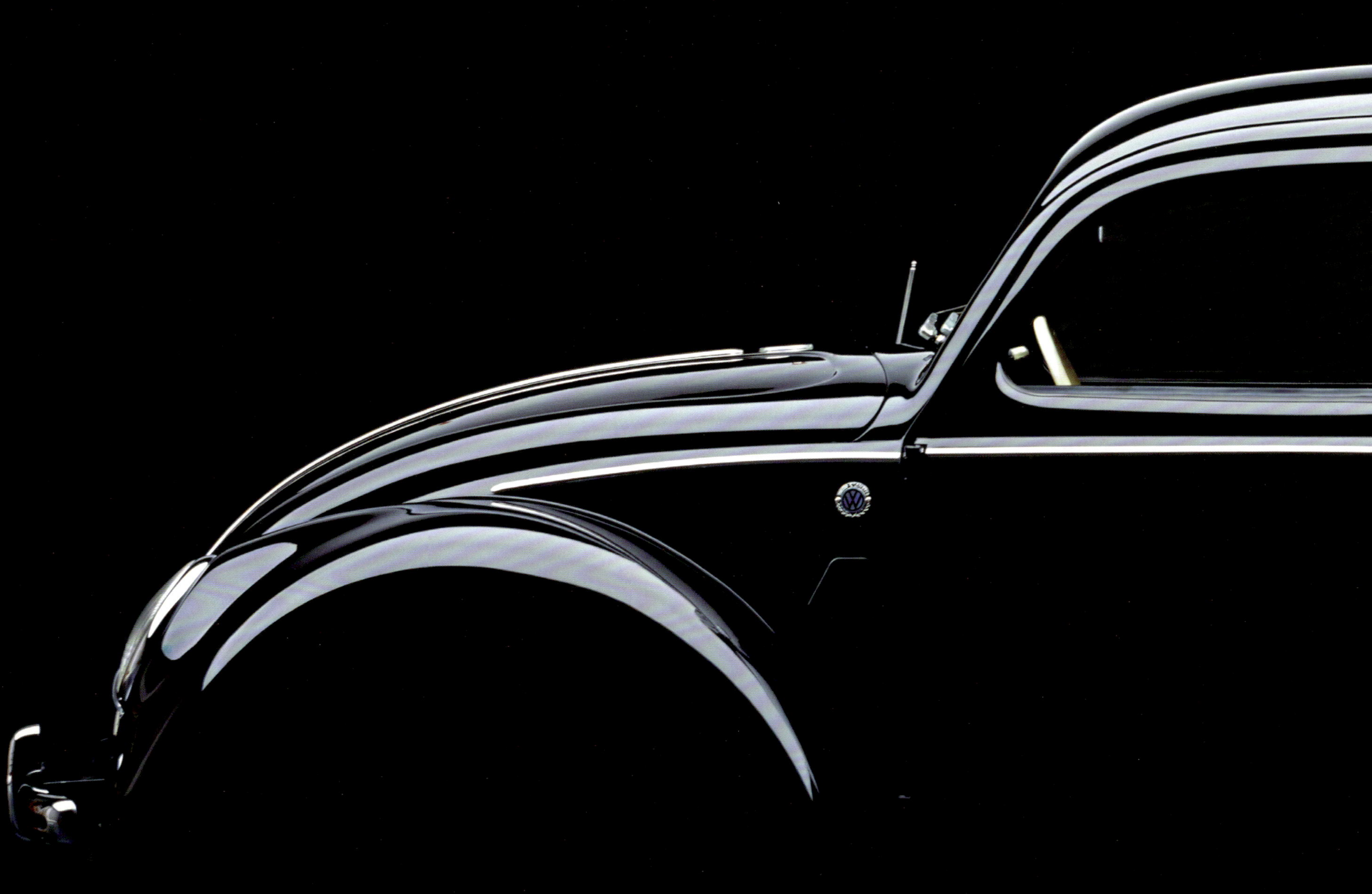

CHAPTER 1

When Cars Learn To Run

The Mercedes Simplex (40/45 CV), which was built starting in 1902, was probably the first vehicle to generate the Mercedes legend. Weighing less than 1000 kg (2204 lbs.), it was also a successful race car.

Left Carl Benz and his daughter Clara portrayed here during an outing in a 1893 Benz Victoria, a single cylinder 2.9 liter engine; basically a carriage. It was the first four-wheeled Benz, and could reach 15.5 mph (25 km/h).

They say that success has many fathers, but with respect to automobiles we can rightly speak of grandfathers and great-grandfathers. Without the preliminary efforts of persons like the Frenchman, Nicolas Joseph Cugnot (1725-1804), who with his steam engine first built a self-propelling vehicle; without the Swiss, François Isaac de Rivaz (1752-1828), who in 1807 mounted a rudimentary internal combustion engine on a cart; without the French-Belgian engineer, Etienne Lenoir (1822-1900), who in 1859 designed the first truly practicable gas engine; and without the German, Nicolaus August Otto (1832-91), the inventor of the four-stroke engine—the automobile may have never existed, or at best it might have had a totally different appearance.

The German automobile is a symbol of quality and since time immemorial has been synonymous with excellent workmanship. We take it for granted that it was Germany that witnessed the birth of the car; this is a thought that comes almost subconsciously to us. And yet for a hair's breadth things didn't turn out differently, and the Germans barely managed not to be deprived of the title of "inventors of the automobile." In any case, there is no doubt that in the autumn of 1885 Carl Benz constructed the first engine-powered vehicle, that is, what we commonly think of as the automobile.

In 1889, a certain Ludwig Czischek, in an article of the Austrian corporation of architects and engineers, attributed the invention of the automobile in 1875to Siegfried Marcus (who was born in Malchin-Mecklenburg and resided in Vienna). From 1910 to 1912 the German historian Franz Maria Feldhaus, an expert in technology, wrote various articles that helped to promulgate this error. Czischek had simple mistaken the date of two photographs, and this was discovered only around the 1960s.

But why do we take for granted that the automobile was invented in Germany? At that time, that is, in the late nineteenth century, many of the significant inventions came from the United States, England and France. In the case of the automobile there occurred a series of coincidences. Otto's prototypes and Benz's far-sighted vision, the brilliant engineers Gottlieb Daimler (whose real family name was Däumler, 1834-1900), and Wilhelm Maybach (1846-1919), such industrialists as the Opel brothers, inventors like Ackermann (stub axle steering) and Bosch (ignition). Yet at the dawn of the automobile Germany soon, and once again, lost its crucial role to France and the United States. True, before the Second World War Mercedes and Maybach, as well as Horch, boasted some of the most exclusive products in the world, but Germany succeeded in surpassing its rivals again only after the war.

Is the correct spelling Carl or Karl Benz? In the vital statistics bureau of the town of Mühlburg, where he was born on 25 November 1844, he was registered as Karl Friederich Michael. And he enrolled at the Karlsruhe polytechnic, where he studied, with the name Karl. In his first description of a patent written in 1880 he also spelled his name with a 'K'. Yet in 1882 he had himself called Carl Benz, and his company at Ladenburg was named Carl Benz Söhne KG.

Whatever the case may be, Carl or Karl Benz was one of the most important figures in the prehistory of the automobile. In 1879 he designed a two-stroke internal combustion engine without compression and later worked on a four-stroke engine. In 1885 he built his first automobile, a three-wheel vehicle propelled by a small motor with 0.8 hp mounted horizontally, and with electric ignition and mechanically operated valves. Two roller chains transmitted power to the rear axle. At first Benz was content with driving within his establishment, and ventured onto the street outside (on the Ringstrasse in Mannheim) only in June 1886.

On 29 January 1886 he had already obtained imperial patent no. 37/435 for a 'vehicle powered by a gas motor', that is, the first 'self-propelled machine'. However, this was not very rewarding for him, in that the vehicle was classified as a 'horseless carriage' and the invention was also unsuccessful from an economic standpoint.

It was only in 1888, when his wife Berta, accompanied by their sons Eugen and Richard, took an adventurous trip from Mannheim to Pforzheim and back again, that a more large-scale public began to show interested in the automobile. The vehicle did not run on gasoline but on ligroin, which was supplied by a pharmacist from Wiesloch. This car was already two horsepower and ran on wooden wheels, not wire wheels.

Around 1893, Benz succeeded in solving the steering problems, which were the reason why his first car had three wheels instead of four.

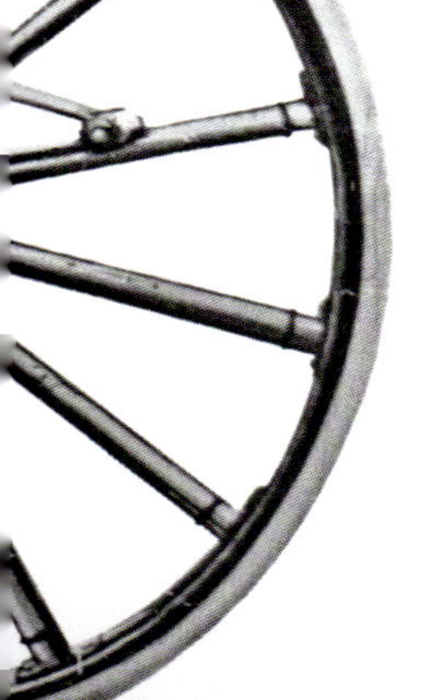

Right For the 'Velociped' by Benz, at least 381 units were built between 1894 and 1897. It could be considered the first car to be mass-produced. The 'Velo' was already equipped with axle-pivot steering.

Top left Gottlieb Wilhelm Daimler (1834-1900) was probably the liveliest of all the German auto pioneers. He developed the first gasoline engine capable of generating high speed and was the world's first four-wheeled automobile.

Bottom left Gottlieb Daimler built the world's first motorcycle, first motor boat, first four-wheel automobile, first streetcar and first truck. Here, Daimler is portrayed in front of a 5-ton truck (1898).

Right The first British auto manufacturer, 'The Daimler Motor Company', began production in 1896. The company name was due to the license that the German Daimler had granted to build engines.

HUTTON & SONS
COACHMAKERS TO
HER MAJESTY THE QUEEN &
THE PRINCE OF WALES
DUBLIN
GRADE
1 IN 4¼
Hudson

Bottom right In October 1886, Gottlieb Daimler integrated a chassis by Wilhelm Wimpff with his first single-cylinder four-stroke, known as the pendulum engine. For the first time in history, autos had four wheels.

Top center Wilhelm Maybach (1846-1929) was an important designer among the first German auto makers. He worked alongside Gottlieb Daimler for a long time (from 1870 circa), and in 1907 he founded his own company.

Top right Gottlieb Daimler portrayed here in 1895 driving his car. Daimler was a brilliant designer, but as a businessman he was never successful, and he never witnessed the Daimler company's success.

Bottom right Wilhelm Maybach built this Mercedes 35 hp in 1901 for the Daimler Motoren Gesellschaft. The name Mercedes came from the daughter of Daimler's most important dealer, Emil Jelinek.

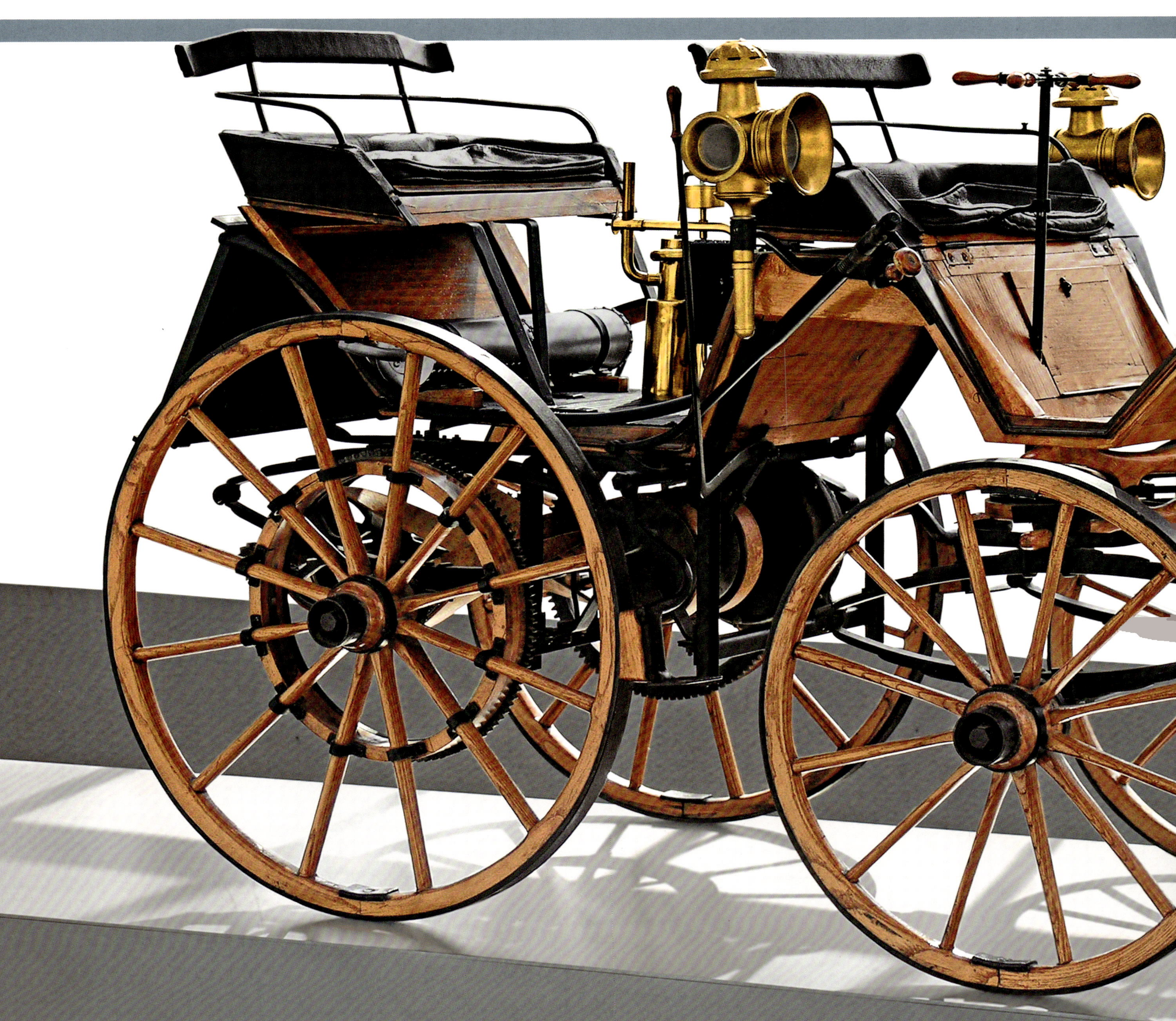

In the meantime, only a few kilometers away the automobile took its first steps. Obviously, at this time Karl Benz and a certain Gottlieb Daimler were not yet aware that the two most important names in the prehistory of the German automobile would eventually merge to create a single company.

Gottlieb Daimler, the son of the baker Johannes Däumler, studied gunsmithing as a youth. This was an interesting choice, since gunsmiths worked in such a painstaking and precise manner that they were also able to build spare parts, which is exactly what the automobile industry of the time—with few exceptions—could not manage to do, even twenty years after the first attempts to construct these vehicles. After a rather restless career that took him to England for two years, in 1872 Daimler went to work in the Deutz gas engine factory owned by Otto and Langen, along with his dear friend Wilhelm Maybach. Daimler felt that the internal combustion engine could be improved to quite a degree, and this is the reason why he was fired.

In 1885, he founded an experimental plant at Cannstadt together with Maybach. In 1883 the two engineers built a four-stroke single-cylinder engine that ran on gasoline. On 3 April 1885 Daimler was granted imperial patent no. 43/926 for his construction, which became famous as the Standuhr-Motor or grandfather clock. That same year Daimler and Maybach built the Reitwagen or 'riding car', which was the world's first motorcycle. The following year saw the construction of the first motorboat in the world. And in October 1886 the single-cylinder engine was mounted on a stagecoach built by Wilhelm Wimpff, the first four-wheel automobile in history. But this is not all. The engine was then mounted on a prototype streetcar in 1887, and at the same time on the world's first truck and, in 1888, on a hot-air balloon. But Daimler and Maybach were still not satisfied, so in 1892 they built a straight two-cylinder engine.

However, the two were earning no money with their enterprise and so they had to have other partners in the firm. After many a dispute with the latter, in 1893 Daimler resigned, only to return a year later as the president of the board of statutory auditors. In this capacity he had a racing vehicle built in 1899 that was named Mercedes, thus closing another circle.

One concept should be clarified at this stage. Around 1900 Benz & Co Rheinische Gasmotorenfabrik Mannheim was the world's largest automobile plant. In 1926 the company merged with Daimler Motorengesellschaft, becoming Daimler-Benz AG.

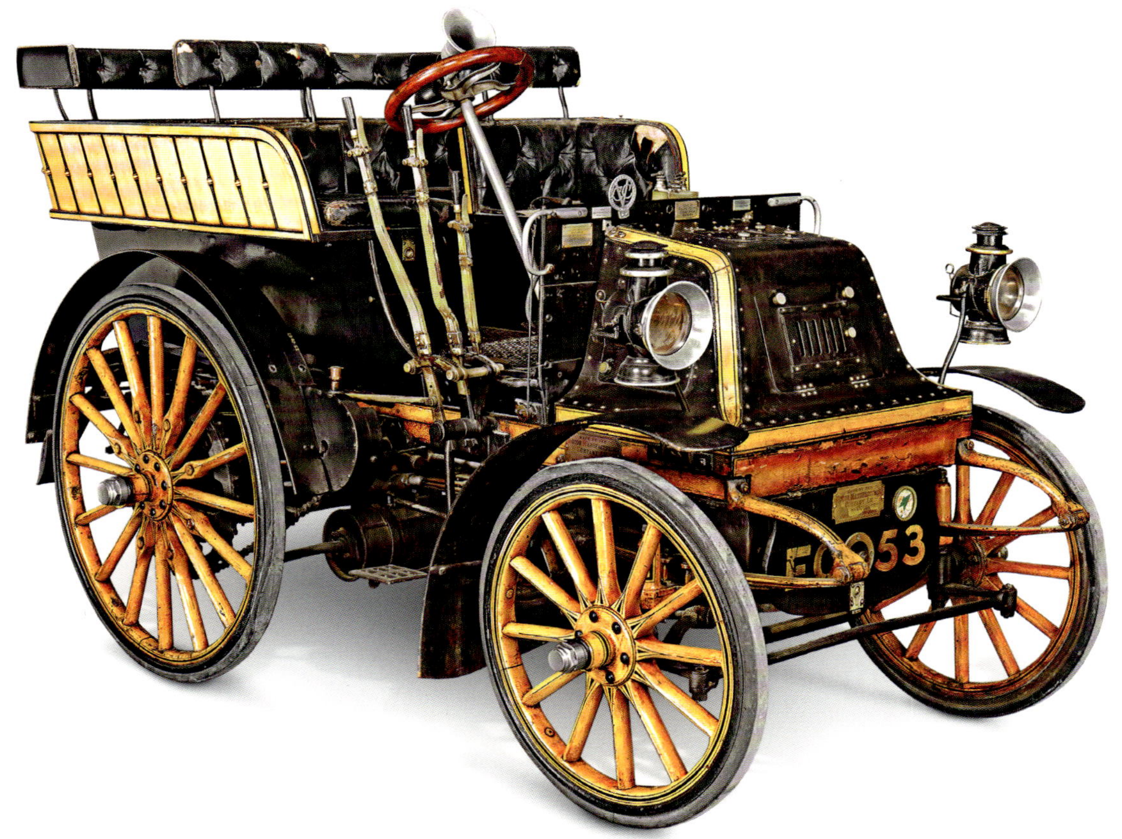

Top left In this picture we see an example of a British Daimler (1899). The twin-cylinder, water-cooled, 1.65 liter produced 6 hp at 700 rpm, and was built under license from the German Daimler Motoren Gesellschaft.

Bottom left Even though as early as the nineteenth century, cars moved progressively further from the carriage, (like this 1895 Daimler), they were still far from being elegant. Chassis builders came into play much later.

Right This air-cooled twin cylinder was built in 1895 by Wilhelm Maybach. Propulsion already worked with a 4-gear shift (plus rear), and its maximum speed was 12 km/h (7 mph).

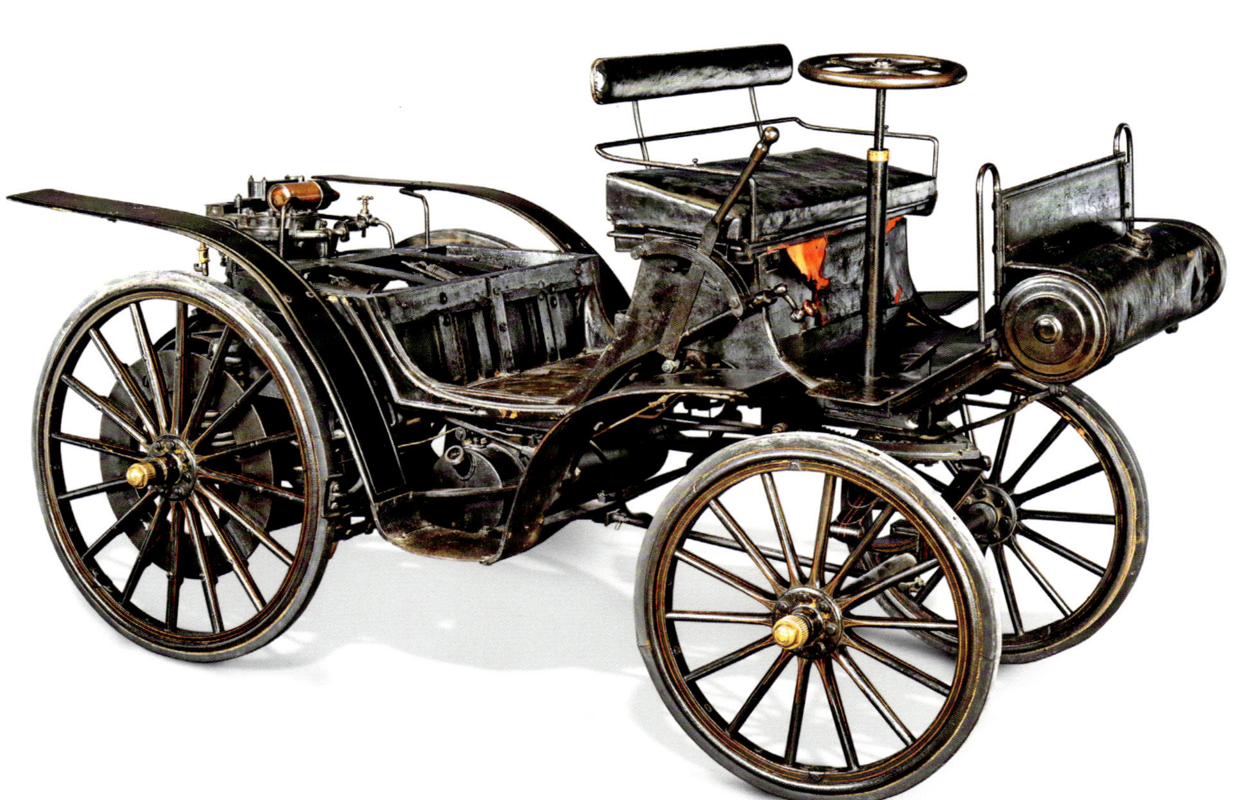

GESELLSCHAFT
Cannstatt
PATENT
464

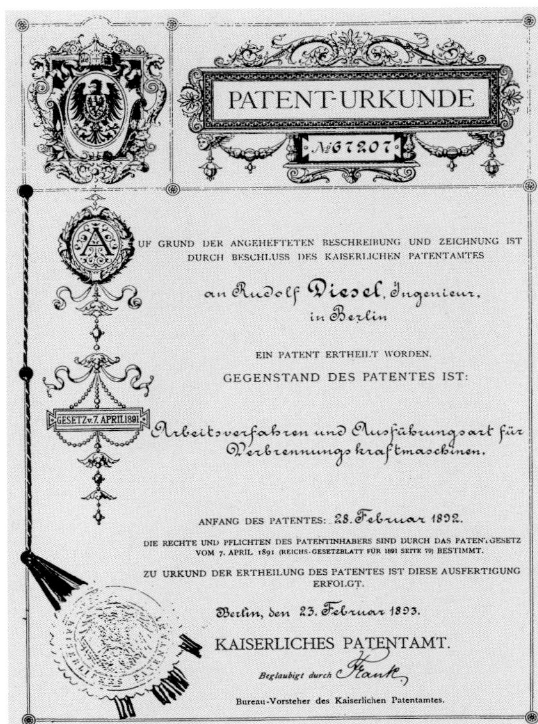

PATENT-URKUNDE

№ 67207

AUF GRUND DER ANGEHEFTETEN BESCHREIBUNG UND ZEICHNUNG IST DURCH BESCHLUSS DES KAISERLICHEN PATENTAMTES

an Rudolf Diesel, Ingenieur, in Berlin

EIN PATENT ERTHEILT WORDEN.

GEGENSTAND DES PATENTES IST:

GESETZ v. 7. APRIL 1891

Arbeitsverfahren und Ausführungsart für Verbrennungskraftmaschinen.

ANFANG DES PATENTES: 28. Februar 1892.

DIE RECHTE UND PFLICHTEN DES PATENTINHABERS SIND DURCH DAS PATENTGESETZ VOM 7. APRIL 1891 (REICHS-GESETZBLATT FÜR 1891 SEITE 79) BESTIMMT.

ZU URKUND DER ERTHEILUNG DES PATENTES IST DIESE AUSFERTIGUNG ERFOLGT.

Berlin, den 23. Februar 1893.

KAISERLICHES PATENTAMT.

Beglaubigt durch Frank

Bureau-Vorsteher des Kaiserlichen Patentamtes.

Left This patent was given to Rudolf Diesel on 23 February 1893. In it, the inventor describes a 'new and rational thermic engine' that today is known as the diesel engine.

Right Rudolf Diesel (1858-1913, center, standing, in a white hat), was one of the great German engineers in the early days of automobile history. His technical talent was much more developed that his business sense.

Rudolf Diesel, born in Paris in 1858 is yet another very illustrious German engineer who earned success at the very beginnings of the automobile. But Diesel only gained true recognition in recent years, since Diesel engines have embarked on a magnificent triumphal march in the automobile world and seem to be at the point of overtaking the traditional petrol engine.

The fact that Diesel engine won such respect after such a long time of its inventor's death is in some way symptomatic of Rudolf Diesel's life. He was very clever and he graduated from the Technischen Hochschule (polytechnic) in Munich with the highest marks ever given since the foundation of the institute. In 1892 he filed 'working method and design for combustion engines'" at the patent office in Berlin. From 1893 he continued to develop his engine for the MAN AG Engineering Equipment factory in Augsburg, but four long years went by before the engine finally came to light. Perhaps without the help of the MAN engineers, Diesel would never have reached his objective and little remains of his original patent. The processes to violate a patent ruined Rudolf Diesel's health and he also suffered financial ruin; the brilliant engineer completely lacked business sense. Diesel died in 1913 on the crossing from Antwerp to London. The circumstances of his death are the subject of heated discussions and there was (and still is) speculation as to whether it was murder or suicide.

In the Diesel engine, unlike the Otto cycle engine, it is not an inflammable mixture of air and petrol that gets sucked into the cylinder, but just air. Air is compressed in the cylinder which causes it to heat up to about 700–900 degrees. Just before top-dead center of the piston, fuel is injected and distributed in this incandescent air. The high temperature is enough to evaporate the fuel and to ignite the resulting mixture of fuel vapor and air. It is for this reason that the Diesel Engine is sometimes referred to as a spontaneous ignition engine. A diesel engine is more efficient than an Otto cycle engine which makes it consume less fuel.

In 1903 the first Diesel engines were used on ships, from 1912 onwards they were also used on locomotives. In 1933 Citroën was the first car manufacturer to experiment with a Diesel engine (however using a version created by the English pioneer Sir Harry Ricardo) but the vehicle was never mass produced for legal reasons. In 1936 Mercedes produced the first standard production vehicle with a Diesel engine with the 260 D.

Until about the mid 90s, Diesel engines were undoubtedly regarded as economical and reliable but four stroke engines were considerably superior in terms of performance and noise levels. Only the increased diffusion of turbos and the use of common rail injection (used for the first time in 1988 on the Fiat Croma TD I.d.) changed this state of affairs. In 2004 in Western Europe for the first time more than 50% of cars sold were diesel, a trend in constant growth. Some of the most advanced Diesel engines today are produced by the Volkswagen Group and BMW whereas the pioneer Mercedes still has room for improvement.

Kollekt
Eingang.

Top left. The design of the Lohner-Porsche (1900), with its twin electrical engines mounted on the wheels, was quite interesting. One year later the 'Semper Vivus' was born, which also had a gasoline engine.

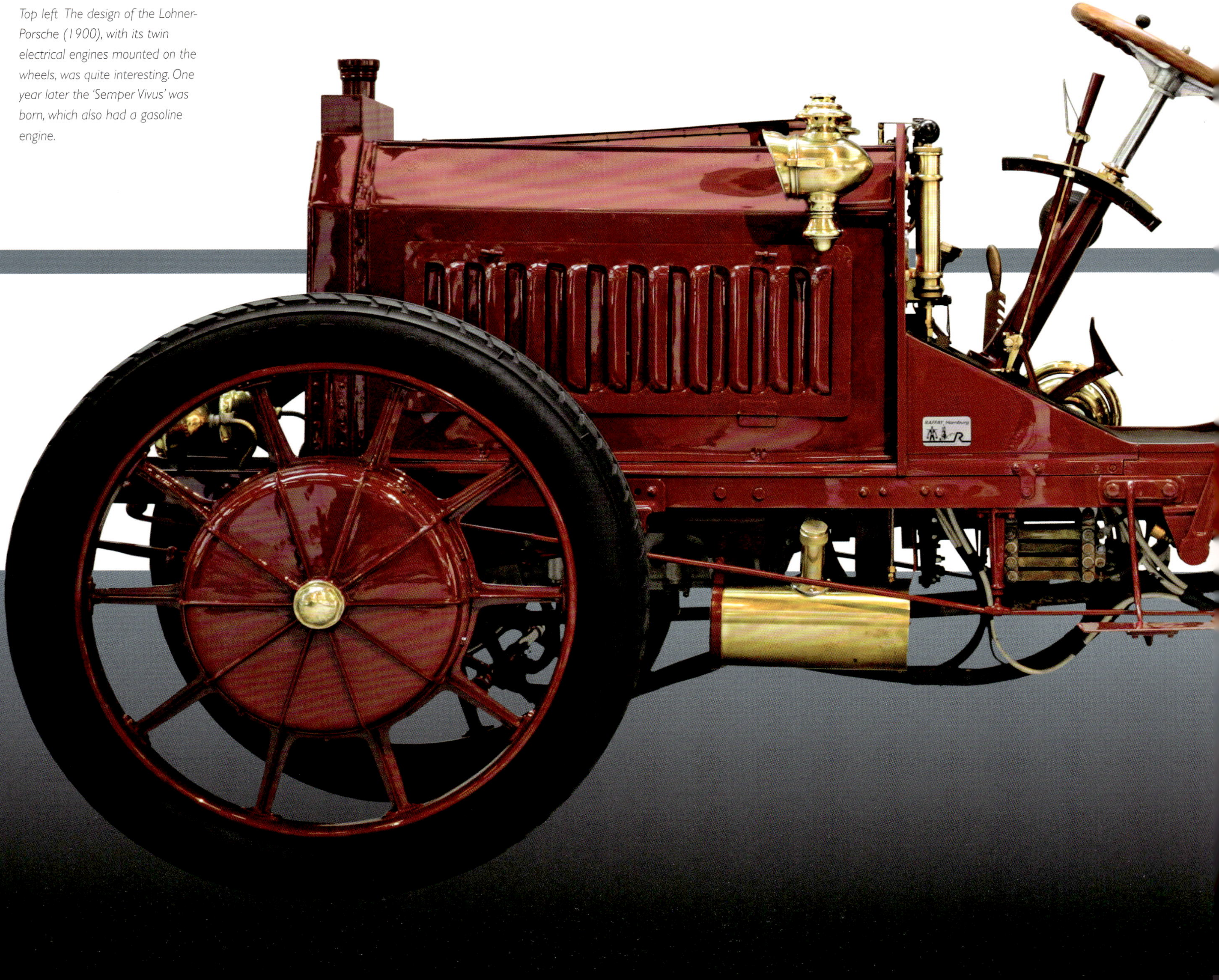

Naturally, there were other famous persons whose names are household words today, even amongst children. Ferdinand Porsche, who was born in 1875, began his career at an early age at the Elektro-Unternehmen Egger Company in Vienna. Egger supplied electric motors to the coachbuilder Lohner, who firmly believed in the future of the automobile and made large investments in this field. Porsche, who had been trained as a gunsmith at his father's workshop, grew from the post of simple laborer to director in only four years, while auditing courses at the Vienna polytechnic. He was a tireless worker, and in only two years he was able to submit his design for an electric transmission to Lohner. The advantage of this device was obvious. The new motor could be mounted directly onto the wheels (and not on the hubs, as was erroneously reported). However, this first Lohner-Porsche model also had drawbacks. It weighed too much, and it had very limited autonomy since it could not go for more than 50-60 kilometers (31-37 mi.).

The first Lohner-Porsche model was driven in 1900. A year later the Semper Vivus model came out, equipped with an alternative additional internal-combustion engine. This was a 'hybrid', as the motor worked as a generator to drive the electric hub motors on the car. It won the first prize in its category at the Exelberg races.

However, the Lohner-Porsche was not the first hybrid model. This honor belonged to the Spaniard Emilio de la Cuadra, who had by 1898, in his small Barcelona garage, used an additional alternative De-Dion internal combustion engine to drive an electric motor. It seems that de la Cuadra was not pleased with the result, since he later concentrated on gasoline-powered motors, together with another famous figure in the automobile industry, Mark Birkigt, who achieved fame with his Hispano-Suiza company. But Germany had once again won a victory recently, creating the first 'hybrid' automobile in the modern age. In 1997 Audi presented its A4 Duo model to the market, long before the Toyota Prius.

Bottom center Ferdinand Porsche, who was only twenty-five years old then, also built a light two-seater for Lohner, with engines on the front wheel hubs, which in 1900 was actually used in races.

Top right These weren't the engines that Ferdinand Porsche mounted on the wheel hubs of the Lohner. Besides Porsche was not the one who created the first hybrid traction, but the Spaniard De la Quadra in 1897.

Center right This Lohner-Porsche with four engines mounted on the wheel hubs was commissioned in 1900 by the British E.W. Hart, and the then twenty-five year old Ferdinand Porsche (next to the driver) personally delivered the car to its owner.

This is not the end of our list of famous Germans, all of whom are obviously in the Automotive Hall of Fame, thanks to their significant contribution to the automobile industry. The Opel Company was founded in 1862 by Adam Opel at Rüsselsheim in Hessen. At first his firm built sewing machines, and then in 1886 began producing bicycles as well. In 1898, three years after the death of its founder (who had always refused to produce automobiles), Opel's sons began to make cars. They bought the vehicle-manufacturing company of Friedrich Lutzmann, master blacksmith at the Dessau court, and named him director, thus creating the Opel Patent-Motorwagen System Lutzmann firm, whose products Lutzmann had already exhibited at the first Auto-Revue show in 1897.

Top left and right The history of the Opel company was typical for the first years of the auto industry: they first produced bicycles (and sewing machines) and slowly moved on to produce cars.

Bottom left The invention of the assembly line (the first step was taken by Ransom Eli Olds, but was perfected by Henry Ford) came only a few years later. With Opel, before the turn of the century, everything was hand-assembled.

Center right The first cars were single units, there were no spare parts. If the engine or the gearbox were damaged, they needed to be replaced completely. In the beginning only men worked in production.

Bottom right An ad from the day reads: "Adam Opel, the mechanic from Männheim, recommends his own wheel machines, in all varieties, of the latest design, at low stable prices."

Adam Opel, Mechaniker
22) **in Rüsselsheim**
empfiehlt selbstgefertigte Nähemaschienen aller Art, nach der neuesten Construction, zu festen und billigen Preißen.

Top left In 1862, in Rüsselsheim, Adam Opel founded a sewing machine factory. His five sons Carl, Wilhelm, Heinrich, Fritz and Ludwig, took over in 1895. In 1898 they started producing cars.

The first patented Opel System Lutzmann vehicle was ready in the spring of 1899. It was driven by a posterior mono-cylindrical engine with a displacement of 1.545 cc (cylinder bore per stroke: 122 x 132 mm, 4 in. x 5 in.) and had a maximum of 3.5 hp at 650 rpm. The body of the piston rod and the crankshaft were unidirectional and lubricated with a simple oilcan. The crankshaft box was made of bronze and the cylinder of cast iron. The fuel feed valve was not motorized, but was strained simply by a spring (the so-called safety valve), while the exhaust valve was provided with an eccentric and a rocker arm (500 mm long, 20 in.!). An electric rocker arm, which was also activated by an eccentric, sparked the aspirated mixture of air and gasoline. Naturally, this elementary carburetor made it difficult to adjust the blend to the gear conditions with any degree of precision, so that the single-cylinder engine could function without any problems, only in a limited range of revolutions. The number of revolutions had to be regulated by leaving the fuel-feed valve more or less open. The gasoline tank was under the driver's seat. In the back, at both left and right, were the two water-cooling tanks. The two axles were rigid and had leaf springs. The semi-elliptical spring clips were positioned on a carriage chassis made of forged steel and elaborately decorated. The structure was made of ash wood. The steering was governed by a chain, and the pedal brake functioned by means of two outer belts linked to two drums on the rear wheels. There was a hand brake also. There were other technical features as well. For example, the Opel was fitted out with a two-gear epicyclical transmission inserted between the belt transmission, and the rear wheel transmission. Each of the rear wheels were propelled by their own chains. This small vehicle weighed 427 kg (941 lbs.), was 215 cm (85 in.) long and 144 cm (57 in.) wide. The wheelbase measured just 135 cm (53 in.). This automobile was not very safe and the design was rather old-fashioned compared to the other leading automobiles such as Daimler, Renault, Panhard et Levassor, De Dion, Peugeot and Darracq. In 1901 the company again manufactured only 65 Lutzmanns. The designer was fired and was assigned the task of bottling mineral water. Opel began to look about for ideas, and in 1902 made a fresh start by producing a Darracq model under license.

OPEL Motorwagen

ADAM OPEL
Rüsselsheim b. Frankfurt a. M.

Dem Zuge der Zeit folgend habe ich die Fabrikation von Motorwagen aufgenommen.

Um meinen geschätzten Abnehmern keine Versuchsobjekte zu liefern, sondern auch in diesem Zweige den guten Ruf, der sich an alle **„Opel"**-Fabrikate knüpft, zu befestigen, habe ich die ganze

Patent-Motorwagen-Fabrik
F. Lutzmann, Dessau

eine der **ersten und ältesten** Deutschlands, deren Fabrikate sich durch ihre Leistungsfähigkeit und Solidität in allen Weltteilen des besten Rufes erfreuen, käuflich erworben und incl. aller Arbeiter nach Rüsselsheim verpflanzt.

Ich bin dadurch in den Stand gesetzt, Motorwagen in jeder gewünschten Stärke und Ausführung in kürzester Frist zu liefern.

Unter persönlicher Leitung eines Fachmannes, wie dies Herr Direktor Lutzmann ist, und gestützt auf einen Stamm alter, in der Motorbranche durch und durch geschulter Arbeiter und die reichen Erfahrungen, die ich durch 35jährige Thätigkeit in der Maschinenbranche erworben habe, hoffe ich meinen Abnehmern ein Fabrikat bieten zu können, von dem es, wie bei meinen Nähmaschinen und Fahrrädern heissen soll:

„Opel-Motorwagen sind die besten".

*Die **Motorwagen-Fabrikation** ist von meinen übrigen Fabrikationszweigen **vollständig getrennt** und wolle man **Correspondenzen lediglich an die Motorwagen-Fabrik ADAM OPEL** adressieren.*

Bottom left and right The first Opel was built in 1899 by Friederich Lutzmann (1859-1930) and it was called the 'Patent Lutzmann'. However, this car was never successful and after two years Lutzmann was fired.

Top left In 1902 Opel took a risky step. They started producing Darracq under license, and thereafter started producing its own cars, the 10/12 hp. In just a few years, Opel was among the leading auto makers in Europe.

Bottom left Cars were toys that only rich people could afford. Soon after the turn of the century, during those rare family trips, there were still fewer cars than carriages and horses.

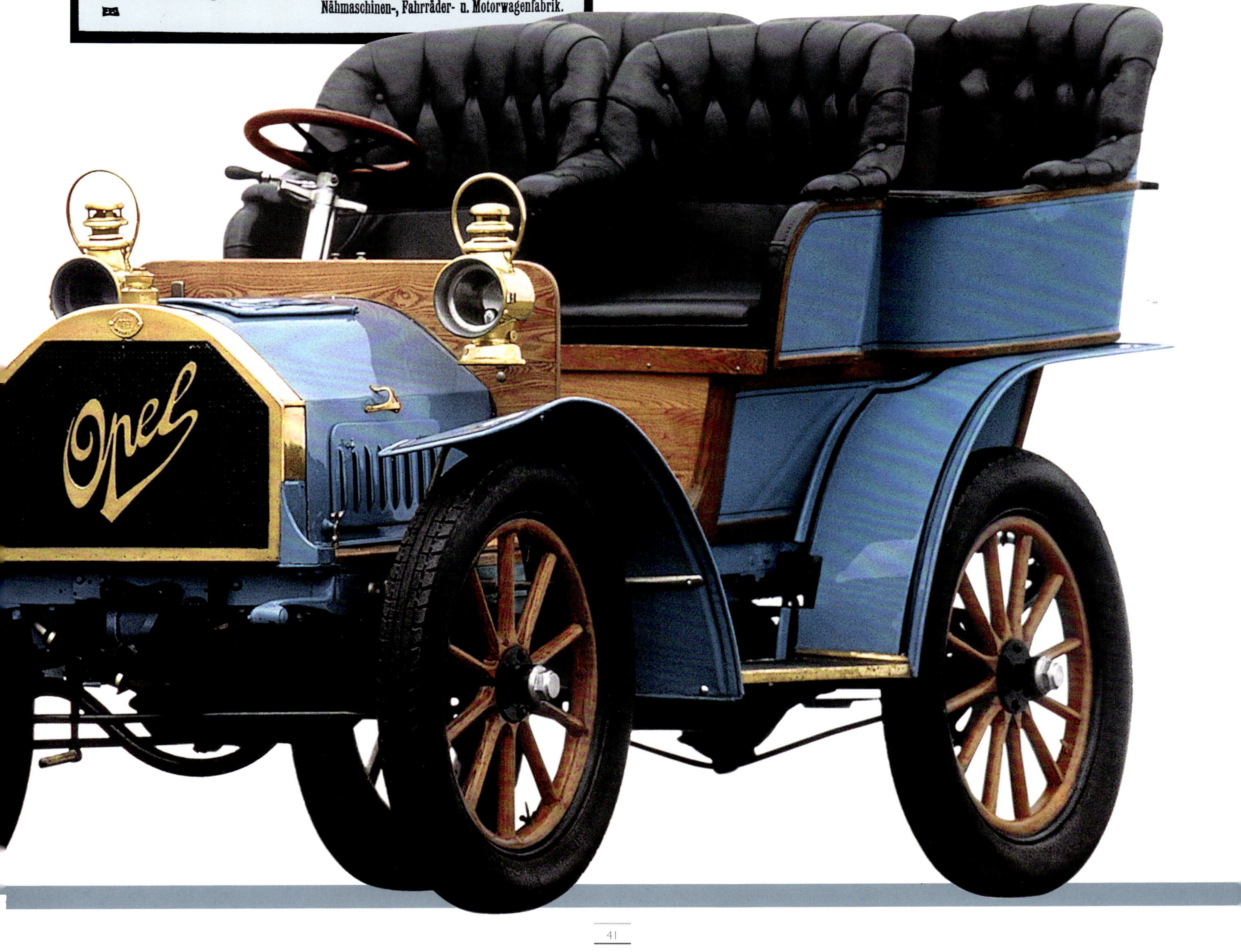

Bottom right The collaboration with Darracq ended in 1907, but the reliable cars granted Opel its first achievements in the auto market. In the meantime it still produced bicycles and sewing machines.

Top center Being one of the first auto makers, Opel understood that taking part in sports events would bring great publicity to the company. It had already worked with bicycles.

Top left The first auto race took place on 22 July 1894 on the Paris-Rouen. Soon after the turn of the century, races started taking place on actual race tracks, and Opel was often a winner in those days.

Bottom left These were the bold men who, in the early years of car races, would face the tracks in their flying jalopies. Truly daring, considering the fact that reliability was a far-fetched concept in those days.

Top right Naturally, Opel's race cars were by all means round. The impression that they are 'oval' is due to the long exposure of the cameras of those days.

Center right Racing events didn't always go the right way, but in this case, it looks like the only accident happened to Opel. Carl Jörns was the most famous driver of the day, and he was also a fast bicycle and motorcycle driver.

Bottom right Just what the driver (and a driver he is indeed: just look at his cap and goggles) is doing here is hard to figure out. Maybe his Opel lost its engine?

Very soon the Opel company became competitive, quite simply because they also constructed bicycles, and at that time races were the best occasion to publicize one's products. The most famous and fortunate Opel racing car pilot in this initial phase was Karl Jörns, who in 1907 won the Kaiserfahrt race. Actually, the real winner was Nazzaro, who was behind the wheel of a Fiat, but Jörns was awarded the cup as the best German driver of a German vehicle by the emperor Wilhelm II, which was a great honor indeed. In fact, motor races were already very 'patriotic'. Jörns was one of the most successful pilots of the time. In all, he won 288 trophies, the last one in 1924 when he was forty nine years old.

Despite the fact that they had begun experimenting with automobiles at an early stage, the Germans were not the leaders in this period. The first car race in the world was organized in 1894 in France and was run from Paris to Rouen. The winner was Count Albert de Dion, who drove a steam-engine vehicle, covering the 127 km (79 mi.) course in less than seven hours. During this first event there was also the first scandal in the history of car racing. The winner was not awarded the trophy because his car did not comply with the race regulations.

Daimler had already built the first racing car, which they named Mercedes, in 1899. This name was the christian name of the daughter of the Daimler company importer in southern France, Emil Jellinek, and it turned out to be quite useful because it helped Daimler to avoid the various disputes regarding name rights (which by the way have not yet been totally resolved). The first racing car under the name of Mercedes was the Simplex, which was built from 1902 onwards. It was much lower than the average cars of the time, weighed only 950 kg (2094 lbs.) and had an output of 45 hp, which was amazing power for the time, powered by four 6.8-liter cylinders. The Belgian Camille Jenatzy, known as the Red Devil, won the Gordon Bennet Cup on a Simplex in 1903. This victory led to the first Grand Prix being held in Germany the following year, and the Germans' love for car races was thus born.

Not all the attempts at manufacturing automobiles were successful in Germany. In 1858 a certain Bernard Stoewer opened a precision machinery repair shop in Stettin. In 1893 he began to produce bicycles, and in 1903 typewriters as well. His sons made their appearance in the world of automotive manufacturing in 1899. The Grosse Stoewer Motorwagen (the large Stoewer engine car) was one of the most advanced vehicles of its time. It was powered by a 2.1-liter single cylinder engine and the transmission worked by means of chains thanks to a three-gear box with differential. The P6 model caused a sensation in 1906 with its six-cylinder engine in which the cylinders, welded in pairs with the side valves, were placed in a 'T' shape. Stoewer was then compared to the best car manufacturers of the time, and upto the mid-1920s the company was at par with Maybach and Horch. The leading model from 1919 on was the D7, which featured an 11.2-liter aero engine, an absolutely superb automobile.

Stoewer passed through the great 1929 economic crisis without any impact, and in this period most of its cars were exported to South America and Australia. Indeed, the percentage of exported autos was much greater than that of those sold in Germany. The company's solid financial basis allowed it to produce automobiles for the mass market as well. In 1930 production began on the V5 model with front-wheel drive and a 1.2-liter engine; 2,100 of these were constructed up to 1932, quite a number indeed! Even more successful was the R149 with a 1.4-liter engine; 2,310 of these were built and sold in a short time. Then the larger models were revived, among which was the much admired Greif (griffin) featuring a V8 2.5-liter, 57 hp engine, as well as front-wheel drive. During the Second World War, Stoewer went back to producing rear wheel drive autos – the Sedina and Arkona models.

In 1935 Stoewer began to produce military vehicles with central steering. From 1935 to 1945, 11,000 LEPKW (Leichter Einheits-PKW, light command field cars) were manufactured for military purposes. The same model was also built by BMW and Hanomag. When the war ended, the city of Stettin became part of Poland, which meant the end of automobile production. The Stoewer plants were dismantled and taken to the Soviet Union.

Left This must have been a rich family, pictured here on a field trip in 1900 with not one, but two cars. In front, a Benz race car from 1900 - there wasn't much of a difference between the latter and a street car.

Right The Benz Parsifal (12/18 hp) was conceived to compete with the Mercedes Simplex and was launched in 1902. Even Prince Henry of Prussia was a Benz customer (Daimler-Benz was founded only in 1926).

CHAPTER 2

Quality as a Sign of Distinction

The first International Motor Show (IAA, Internationale Automobil Ausstellung) took place in 1897 at the Hotel Bristol in Berlin. Berlin was the setting for the IAA until 1951, after which the most important car show moved to Frankfurt.

The history of the automobile begins in Germany, but the German constructors soon found they had lost their place as leaders in this field. For the most part it was their fault. In 1889 Daimler had sold the license to produce their engines to the French industrialist Emile Levassor, who was a very shrewd businessman. He in turn sold the engine to Peugeot and together these two manufacturers had sales proceeds that Daimler could only dream of earning. Probably the German designers and inventors were more inclined to improve their products rather than sell them. In 1908, when Henry Ford began manufacturing his Model T on a large scale, the annual production in Germany was just 9,444 vehicles.

The First World War (1914-18) nearly annihilated the European automobile production, but in Germany it had the opposite effect and brought success to the auto industry. In 1921 almost 60,000 cars were circulating in Germany, and in 1923 this figure had already jumped to over 100,000, despite the fact that the nation was crippled by terrible inflation (a liter of gasoline could cost as much as DM 686). In 1908 Cadillac won the Dewar Trophy in England. Three automobiles were completely dismantled, the individual parts were mixed and then the three autos were reassembled. This was a sensational event at the time, because until then every automobile was unique. For example, if a piston broke, the engine had to be thrown away. In fact, there were no spare parts as we know them today. Cadillac was the first auto manufacturer that grasped this problem and then solved it. Leland, the Cadillac founder, had borrowed the principle that spare parts were necessary from the firearms industry, which for decades had based its production on the concept of replaceable parts.

The precision work carried out by Cadillac significantly influenced the automobile industry, especially in Germany, where the manufacturers began to concentrate on quality. During this early phase of the history of automobiles, Mercedes and Maybach (which since 1909 had been independent with its own trademark), Horch, Stoewer, and other German automakers had the reputation of being particularly reliable. There was strong rivalry to gain supremacy in the highest price sector, and the German manufacturers managed to compete with such companies as Rolls-Royce (active since 1906), Isotta-Fraschini (1903), Hispano-Suiza (1904) and Cadillac (1902). And with time the 'Quality made in Germany' concept became virtually synonymous with total commitment and great reliability in auto-making.

Only in 1919 was the first Maybach car was put on the market. But the company soon became one of the most exclusive builders of upper tier sedans, as seen in these ads from those days.

Der neue
Maybach
mit Schnellgang

Top right Although as early as 1883 photographs could be printed in newspapers, drawings stayed fashionable for a long time. Here is an example by Herbert Schlenzig for Adler, dating back to 1905.

Center right Even the German auto sector witnessed the flourishing of certain tendencies (patriotic or nationalistic). Pictured here, for example, is the Adler Standard emblem used during the mid-thirties.

In 1902 the German author Otto Julius Bierbaum (1865-1910) took a trip in an automobile from Germany to Vienna via Prague. He then went to Italy and from there, returned to Germany crossing through Switzerland. Bierbaum, who is known for his novel *Stilpe* (1897), described his adventure in a very interesting piece written in 1903, *A Sentimental Automobile Journey*.

Behind the wheel of his Adler, Bierbaum was the first person to cross St. Gothard Pass in Switzerland in a car. At that time the famous tunnel was still an idea. Adler had already begun to build automobiles in 1899, first a *voiturette* of French inspiration powered by a De-Dion engine.

Bierbaum's car was larger, but still had a De-Dion engine. It was only in 1903, when the young engineer Eduard Rumpler (who will be discussed further on) began working for the Adler factory, that the company began to produce its own engines, with very good results. In 1914, before the First World War broke out, almost 20% of all the automobiles manufactured in France bore the Adler of Frankfurt trademark.

One of the most famous models of the period between the two wars was the Standard 6 (first built in 1926 and greatly influenced by Chrysler), around 20,000 of which were manufactured up to 1934. This then served as the model for the eight-cylinder Standard 8 and the four-cylinder Favorit. There was also the famous Trumpf model, which had independent suspension on all the wheels, and a front-wheel drive. The period from 1934 to 1939 witnessed the production of the small Trumpf Junior, 10,000 of which were sold.

In 1930 Walter Gropius, the founder of the Bauhaus, designed some bodies for the Adler company, but they were not well received by the public. This was not the only case of a famous architect's lack of success in the automotive industry. Le Corbusier's ideas for the French Voisin were not put into practice. After the Second World War all the automobile plants were requisitioned by the occupying armies, which led to the end of a major automobile manufacturer.

Top left Ads and posters of the early days were something rather innovative and artistic compared to today. Here, a drawing for Adler, 1914.

Bottom center The Standard, which is esthetically reminiscent of the American Chrysler models of the 20s, was one of the most successful high-end models in Germany in between the two world wars.

Top center The picture shows a work of art by Herbert Schlenzig for Adler, in 1910. In this period, cars made huge technical progresses, differently from carriages, which slowly disappeared.

Top left The Protos by Koeppen, during the 1908 New York-Paris, was days ahead when it entered Berlin (in Kochstrasse in this illustration). At this point the lieutenant had the feeling that he would be the victor in Paris.

Bottom left The starting line of the New York-Paris, which is 19,000 kilometers (11,806 mi.) long, was on Broadway, and people flocked to come and watch, as this type of car race, was truly something new.

Long journeys such as the one made by Bierbaum in his Adler, which were described in detail by the newspapers of the time, which was not only great publicity, but also brought another German automaker to the limelight. That company no longer exists but was world-famous up to the early twentieth century.

On 12 February 1908 it was snowing in New York, and the weather got worse the following days, with snowstorms and whirlwinds. The six automobiles that had left New York on 12 February for Paris via the Bering Strait, for what was called the greatest race in the world, had difficulty in moving. Of the seventeen cars that had been scheduled to race, more than half did not even make it for the start of the competition. At that time, roads were few and far between, and there was a great deal of mud as well.

Two thousand kilometers (124 mi.) from San Francisco the prototype of Hans Koeppen caused a great hubbub. Its cardan shaft was broken. Koeppen continued his trip by train and ship. He managed to have the automobile repaired only in Vladivostok, Siberia, and from there proceeded at full speed, succeeding in arriving a few days before two other competitors; an American, Thomas, and an Italian, Züst. When he arrived in Paris on 26 July 1908, the Thomas was still in Berlin and the Züst somewhere in the Siberian steppe. Yet Koeppen was not awarded the victor's cup, which was given to Georg Schuster Sr., who had driven a Thomas. This was justifiable, since Koeppen had not made the entire trip in his automobile.

In any case, it is worthwhile reading Koeppen's 1902 book, *Around the World in an Automobile*. Koeppen embarked on this adventurous journey on a Protos 17/35PS, 35 hp model. The name itself tells us this was a four-cylinder car with 4.6-liter displacement. The constructor from Berlin, Josef Neuss, had adapted a special body to Koeppen's vehicle, which can be seen today in the Deutsches Museum, Munich. This model which had a gas tank with an 800-liter capacity, and weighed about 2.7 tons, could go more than 100 kilometers per hour (62 mph). The Protos Co. built automobiles from 1905 to 1927. They had a great reputation for reliability, because the German firm originally built trucks, and their cars were modeled after these 'giants'. The E2 model with a six-cylinder engine (6.8-liter displacement, 65 horsepower), which was manufactured from 1908 to 1914, was the favorite automobile of the German crown prince Wilhelm.

Bottom right *On 12 February 1908, the New York-Paris took off. The future winner, a German Protos with Lieutanant Hans Koeppen at the wheel, is portrayed here valiantly waiting in second line.*

Top right *The 1910 Mercedes Prinz-Heinrich-Wagen was certainly not a gorgeous car, but underneath the original chassis was one of history's first 4 valve engines, which produced 100 hp.*

Together with the Protos, there was another famous automobile of the time that was extremely popular, mostly in the United States; the Blitzen-Benz. Ironically, this nice name was not coined in Germany but in the United States. It was originally called Lightning Benz and was later changed to Blitzen-Benz, and was actually decorated with an imperial eagle. Its German manufacturers had been quite sober in their choice of the original name of this car, as was the custom at that time. The 'monster' was baptized Benz 200 PS.

In 1909 the board of directors of Benz & Cie asked its constructors to design an automobile that could go 200 kilometers per hour (124.26 mph). It was decided use the Benz Grand-Prix model, which had 150 hp, as the basis for the new model. The displacement was increased to 21.5 liters and by dint of hard work the longed-for 200 hp was achieved.

In the first race in which this car competed, from a flying start one kilometer (0,6 mi.) long, the pilot Fritz Erle reached an average speed of 159.3 km per hour (99 mph). In 1909, in the same type of competition, Victor Héméry reached an average speed of 202.7 km per hour (126 mph) with a Blitzen-Benz in the new motor racing circuit of Brooklands, England.

For that time, the aerodynamic body that was tapered in the rear, which Erle and Héméry had specifically requested in their attempts to set a record, was very special indeed. In any case, things went even better. The first Blitzen-Benz was sold in America in 1910 (where it was renamed) and records continued to be broken. In March the speed obtained was 211.97 km/h (132 mph). On 23 April 1911 at Daytona Beach, Bob Burmann reached 228.1 km/h (142 mph) from a flying start in a one-kilometer (0,6 mi.) stretch – a record that was broken only in 1919.

All told, six Blitzen-Benzes were constructed—or better, seven, because in 1935 another one was assembled with spare parts, and is now on display in the Mercedes-Benz museum in Stuttgart.

However, only the first Lightning Benz, which was dismantled into single parts in 1923 by the owner, Count Louis Vorow Zborowski – truly honored its name, since the others never managed to go faster than 200 km per hour (124 mph).

Top left In 1911 Robert 'Bob' Burman was the absolute king of speed records. Even on the legendary Indianapolis oval, as seen on this picture from 29 May 1911, he was crowned the winner for the umpteenth time, driving a Blitzen-Benz.

Bottom left The 1909 Blitzen-Benz produced an astonishing 200 hp: a huge capacity, 21.5 liters. In 1911, in Daytona Beach, this car set the world record for speed at 228,1 km/h (142 mph).

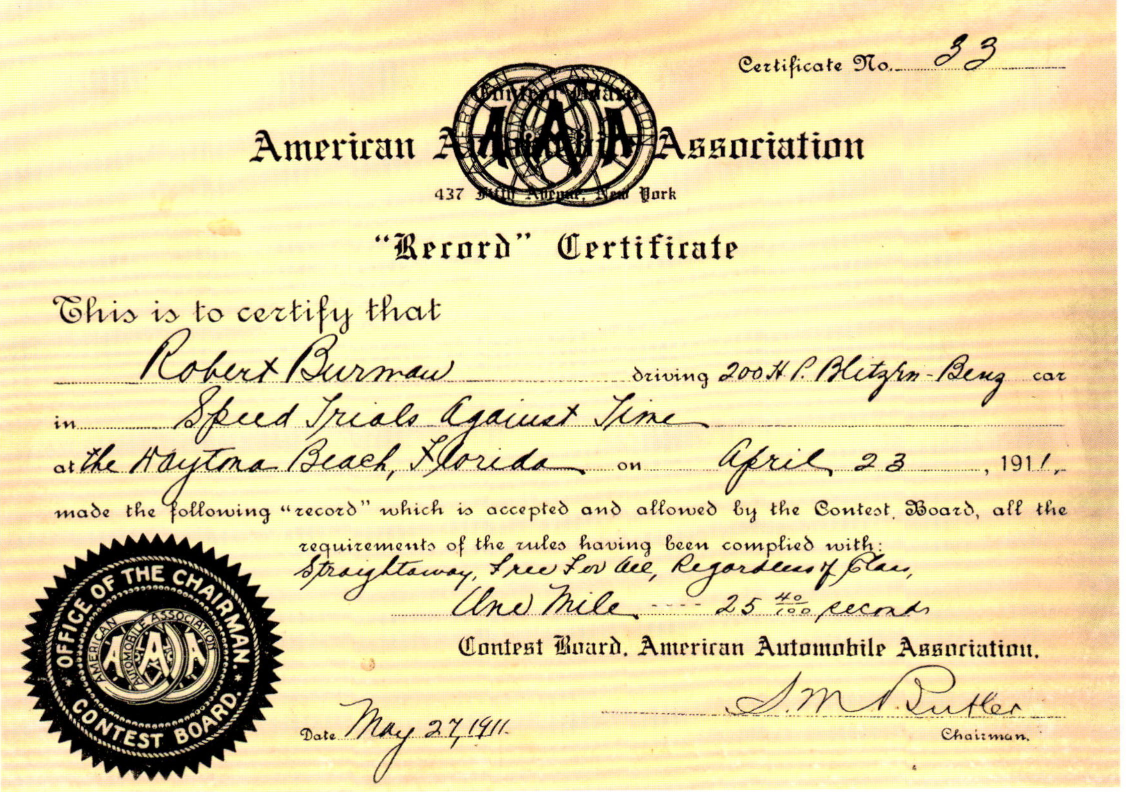

Certificate No. 33

American Automobile Association

437 Fifth Avenue, New York

"Record" Certificate

This is to certify that Robert Burman driving 200 H.P. Blitzen-Benz car in Speed Trials Against Time at the Daytona Beach, Florida on April 23, 1911, made the following "record" which is accepted and allowed by the Contest Board, all the requirements of the rules having been complied with:

Straightaway, Free For All, Regardless of Class,

One Mile --- 25 40/100 seconds

Contest Board, American Automobile Association.

Date May 27, 1911.

S. M. Butler

Chairman.

Top right Even in Europe, the Blitzen-Benz were record-hunters, as seen here on the legendary Brooklands circuit. This car (a total of seven units were built) belonged to the Hon. L.G. 'Cupid' Hornsted.

Center right This picture shows one of the Blitzen-Benz's first appearances in 1909. The car was very hard to drive: taming a 200 hp on unpaved roads must have been really difficult.

Bottom right This certificate confirmed that on 23 April 1911, Bob Burman, had actually broken the speed record in Daytona Beach, in a Blitzen-Benz. In those days, these records were all the rage.

Top left and right The Rumpler-Tropfenwagen caused a sensation in 1921. Its teardrop shape was very aerodynamic and offered a lot of room. Its V6-W engine was extraordinary, but also very unreliable. It was never very popular.

Bottom center Ferdinand Porsche designed the 'Sascha' in 1921. It should have actually been a 'people's car', small, light and cheap; but they were only produced as race cars, which in 1922 garnered quite a few victories.

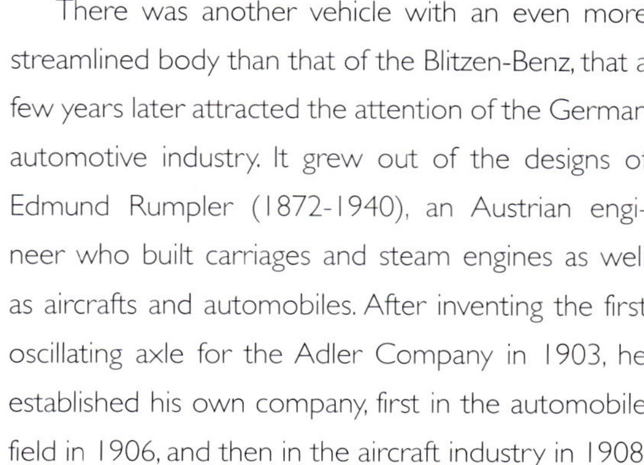

There was another vehicle with an even more streamlined body than that of the Blitzen-Benz, that a few years later attracted the attention of the German automotive industry. It grew out of the designs of Edmund Rumpler (1872-1940), an Austrian engineer who built carriages and steam engines as well as aircrafts and automobiles. After inventing the first oscillating axle for the Adler Company in 1903, he established his own company, first in the automobile field in 1906, and then in the aircraft industry in 1908.

His most famous airplane was the Taube (dove), a monoplane that he had not conceived, but had built under license from the Austrian aviator Igo Etrich (however, Rumpler never paid for the royalties).

In 1921 Rumpler exhibited his Tropfenwagen (teardrop car) at the Berlin automobile fair. When viewed from above, the shape of this auto actually reminded one of a drop of water. As the Volkswagen company demonstrated many years afterwards, by means of a wind tunnel test, the Tropfenwagen had an extremely low air-resistance coefficient of 0.28, thanks not only to the particular shape of the body, but also due to the smooth surface. But this was not all. Rumpler mounted a central engine immediately in front of the back axle of his vehicle, which according to his calculations was the most favorable position. The transmission and differential were placed behind this, while the traction wheels had an independent elastic suspension. In 1921 the magazine *Motor* wrote the following concerning the Tropfenwagen: "The widespread opinion according to which it would be impossible to improve an automobile any further is erroneous and is in fact refuted by this type of construction." However, Rumpler's automobile was not a success with the public. The six-cylinder V engine was not reliable, there was no trunk, it was very to difficult to steer because of vibrations, and the rear wheels wobbled. The car was popular in Berlin only as a taxi, because it was easy to get into. It also had a brief career in the cinema. The great director Fritz Lang had two of Rumpler's creations burn in the last scene of his famous film *Metropolis*. In all, perhaps 100 'teardrop cars' were built. The only remaining one is on display in the Deutsches Museum, Munich.

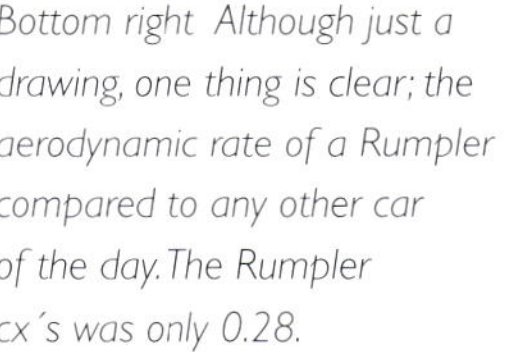

Bottom right Although just a drawing, one thing is clear; the aerodynamic rate of a Rumpler compared to any other car of the day. The Rumpler cx's was only 0.28.

Nowadays we often read that the German automobile manufacturers have to defend themselves from Chinese piracy. However, even the German automotive industry was not blameless in this respect. Unlike what occurred with Rumpler, this type of copying brought fortune to the industry.

The most obvious, and most felicitous, example of this is the Opel 4 CV, produced from 1924 to 1931. This was the first German automobile manufactured in an assembly line. The 'car for everybody' cost DM 4,500, which was not much compared to most German cars being made at the time, but it was still the equivalent of the cost of a private home. People called it the *Laubfrosch* or tree frog because it was small and green, while the others were rather large and black. In any case, the color green was the distinguishing feature with respect to the original, the Citroën 4hp, which made its debut in 1921, and was lemon yellow. Citroën attempted to sue Opel for having copied their patented automobile, but the German courts of law dismissed the petition of plagiarism on the basis of the different shape of the radiator grill. Whatever the case, the customers soon found out about the origin of the so-called new invention, hence the German expression 'the same in green', which most probably alluded to the Opel Laubfrosch.

The first Laubfrösche (known as the 4/12 hp) were available only with the so-called boat stern rear section and with a canvas roof. Other variations followed at a later stage. The two, three and four-seater Opel Cabrio, or the sedan with three or four seats, and even a van. The small Opel could attain a speed of 60 km per hour (37 mph) with a six-cylinder one-liter engine. One hundred and twenty thousand of them were sold, which was a great success for that time. In 1931 the Laubfrosch was replaced by the 1.2-liter Opel, the precursor of the P4 and Kadett models.

Bottom left *Opel was bought out by General Motors in 1929, and the brand was strongly influenced by American innovations such as customer service, which wasn't as widespread in the Europe of those days.*

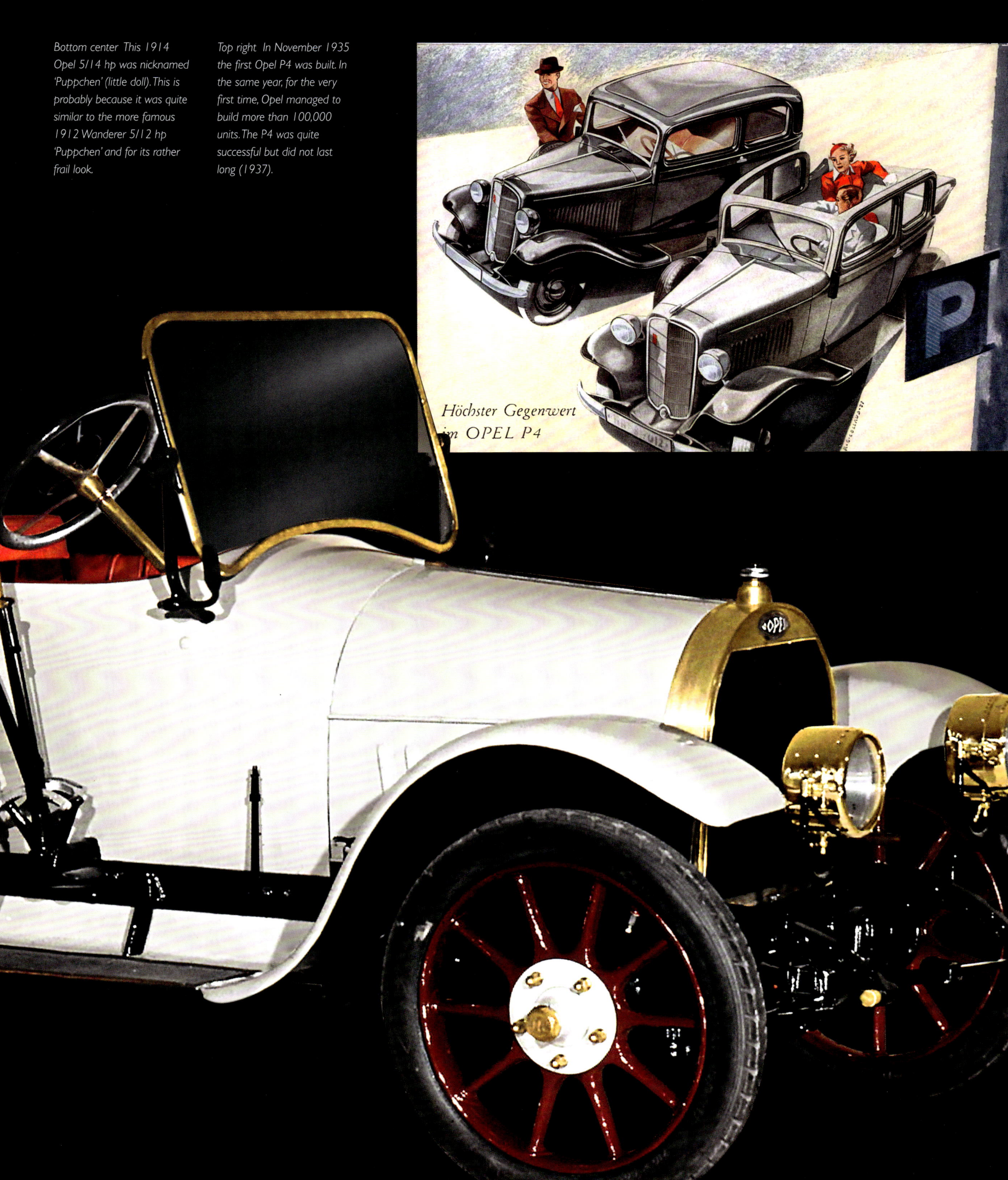

Bottom center This 1914 Opel 5/14 hp was nicknamed 'Puppchen' (little doll). This is probably because it was quite similar to the more famous 1912 Wanderer 5/12 hp 'Puppchen' and for its rather frail look.

Top right In November 1935 the first Opel P4 was built. In the same year, for the very first time, Opel managed to build more than 100,000 units. The P4 was quite successful but did not last long (1937).

Top left. In 1919 Germany adopted the US assembly line concept as early as the mid-twenties. Left is the Eisenach car factory. Surely the Dixi plants managed to survive World War I, but due to the obsoleteness of the products in 1919, they never obtained the success they had before the war.

Bottom center The car factory in Eisenach produced the Wartburg at first and then, from 1904 on, the Dixi cars which included classy sedans and trucks. Dixi is a Latin expression for "I said."

Right The original draft of an Austin 7 (1922-1939), the basis for the Dixi 3/15 hp, which was built from 1927 onwards. German cars, following the dictates of left-hand traffic, were built completely in reverse, including the engine.

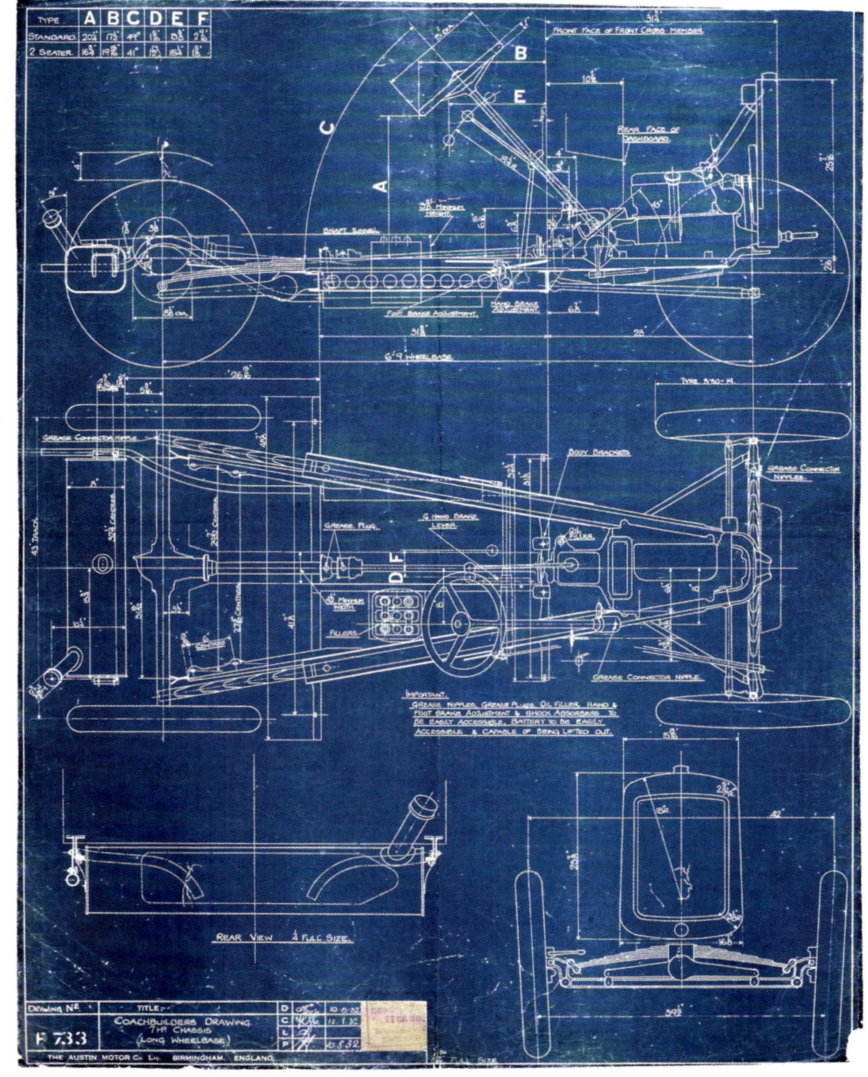

The famous BMW Dixi ('I said' in Latin) is another instance of a car that was not an original creation. However, here the 'plagiarism' was not so blatant as was the case with the Opel model. The Dixi 3/15 was made by the Eisenach car plant and in 1927, thanks to a licensing agreement with the Austin Car Co., a version of the Austin 7 (1922-39) was produced and BMW paid royalties for every car manufactured. The first models had right-hand drive. In 1928 the 3/15 DA came out. This model not only had left-hand drive, but its 'German version' also had an inverted engine. The small engine had 743 c. cm (292 in.) displacement and 15 hp, as its name itself tells us. It was only 3.25 meters (11 ft) long but there was enough room for two adults and three children. Unlike the Austin 7, the Dixi had brakes on all four wheels.

The Dixi was the first Bayrische Motoren-Werke automobile but it was not a success for the company. The model cost too much, the sales indexes were too low, and the license royalties to be paid (not only to the Austin company but also to Rosengart, which had the patent for the all-steel body) were too high. The first automobile entirely built by BMW came out only in 1932. This was the 3/20 AM1 (AM stands for Ausführung München or Munich version). There was also a lovely small racing car version of the Dixi, the BMW 3/15 PS DA3 Wartburg, only 150 of which were manufactured from 1930 to 1932. The cost of this model was high in proportion, RM 3,100 (but even the basic version cost RM 2,500). Yet this was still the beginning on a large scale, of a sport that would prove to be very important for BMW.

Left A Dixi ad from 1917, the model on the bottom is a S16, a large convertible. The scenes from the ad show how to enjoy the car. In those years, symbols were very important.

Right The ads in the mid-twenties (1924 in this case) were still basically artistic drawings. Dixi was still building large sedans, but success was still far away.

6|24 PS.

DIXI

Deutsche
Edelarbeit!

Dixi-Werke
EISENACH.

Top left Beginning in 1928, the Tempo company (Vidal & Sohn) built tricycles which at first looked like a combination between a motorcycles and a cargo bed. In the following years, the third wheel moved forward, in order to improve maneuverability.

Bottom left A bit of sheet metal and some paint, and there you have it, the Hanomag! This is how it is commonly known. But the Hanomag 2/10 hp, called 'Komissbrot' (sandwich), built from 1925 to 1928, never managed to succeed. The image shows a converted sedan.

Bottom right Cruising through the Silesian mountains in a 1913 Apollo. Carl Slevogt is at the wheel. The Apollo brand only built cars until 1927, despite the fact that they were much appreciated for their moderate price and high quality.

Tempo Pony
Der Lieferwagen
für nur Rm. 860
führerscheinfrei, steuerfrei
VIDAL & SOHN
TEMPO-WERK HAMBURG 1

Of a wholly different elegance compared to the Dixi roadster was another vehicle that was destined to become important for the German automobile industry; the three-wheel Tempo. The Vidal & Sohn Tempo plants were founded in Hamburg in 1928 (1924?). Their first car, which was assembled in the father's coal establishment, was a very simple three-wheeler with a cargo-carrying surface in front of the driver's seat. A short time later the structure was modified. The cargo surface was put in the back and the driver's area was completely covered and roofed. These models, which at times were quite impressive, were powered by one or two-cylinder engines that propelled the front tire by means of wheelwork and a chain. Thus it was necessary to mount the engine so that it could rotate, in order to maintain the front wheel steering potential.

The Tempo was famous for the appealing advertising slogan, which went more or less like this: 'Tempo, Tempo schreit die Welt! Tempo, Tempo, Zeit ist Geld'! (Tempo, Tempo, the world goes forward! Tempo, Tempo, time is money). The three wheels, both before and after the Second World War, were synonymous with very simple maintenance, a robust structure and absolutely reliable and safe service. Small firms in particular appreciated the three-wheelers (and also, in a later period, the Matador, a small four-wheel commercial van) because they were very versatile in that they allowed for any type of superstructure and also because the three-wheel Tempos were excellent vehicles for publicizing one's products. It must not be forgotten that after the war the three-wheel Tempo models were the precursors of the German cabin motor scooters, which were quite popular. The steering traction wheel served as a model for many automakers.

In 1962 this interesting chapter in the history of the German automobile continued in India, and ended in 2000 with the Lombardini diesel engines. Only a few of these models have come back to Europe.

Before the outbreak of the Second World War there were many automobile manufacturers in Germany that no longer exist, and almost nobody even remembers them. However, some of these firms do not deserve to be forgotten.

For example, there is Steiger. This was founded in 1914 at Ulm by the German constructor Walther Steiger (1881-1943), who had a diploma in chemistry. The Steiger company repaired vehicles and airplane engines during the First World War. In 1920 it produced the 10/50 PS with a four-cylinder, 2.6-liter engine, the features of which were the spiral-toothed bevel gear wheels that propelled the camshaft placed overhead. For its time this vehicle was considered the most advanced German assembly line-produced automobile, and was often compared to the Bugatti. Upto 1926, when the company went bankrupt, 3,500 of these cars were manufactured.

At a slightly lower lever, there was the Grade 4/16 PS economy car, which in 1924 was the one with the most sales in Germany. Of particular interest were the body, which reminded one of a boat, and the two-cylinder engine of in-house design. Hans Grade (1879-1946), who had his own company, was a former airplane constructor. Despite the success of his small firm, he had to declare bankruptcy yet another time, after having built 2,000 automobiles.

The Röhr Company was founded in 1926. The following year it launched its Röhr 8 model, a very good automobile that won the approval of the public because of its good grip on the road. With time, the model was continuously improved, especially the engine which was made more powerful. In any case, by 1931 the company had to declare bankruptcy despite attempts to save it with the bodywork designed by Professor Ferdinand Porsche.

Apollo built motorcycles in 1903 and in 1904 began to produce a small four-wheel car, the Piccolo. Two years later, again using the same name, the company presented a four-cylinder auto with an air-cooled engine, which at that time caused a sensation. The company changed its name to Apollo in 1910. It managed to hire as its designer the talented Carl Slevogt, who created racing cars, some of which were quite popular. Yet the company could not cope and stopped production in 1927.

The Limelight Years and The Dark Years

This image highlights a detail of a Mercedes Roadster 540 K. Before the war the 540, which produced 115 hp, was one of the most technologically advanced vehicles, and the chassis had very elegant details.

CHAPTER 3

Despite its defeat in the First World War, with the sacrifice of a great many human lives, in the immediate post-war years Germany's economy and industries made a surprisingly strong and rapid comeback. In 1924, Opel introduced the assembly line (which had been initiated the year before by Henry Ford), in 1926, Benz & Co. merged with Daimler Motoren-Gesellschaft to become Daimler-Benz AG which, in 1931, presented its DKW F1 model, the first assembly-line produced automobile with front-wheel drive.

By the late 1920s, German automakers had once again become among the most important in the world. Horch, Maybach and Mercedes regained their great reputation and were able to compete with the most important auto manufacturers of that time. In the 1930s the German firms, Mercedes, and Auto-Union, were also number one in car racing. From 1934 to 1939 their domination was absolute, even though they had such formidable rivals as Alfa Romeo and Bugatti.

Although the prevailing political atmosphere of Nazi Germany certainly did not lend it honor, it was the project known as KdF (Kraft durch Freude, or 'strength through joy', the name of the leisure time organization that was part of the German labor front), that indicated the future of the automobile industry in this country. In 1933 Hitler asked Ferdinand Porsche to build a Volkswagen (people's car) that could seat two adults and three children. It was to be able to reach a speed of 100 km per hour (62 mph), consume seven liters of gasoline for every 100 km (62 mi.), and cost no more than 1,000. Before the war broke out, in 1939, 330,000 Germans had begun to take part in the savings scheme established to allow working people to purchase a Volkswagen. To this end, the government issued passbooks on which saving stamps could be glued. At the beginning of the war, at the Arbeitsbank of Berlin 278,000,000 had been registered in this account, which shows how many people had already filled their passbooks and were trustingly waiting for the car of their dreams. And yet, instead of the passenger cars that had been promised, the Volkswagen plant in present-day Wolfsburg (where Hitler himself had laid the foundation stone on 26 May 1938) continued to produce only military vehicles, especially utility vehicles and amphibians.

Left This picture highlights the lines of one of the three BMW 328 roadsters which, in 1940 took part in and won the Mille Miglia. The racing versions had a power of approximately 120 hp and reached a maximum speed of 220 km/h (137 mph).

Top right Adolf Hitler is about to visit an auto and motorcycle show in Berlin on 20 February 1937. He is portrayed here saluting the pilots of the Auto Union team. The Third Reich supported sports events in order to keep up its image.

Bottom right Before World War II, the Avus high speed circuit in Berlin was definitely the most famous in Germany. This is a typical image showing Auto-Union and Mercedes dominating the scene.

Wilhelm Maybach (1846-1929) was one of the most important pioneers in the German automobile industry. For many years he was a partner of Gottlieb Daimler. Their collaboration began in the orphanage where Maybach had grown up and studied.

Maybach went on his own only in 1909, together with his son Karl. He began by making engines, including models for the Zeppelin airships. His first automobile, the W1, came out in 1919 with a Daimler chassis, while the W3 luxury car, which was presented in 1921, was entirely produced by Maybach. This limousine soon became a status symbol for the rich and powerful, especially the Zeppelin model, which arrived on the market soon after Maybach's death. The Zeppelin was powered by a twelve-cylinder, 7.9-liter 200 hp engine, thanks to which the car, which was 5.5 meters (18 ft) long and weighed more than three tons, could reach the speed of 170 km per hour (106 mph). This car could be purchased directly from the plant with its bodywork, but at that time if anyone wanted a particular detail he could order a custom-built body from a leading designer. Among the most famous of these latter were Erdmann & Rossi, or Hermann Spohn, who designed the marvelous Zeppelin DS8 that is now on display in the Mercedes Benz museum in Stuttgart. 'Only the best from the best' was the slogan used in the 1934 Maybach brochure, adding; 'The Zeppelin Maybach is the latest automobile dream come true, with its distinguished elegance and great power'. It is therefore not surprising that the upper echelons of the Nazi regime were only too happy to be behind the wheel of a Maybach.

In 2002 Daimler bought Maybach and revived one of its luxury models, the S class. However, sales of these new generation Maybach models were not significant, since the design was too 'normal' and the price too high. Wilhelm Maybach, who had excellent and inventive designers whose merits were undervalued, would not have been very happy with this revival of 'his' brand, because his main preoccupation was always the search for the unusual.

Top left and center The Zeppelin Maybach (left) was one of the most important vehicles of the 30s. It was propelled by a 7.9 liter 12 cylinder engine, which delivered up to 200 hp that pushed the car to 170 km/h (106 mph). Whoever wanted to stand out would commission a custom chassis. Tradition saw its maximum splendor in the 30s; right, a gorgeous Zeppelin Maybach.

Bottom left Wilhelm Maybach (second right, in front of a W3 and his factory in circa 1924-25) was one of the pioneers of the German auto industry. The first of its official vehicles was put on the streets in 1919.

Right When there were still no three-lane highways crossing the Alps, a car ride through the mountains was definitely and adventure.

BERGBEZWINGER
MAYBACH 12
TYPE ZEPPELIN
MAYBACH
Maybach-Motorenbau G.M.B.H. Friedrichshafen a.B.
Fernsprecher 174, 230, 231 • Telegr.-Adr.: Maybachmotor
Verkaufsbüros und Vertretungen in Berlin, Dresden, Frankfurt a. M., Köln, Hannover, Stettin, Bremen, Hamburg, München, Nürnberg, Stuttgart, Freiburg, Pforzheim, Danzig, Basel, Zürich, Den Haag, London, Prag, Warschau, Budapest, Wien, Belgrad, New York

Along with Horch and Mercedes, during the 20s and 30s, Maybach was on top of the German auto industry. These pictures show a beautiful specimen of a 1936 Zeppelin DS8. The vehicle weighed almost 3 tons but moved rather easily.

The hydraulic shocks guaranteed comfort, and the drum brakes braked homogeneously thanks to its negative pressure servo-system. Notice the long wheelbase of 3.74 meters (12 ft). In total the car is longer than 5.5 meters (18 ft).

ZEPPELIN

55

Top left August Horch (leaning on the car), portrayed with a 11/22 hp with its four in-line cylinders, in a 1906 version, the year in which Horch managed to win the Herkomer Fahrt with this car.

Top center August Horch (sitting, with cap and goggles) with the first collaborators, hired in 1899 for his Köln-Ehringfeld factory.

Bottom left August Horch at the wheel of a 11/22 hp, whose 2.7 liter four-cylinder engine produced 22 hp. The vehicle was used in the 1908 Prinz Heinrich Fahrt but never managed to bring home a flower bouquet.

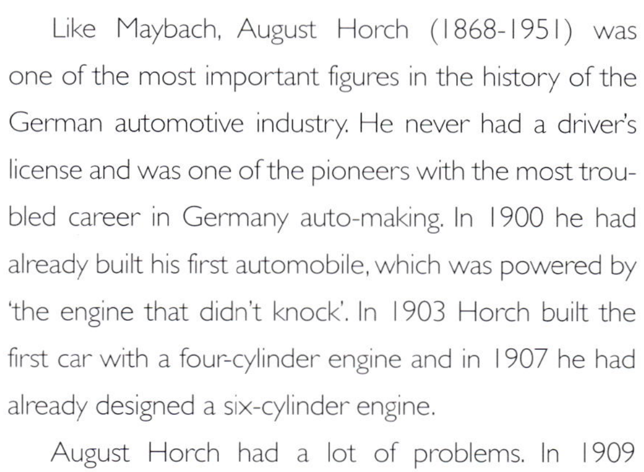

Like Maybach, August Horch (1868-1951) was one of the most important figures in the history of the German automotive industry. He never had a driver's license and was one of the pioneers with the most troubled career in Germany auto-making. In 1900 he had already built his first automobile, which was powered by 'the engine that didn't knock'. In 1903 Horch built the first car with a four-cylinder engine and in 1907 he had already designed a six-cylinder engine.

August Horch had a lot of problems. In 1909 in-house issues forced him to leave his company. He later established a new auto-making firm of his own whose name caused him more trouble, since he was not legally allowed to use 'Horch'. The story goes that a Latin teacher who happened to be with Horch suggested the solution. The imperative singular in Latin of the German word *horch* ('hark, listen') was Audi, which he adopted. In any case, Horch remained with the Audi Company only until 1922, and after the Second World War he concentrated on reviving the Auto-Union company.

The Horch automobile industry activities flourished even without August. The peak was reached with the 850 model, which was placed on the market in 1935. This fine Horch car had an eight-cylinder, 4.9 liter, 100 hp engine. It was continuously improved. Innovations included transmission with overdrive (with a second gear-shift), a rear axle with a double ball joint, and a more powerful engine (120 hp). Several types of bodywork were available, from the two-seater Roadster (the 855, also with a reduced wheelbase) to the large Limousine 951. The Horch automobiles of the time could not compete at par with the large Mercedes and Maybachs, but at a technical level they were quite interesting and very reliable.

Horch ended its production in 1940. Fortunately, so far the Audi Company has resisted the temptation to revive this model.

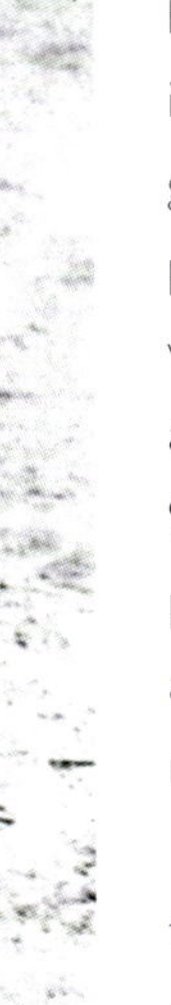

Top right A Horch roadster from the 30s with a special chassis. Today, it is no longer possible to find out what moved designers to make such elongated cars.

Center right Here is design that is removed from reality. Notice the huge headlights, and the wheels that seem small in comparison. Even its wheelbase seems somewhat surreal.

Bottom right An illustration by the Berlinese Casparry that portrays a Horch Limousine. Horch left the company that carried his name as soon as 1909 and therefore couldn't share its moments of glory.

Nowadays most people think that the Mercedes Benz has always been the German luxury car. This is simply not true. It took a long time for this star to reach the zenith of Maybach and Horch. The first step in this direction was with the Mercedes S, which came out in 1926 as a racing car variant of the K model. The W06 series was powered by a six-cylinder, 6.8-liter, 120 hp engine; a Roots compressor made it possible to rapidly increase the horsepower to 180. The SS model, introduced in 1928, had already attained 200 hp with its compressor, and the latter versions even went up to 225 hp. This type of engine was also available in the SSK, which stands for *SuperSport kurz* (supersport with short wheelbase). In fact, the SSK wheelbase measured only 290 cm (114 in.), while in the SS it was no less than 340 cm (134 in.), which made the car must lighter.

Certainly the most famous model in this sports car series was the SSKL (WS06 RS), which was a spin-off of the SSK; SSKL stands for *SuperSport kurz leicht* (supersport with short, light wheelbase). This roadster not only weighed 200 kg (441 lbs.) less than the SSK, it also had more powerful motorization. Officially it had an output of 240 hp, and reached 300 hp with a Roots compressor, but the first figure is only theoretical because in the SSKL the compressor was always active. The most famous driver of this car was Rudolf Caracciola. In all, three hundred of these cars were produced.

Bottom left The Mercedes SS (project name W06) were built starting in 1928. These were very powerful cars, with a 6 cylinder engine and a compressor that soon increased its power to 200 hp.

Right This historic photograph shows an assembly conveyor of the Mercedes Nürburg, aka 460 (project name W08). Starting in 1928, it was the brand's first eight cylinder, as well as the first 'popemobile', because Pope Pius XI was given one as a gift.

P7

Bottom left This is how one would imagine the typical SSK which stands for 'Supersport kurz', short as it were, because these chassis were mounted on a frame that had a wheelbase of only 2.95 meters (10 ft).

Right A beautiful, classic model of a 1927 Mercedes S, with a white varnish, typical of those days. Today these vehicles are highly priced among collectors, if it is even possible to find one.

Continental

An extraordinary body for a 1929 S. In the late 20s, disc wheels were fashionable. Even in this case, we are in front of a powerful vehicle, oversized for just two seats. It is unusual for an S to have only one exhaust pipe, although in this case the vehicle is no less elegant. Notice the manual projector on the driver's side. Each cylinder of the 6.8 liter S engine has two ignition sparks, hence a double ignition, activated both by the battery and by a magnet. The gearshift was a four-speed.

Left The elegant cover design of the 'Motor und Sport' review, which was supposed to represent the international fame of the Mercedes cars, portrays a Mercedes Mannheim (project name W10).

Right One of the most famous ads of the 20s, the 'lady in red', by the Offelsmeyer Cucuel agency, published in 'Elegante Welten'. The ad publicized the Mercedes S, known also as the 26/120/180 hp.

MERCEDES
BENZ
MERCEDES-BENZ

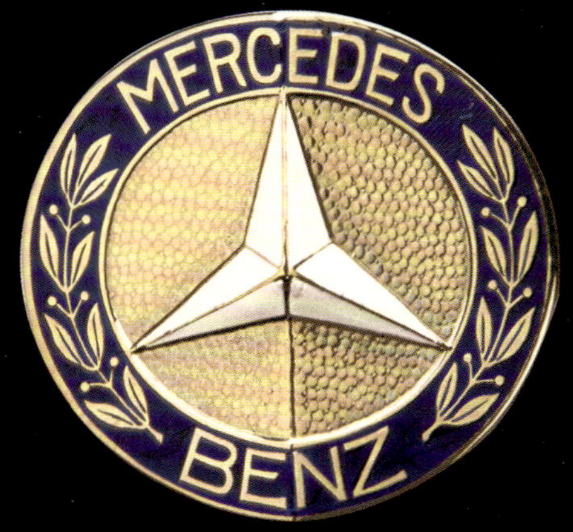

The direct successor of the S/SS/SSK/SSKL automobiles was presented in 1934 at the Berlin auto show. Its name was 500 K; in general the prototype was called W29, the same name already used by Daimler-Benz. It was available with three different chassis; the short version with a 298 cm (117 in.) wheelbase, the normal one with a 329 cm (130 in.) wheelbase, and another 329 cm (130 in.) version but with a rear engine. The 500 K was powered by an eight-cylinder, 5-liter, 100 hp engine, which was nothing really exceptional. Like the W06, the engine was connected to a Roots compressor that boosted the horsepower to 180. One of the many technical features was the hydraulic vacuum brakes on all four wheels. The next model, the 540 K, was already presented in Paris in 1936, with a new 5.4-liter engine

Top left *In the 30s the Mercedes-Benz brand enjoyed great fame, not only for its mass production but for its efforts in the world of racing, which was long dominated by the 'silver arrow'.*

Bottom center *A gorgeous 1937 Mercedes 540 K. In the late 30s these vehicles were the apex of technology, they were very reliable, very fast, and also very expensive.*

that, in normal conditions produced 115 horsepower. In 1939-1940 experiments were made on a 580 K model (only two were manufactured, 5.8 liters and 130-200 hp), but with the outbreak of World War Two production of this series was interrupted.

Although today the Daimler firm is uncomfortable about its 'Nazi' past, the 540 K was of particular significance for the Third Reich. After the attempt to assassinate Reinhard Heydrich in May 1942 in Prague, the Reich ordered twenty armored 540 K models, which were produced in the two-door sedan version (the Mercedes 770 was similar to this and had already been manufactured). The firm also made a dozen 540 Ks with a long wheelbase (388 cm, 153 in.) for the German government, which were produced as six-seat roadsters. These vehicles had the so-called De Dion double coil-spring swing axle in the rear, while a rigid axle was in the front. Mercedes produced three hundred forty two 500 K and four hundred nineteen 540 K models. As usual, their registers were extremely precise.

One of the most elegant W29s was the so-called Autobahnkurier (expressway courier). Only two of these were made, one of which still exists.

crossed the ocean and reached Europe; chrome, which became synonymous with rich. Whoever owned a car like this 540 K surely wasn't worried about finances. The posterior was was definitely not typical of the 30s. Surely it did not correspond to any logical or practical criteria: the cars had to give up their back trunk. And the rear end was very light.

detailed interiors of a 1937 540 K. The first thing that meets the eye is the brushed aluminum frame for every instrument; a detail that has made a comeback today.

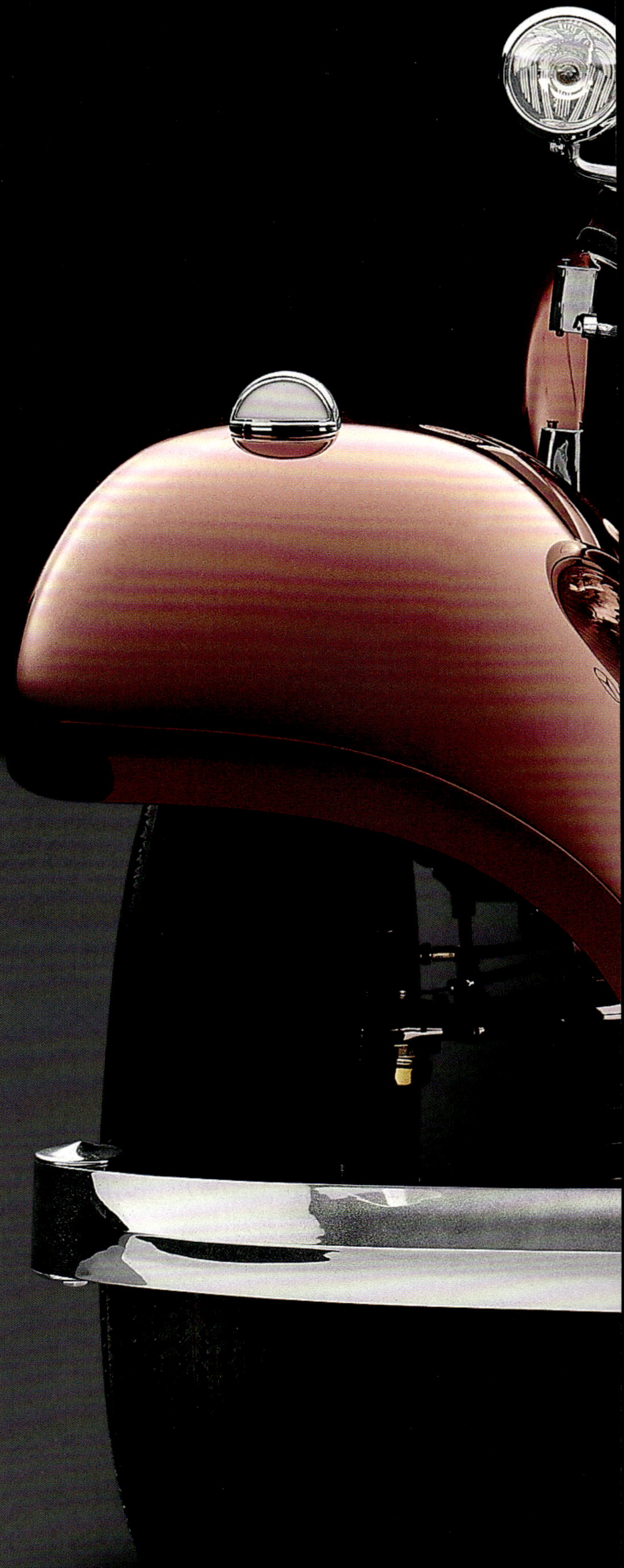

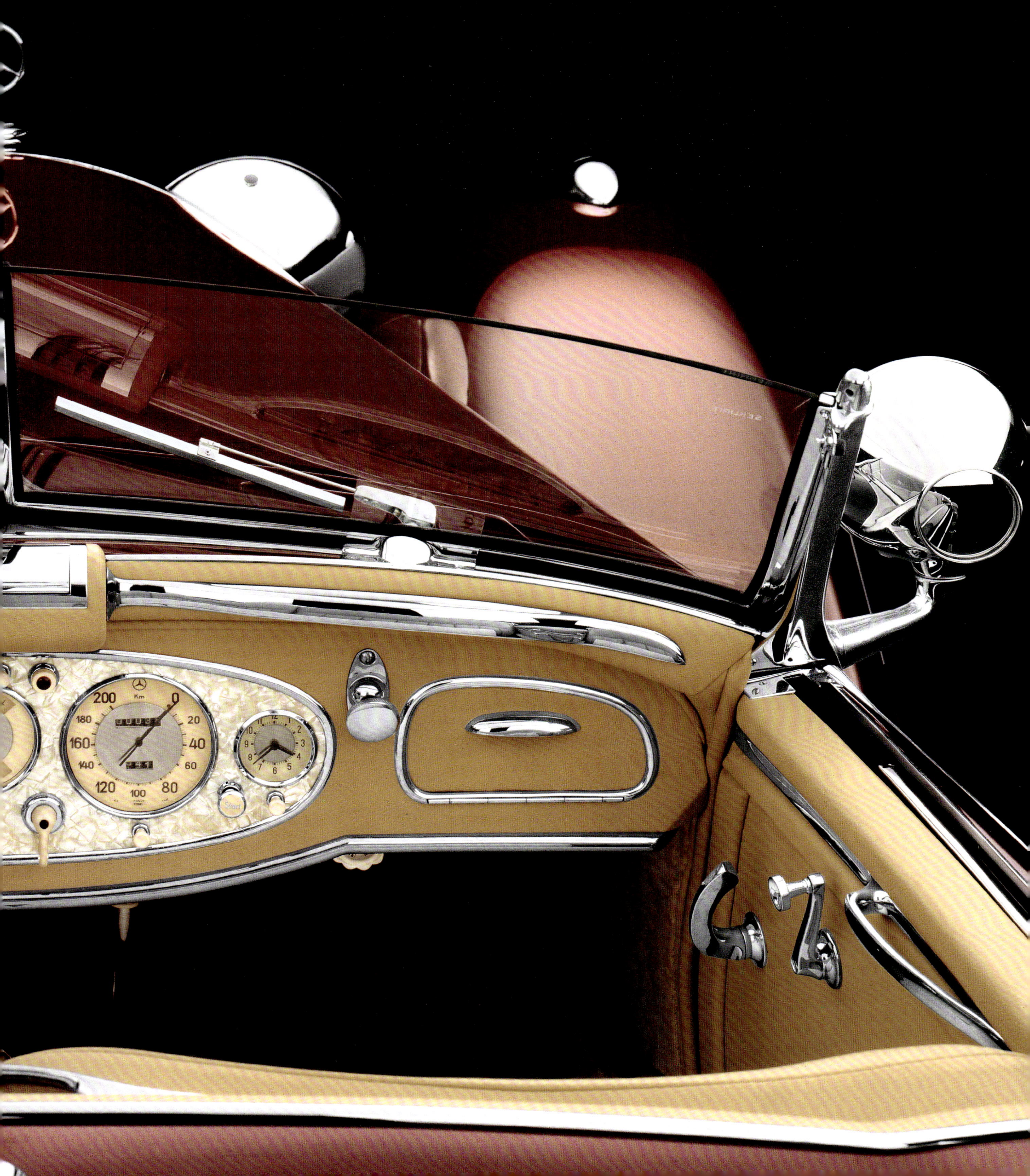
Km
200
180
160
140
120
100
80
60
40
20
0

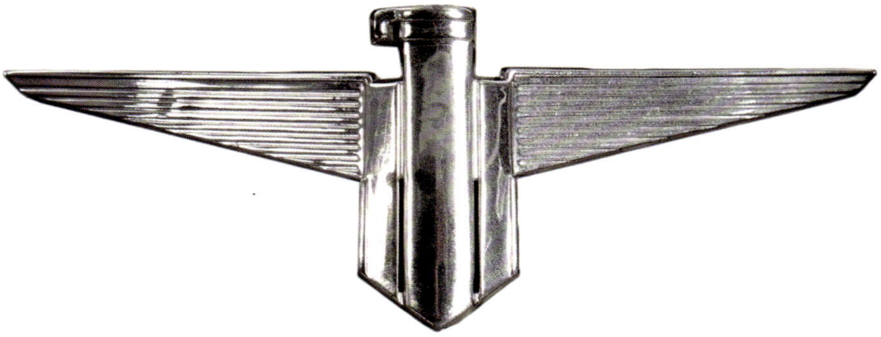

Top left The eagle of the Adler emblem, could be problematic nowadays, but back then, in the late 30s, everything in Germany had to follow certain criteria of style.

Right The Diplomat, produced in 1934 was, with its 2.9 liter, six cylinder, the successor of the fortunate Standard 6 and 8 models. Up until 1938, the economical Diplomat only sold 3,205 units.

During the Third Reich there another automobile that was not particularly successful with the public, despite the fact that it was very advanced technically for its time. In 1932 the Adler Company presented the Trumpf and Primus models, both of which had the same 1.5-liter displacement engine. The Trumpf, unlike the Primus, had front-wheel drive, but it was not Adler that discovered front-wheel drive. The first automobile with this was created in Vienna as far back as 1898 in the Gräf & Stift plant. The Adler system was based on the work done by the French company Tracta, which in the late 1920s sold its invention to both Adler and DKW. The latter company actually came out with this innovation a few months before Adler with its F1 model.

The amazing thing was that the Trumpf with front-wheel drive outdid its more conservative sister model in sales by far. Till 1938 more than 100,000 were sold (from 1936 on it had a 1.7-liter engine). The 'father' of the Adler Trumpf was Hans Gustav Röhr. He equipped it with a differential, the third gear of which was particularly quiet. At first the body was made of plywood covered with artificial leather, while the metal plate arrived at a later stage. Karmann built a very stylish cabriolet. The car was relatively cheap despite the high-quality workmanship. A two-door Trumpf cabriolet cost RM 4,600, while the four-door version came at RM 5,050.

The last Adler model was the 2.5-liter one, which was presented in 1937. It boasted a 6-cylinder in-line engine, while the body was very elegant and streamlined. A special feature was that the headlights were integrated into the body, an innovation that made its appearance in the history of European auto-making for the first time. The American Cord had already introduced this feature in 1936. There was also a version with the rather banal name of *Autobahn* (expressway) that actually won some races. The bombardments in the Second World War totally destroyed the Adler plants. Production was resumed after the war, but the Adler Company limited its output to the product that had made it famous—typewriters.

ADLERWERKE VORM. HEINRI

ADLER DIPLOMAT

3 LTR. 6 ZYL.

Ein Wagen großer Leistungen bei wirtschaftlichstem Verbrauch. Es ist das Fahrzeug Ihrer Repräsentation.

Innensteuer=Limousine, Preis ab Werk **RM. 7500.–**

KLEYER AKTIENGESELLSCHAFT · FRANKFURT AM MAIN

Top left A beautiful interior detail of a Adler 2.5 Liter cabrio. Its gearbox was a 'revolver' type and required a lot of sensibility.

Bottom and top center The Adler 2.5 Liter was born out of a project by Karl Jenschke, who had previously worked at Steyr-Daimler-Puch in Austria, where he had designed the 'Steyr-Baby', a very similar vehicle. The Adler 2.5 Liter, aka Type 10, also existed in the convertible, two-door version. The front windows opened with a pivot mechanism.

Top right The Adler 2.5 Liter arrived on the market in 1937, during an unfortunate time. With its aerodynamic chassis, it was too far ahead of its time. It was nicknamed 'the eagle of the roads' because it reached 150 km/h (93 mph).

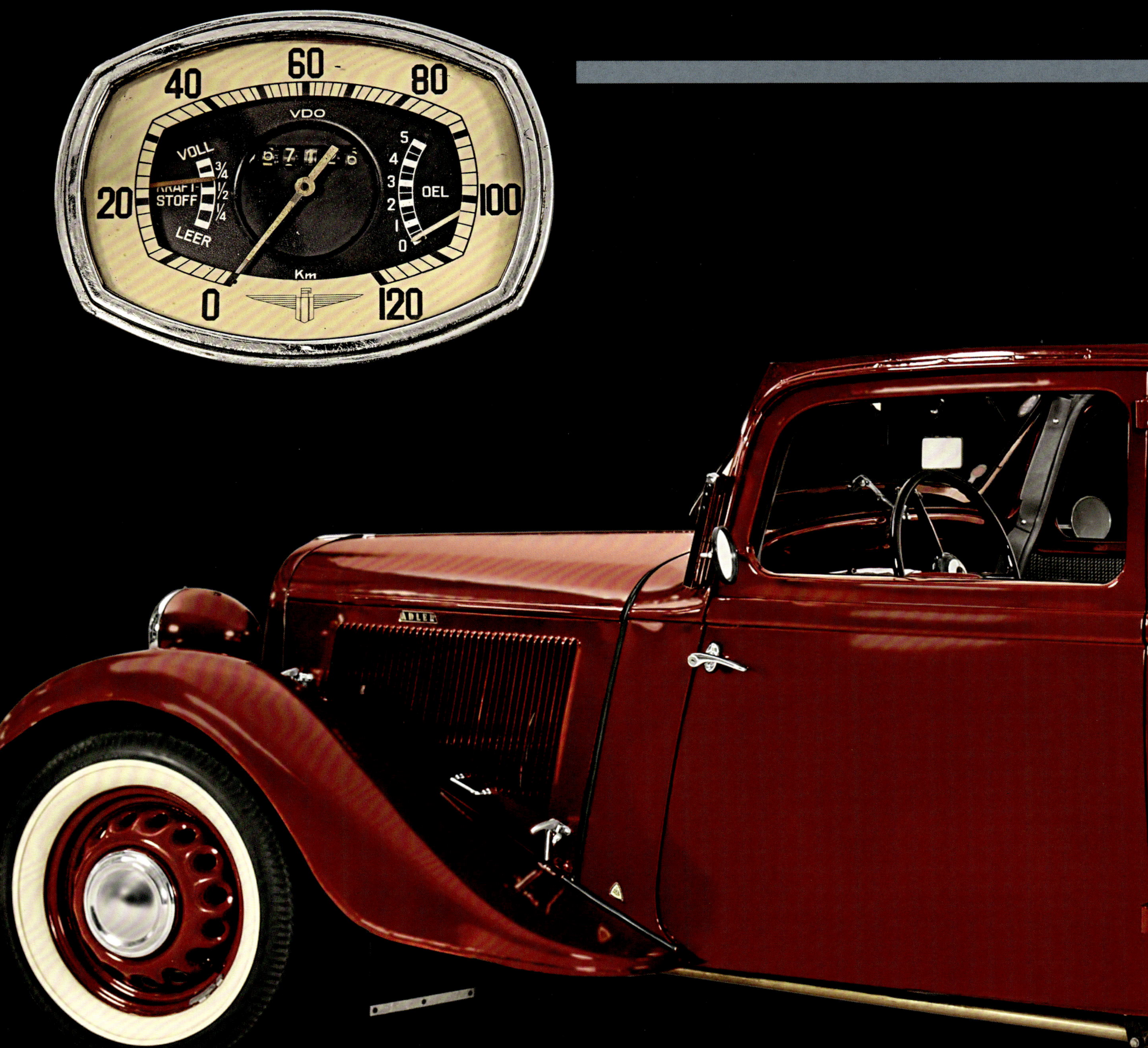

40
60
80
VDO
VOLL
3/4
KRAFT-
STOFF
1/2
1/4
LEER
20
5
4
3
2
1
0
OEL
100
Km
0
120

Top left Before World War II, the Adler brand was one of the most advanced. Consider the instruments, embellished by decorative elements, where other brands were limited to mounting classic round instruments.

Bottom center The Adler Trumpf Junior, built in 1934, was the little sister of the Trumpf. It too had front drive and only mounted a small 1 liter engine, that produced between 25 and 28 hp.

with the Trumpf.
The cars had an aerodynamic chassis; Orssich and Sauerweine obtained class victory and absolute 6th place.

Bottom center *A total of six aerodynamic Trumpf were produced. The chassis belonged to the baron Reinhard von König-Fachsenfeld, who took inspiration from the notions of the aerodynamics researcher Paul Jaray. Today there still are three units around.*

was also a record-breaking car, and a similar vehicle was owned by the director of the Adler plants, Erwin Kleyer. Even Huschke von Hanstein, who later became even more famous, drove a 'Stromlinie'. The ad recites: "Adler's opening victory in the Le Mans auto race, 19/20 June 1937."

ADLER Klassen=Sieg beim schwersten Sportwagen=Rennen der Welt in Le Mans, Frankreich, 19./20. Juni 1937

It is hard to believe, but it actually moved, as shown in this old picture. On 28 May 1928, the Opel Rak2 with Fritz von Opel at the wheel, broke a new world record, at a speed of 238 km/h (148 mph).

The only famous automobiles that were produced in the agitated prewar years were racing cars, despite the continuous technological progress made in the German (and not only German) automobile industry. Obviously, racing cars were also a testing ground, since many of the technical innovations in this field were then applied to the assembly line products, and in any case car racing was useful to the automobile firms (and to the Third Reich project managers) to increase their knowledge and stimulate inspiration. Then as now, winning international car races made and makes for publicity.

Opel got on the wrong track. At Rüsselheim in 1927 the company began to study rocket propulsion in collaboration with the astronomer and publicist Max Valler. The first tests with two rockets mounted on an Opel Laubfrosch went rather badly. The car went only 150 meters (492 ft) in 35 seconds, and fortunately for the firm, this test was not carried in public. On 11 April 1928 Opel invited the public to view the Rak1, a vehicle with an aerodynamic, futuristic body. Behind the wheel was Volkhart, who reached a speed of 100 km per hour (62 mi.) and then had to stop because only seven of the twelve rockets on the car had ignited. In any case, this was a great success for Opel, since it demonstrated that rockets served a purpose. The head of the firm, Fritz von Opel, announced that further research would be carried out and spoke of space flights with men on board. He personally went on to show he was serious on 28 May 1928, at the AVUS testing circuit in Berlin, when he himself drove a Rak2. He ignited 24 rockets in all, each one with 120 kg (265 lbs.) of explosives, and reached a speed of 238 km per hour (148 mph)! The proverbial launch on a cannonball had become reality.

OPEL RAK 2
SANDER

The Opel Rak1 was white, and white was the traditional color of German racing cars. But the year 1934 marked the presentation of the two most prestigious racing cars of the time, both painted silver. They were Mercedes-Benz, and Auto-Union. The German press immediately called them 'silver arrows' (Mercedes-Benz) and 'silver fish' (Auto-Union). To this day it is not clear why this color was chosen.

This is a fascinating story. In October 1932 the international sports authorities had established that the maximum weight for racing cars from 1934 to 1936 had to be 750 kg (1653 lbs.). Mercedes set out to comply with this regulation and thus designed the W25, but when it was weighed for the Eiffelrennen race on the Nürburgring track on 3 June 1934, instead of 750 kg (1653 lbs.) it weighed one kilogram more. The story goes that the sports director was enraged and exclaimed,

"Now we are the ones who have been cheated."

As a result, Manfred von Brauchtisch, the Mercedes pilot, got the idea of scraping the white paint off the car to reduce its weight in order to comply with the regulation. This done, what remained was the aluminum plate with its silver hues. Von Brauchtisch, who went on to win the race, confirmed this legend a short time before his death. The only thing we know for sure is that the notion of a 'silver arrow' appeared for the first time in the newspapers after that race was run, in June 1934. However, other sources state that the W25 was originally a silver color, so we will probably never know what really happened.

The only certainty we have is that the W5 marked the beginning of a new era in car racing. With their weight regulation, the authorities had set out to limit the maximum speed, but their project backfired. For the 1934 season Mercedes had designed a new eight-cylinder, 3.4-liter racing car engine, obviously with a compressor. The aim was to attain about 280 hp, but the first version already produced 354 hp, a horsepower-displacement ratio with 100 hp 'extra'. In the two following years much work was done on the engine unit, which weighed a little over 200 kg (441 lbs.). In 1936, in the final manufacturing stage, the mechanics and designers succeeded in obtaining the impossible; 494 horsepower and 4.7-liter displacement. The W5 won the Grand Prix and other major races sixteen times. For the year 1937 Mercedes had to design a new racing car. The W125 was similar in appearance to the preceding model, but engineer Rudolf Uhlenhaut had revolutionized the union of the chassis with a very simple idea. The W125 no longer participated in the races with rigid suspension and soft, pliant shock absorbers, but with pliant suspension and rigid shock absorbers. The result was very good, except for the fact that in the last race of the season, on the Donington track in England, Mercedes lost to Bernd Rosemeyer's Auto-Union car. The W125 was a fantastic racing car. In running order it weighed 1,097 kg (2418 lbs.) including the driver and the 240 liters of fuel (88% methyl alcohol and 8.8% acetone). The eight-cylinder engine unit obtained a displacement of 5.7 liters and consumed almost 100 liters of fuel mixture for 100 km (62 mi.). The last version of this engine had an output of 646 hp.

Top center *The 1934 Italian Grand Prix took place on 9 September in Monza. Luigi Fagioli (in the picture) and Rudolf Caracciola alternated at the wheel of a Mercedes W25 and together won the race.*

Right *In the German Grand Prix of 25 June 1937, on the Nürburgring, Bernd Rosemeyer in an Auto Union obtained the best starting position, but the race was won clearly by the Mercedes silver arrow.*

Bottom center *As early as 1935, the Swiss GP, near Bern, took place in pouring rain. The 'rainmaster' Caracciola, who always won in these conditions, was unbeatable on wet roads.*

Ein Doppelsieg von Mercedes-Benz

Erster: Rudolf Caracciola
mit einem Stundendurchschnitt von 133,2 km

Zweiter: M. v. Brauchitsch
mit einem Stundendurchschnitt von 132,7 km

(6. Christian Kautz 7. Hermann Lang)

Alle Wagen waren ausgerüstet mit Continental-Reifen, Bosch-Kerzen und Bosch-Zündung

MERCEDES-BENZ

Herausgeber: DAIMLER-BENZ AG. Druck: Chr. Belser AG, Stuttgart

35
31

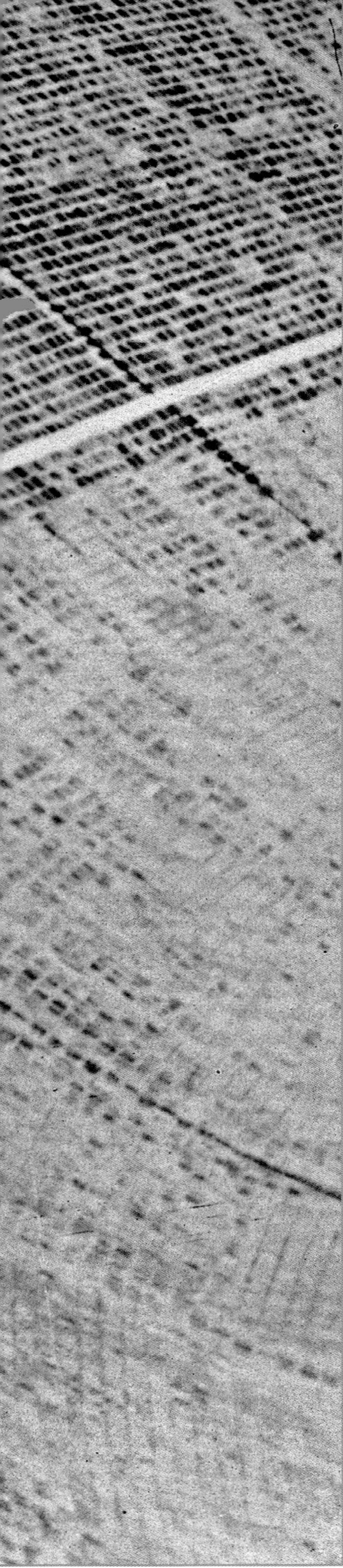

In 1936 the AIACR (Association Internationale des Automobile Clubs Reconnus) had already published the regulation for 1938. A maximum displacement three liters with supercharger and 4.5 liters without supercharger, and minimum weight 450-800 kg (992-1764 lbs.), depending on the class were allowed. Mercedes came up with a lot of ideas, even a V24 aspirated engine with three rows of eight cylinders each. They eventually decided to utilize a V12 with four valves per cylinder, 3-liter displacement and two compressors. In 1938 they reached an output of 430-474 horsepower, which made it possible for Hermann Lang to go 283 km per hour (176 mph) in the legendary Reimst track. For the first time Mercedes used a five-speed transmission. The W154 was the luckiest 'silver arrow'. In 1938, Rudolf Caracciola became champion of Europe by winning three out of the five races. In 1939 the result was the same, but the champion this time was Hermann Lang.

Mention should be made of one more detail. In the W154 the pilot did not sit in a central position but his cockpit was positioned slightly to the right, next to the cardan shaft. In order to improve balance, a second tank was placed between the pilot and the engine.

The history of the pre-war years often neglects to mention another 'silver arrow', the W165, which came out in 1939. It was built for only one race, the 1939 Grand Prix of Tripoli. Here, it was not the title that was important, but fame and honor were at stake. The pilots loved this circular 13-kilometer (8 mi.) track. The new car was completed in only eight months because in Tripoli the race was run with the Voiturette formula, that is, a 1.5-liter engine. The W165 was explicitly based on the W154 but was a smaller version (368 cm, 145 in., long with a wheelbase of 245 cm, 96 in., while the W154 was 425 cm, 167 in., long with a 273 cm, 107 in., wheelbase). The engine was a V8 with 149 cm (59 in.) displacement and with an output of 254 hp thanks to two compressors.

Top left The Avus GP of 30 May 1937, crowned neither Caracciola the victor in his Mercedes, nor Rosemeyer in Auto Union. In front of 400,000 spectators, victory went to the Mercedes driver Hermann Lang, who had already won the season's first races.

Bottom left Operation 'desert' was successful. Hermann Lang managed to win the Tripoli GP, in front of Caracciola, both at the wheel of a W165. Villoresi only placed third, driving one of his favorite Alfa Romeo Type 158.

Right Mercedes mechanics working in May 1937 on a W125. The engineer had revolutionized the chassis; the silver arrow had rather soft suspensions, and mounted rigid shocks.

Top left 11 November 1936, Rudolf Caracciola, at the wheel of this Mercedes race-car with its aerodynamic chassis, broke the world record for speed on 16 km (10 mi.); the average speed was 337 km/h (209 mph).

Center left The car that in 1936 allowed Caracciola to break several speed records, drew on the Grand Prix W25, whose overpowered eight cylinders produced almost 500 hp.

Bottom right On 9 February 1939, Rudolf Caracciola at the wheel of this record-breaking car (a W154 with a overpowered 3 liter engine), broke the two world records for standing starts; 175,695 km/h (109 mph) for the kilometer, and 204.57 km/h (127 mph) for the mile.

Top right The new highways of the Third Reich were perfect for record-breaking. In the picture Caracciola is at the wheel of his W154 Rekordwagen on the highway between Dessau and Bitterfeld, February 1939.

Left The spirit was very nationalistic in Germany in the late 30s, as demonstrated in this cover image of 'Motor und Sport', February 1938. In the center, an Auto Union race car, behind a NSU motorcycle.

Right On 22 October 1934, Hans Stuck in a Auto Union, broke a series of speed records on the Avus track in Berlin (five to be precise). The vehicle was the race car built by Porsche.

The silver arrows of the pre-war years had an interesting and (almost) equal adversary – Auto Union. Their racing car was born in autumn in the mind of Dr. Ferdinand Porsche, who absolutely wanted to build a vehicle for the 750 kg (1653 lbs.) formula, in effect since 1934, but did not have the necessary financial means.

In 1933 he made his initial contact with Auto-Union, whose designs Porsche purchased for RM 75,000 after finding out that Mercedes was also interested. The so-called P Wagen (P stands for Porsche) was built in the Horch racing car plant at Zwickau; Porsche was part of the team but left in 1937 when the 750 kg (1653 lbs.) formula was replaced. Porsche's working procedure is worth mentioning here. He did not want to work in Zwickau, so he would send the designs for the individual parts to Robert Eberan von Eberhorst, who first tested their reliability and then had them built. After leaving Porsche, von Eberhorst saw to the construction of the D type model, which was produced in 1938-39. A feature of the first Auto-Union racing cars was the 16-cylinder engine. In 1934 the A model had a 4.4-liter, 295 hp engine; the 2700 rpm torque was actually 530 Nm. Then, a sixteen-cylinder, 5-liter (375 hp) engine was mounted on the B type model and was once again placed in a central position. The C model, which proved to be the best racing car in the 1936 season with Bernd Rosemeyer at the wheel, was also a strong and dangerous rival of the Mercedes silver arrow (the Stuttgart Company had to withdraw from competition with the season only half finished). It also had a Porsche engine (six cylinders and 520 horsepower); the maximum of the 2500 rpm torque was 853 Nm.

Start Nr
Gefahrene
Runden

The Type D was the last development phase (1938/39) of the Grand Prix race car by Auto Union. The car was propelled by a 3 liter, twelve cylinder, which, thanks to its two Roots compressors produced 485 hp. Originally the Auto Union sports car was built by Ferdinand Porsche. However the Type D was designed by Robert Eberan von Eberhorst, who later worked for Porsche, ERA and Aston Martin.

The C model was the basis for the so-called Bergrennwagen (hill climber automobile), which with its double rear wheels on the rear axle caused quite a sensation. The D model had a twelve-cylinder, 3-liter engine that thanks to two Roots compressors had an output of 485 horsepower.

While Mercedes could count on the skill of several drivers, Auto-Union had only one who attained great success; Bernd Rosemeyer. He had begun as a motorcycle racer, and his first automobile race took place only in 1934. The hero of the prewar years was a tall man with blond hair who was absolutely fearless. Rosemeyer was married to the airplane pilot Elly Beinhorn. On 26 October 1937 he was the first pilot to reach 400 km per hour (249 mph) on a public road. On January 28 1938 he had a fatal crash while attempting to set yet another record on the Frankfurt-Darmstad highway; his Auto-Union R (Rekordwagen) model was struck by a gust of wind while he was going over 440 km per hour (273 mph), causing the car to roll over several times.

Top left An interesting encounter after the Mille Miglia: three BMW 328s, on the left, a Roadster, in the center, the victorious Touring Coupe, and on the right, the so-called 328 'Kamm', a prototype built for aerodynamic tests.

Top center The gorgeous Touring Coupe Superlight built on the BMW 328 victorious at the Mille Miglia in 1940, crosses the finish line. At the wheel, Steuer Huschke von Hanstein (co-pilot Walter Baumer).

Bottom center The BMW 328 sports car made its first appearance on the Nürburgring in late 1936, when it won the race. It was built until 1940 in only 464 units; the 2 liter, six cylinder produced 80 hp.

Following pages The victory obtained at the 1940 Mille Miglia was obviously a good element in the background of the a BMW ad. It must not be forgotten that in 1940, the competition was almost nil and BMW's victory was guaranteed from the start.

Another German racing car built in the prewar years that was not considered part of the elite but still enjoyed much success, was the BMW 328. It was based on the four-seat 326 model and was produced in 1937; it was seen for the first time in the Eiffelrennen race on the Nürburgring track, in which Ernst Henne earned an amazing victory. This car, which weighed a little over 800 kg (1764 lbs.), was powered by a six-cylinder, 2-liter engine with an output of 80 hp. At RM 7,400, it was relatively expensive, and its assembly line version was able to go 150 km per hour (93 mph).

Beside the two-seater roadster, there were other German bodies, the most well-known of which are the two aerodynamic coupes produced by Wendler in Reutlingen. The BMW 328, 464 of which were manufactured up to 1940, was a successful sports car, both before and after the war, that was suitable for very demanding pilots. After the war such manufacturers as Veritas and Bristol built new models based on the BMW 328.

The most famous 328 is the MM. In 1939 BMW asked the Milan car body builder Touring to make the so-called Superleggera (superlight) body on the 328 chassis in order to participate in the 24 Hours race at Le Mans. But in any case, the 328 MM celebrated its greatest victory at the Mille Miglia (hence the two 'Ms' for the 328 model) race in 1940. For the first time, this race was run on a short course (it was usually held on public roads, from Brescia to Rome and back). Huschke von Hanstein and Walter Bäumer won convincingly. In all BMW had entered five cars in this race, two Coupé Tourings and three Roadsters, one of the latter coming in third. These racing versions of the 328 had an output of 120 hp and could go as fast as 220 km per hour (137 mph).

The past models of the 328, the 327 and especially the 326, were, at least from a sales point of view, much more successful than the 328. The 326, a sedan, 15.936 units were sold between 1936 and 1941. The 327, which was launched in 1937 as a convertible and in 1938 as a coupe, had the same 1.9 liter (50 hp) six cylinders as the 326, but its body was noticeably improved. A shorter, boxed chassis with torsion bar springs on the back axis, which was guided by a leaf spring underneath and hydraulic breaks.

Der erfolgreiche de

utsche Sportwagen

Top and bottom left
The BMW 327 was the coupe version of the 326, presented in 1936; it was launched in 1938. However, as early as 1937, there was a beautiful convertible with the same name. The 327 was propelled by a 1.9 liter six cylinder. The 327 was based on a boxed element chassis, which was slightly shorter compared to the 326 and was equipped with elastic torsion bars, a new concept compared to the rear axis. Notice the hidden spare wheel.

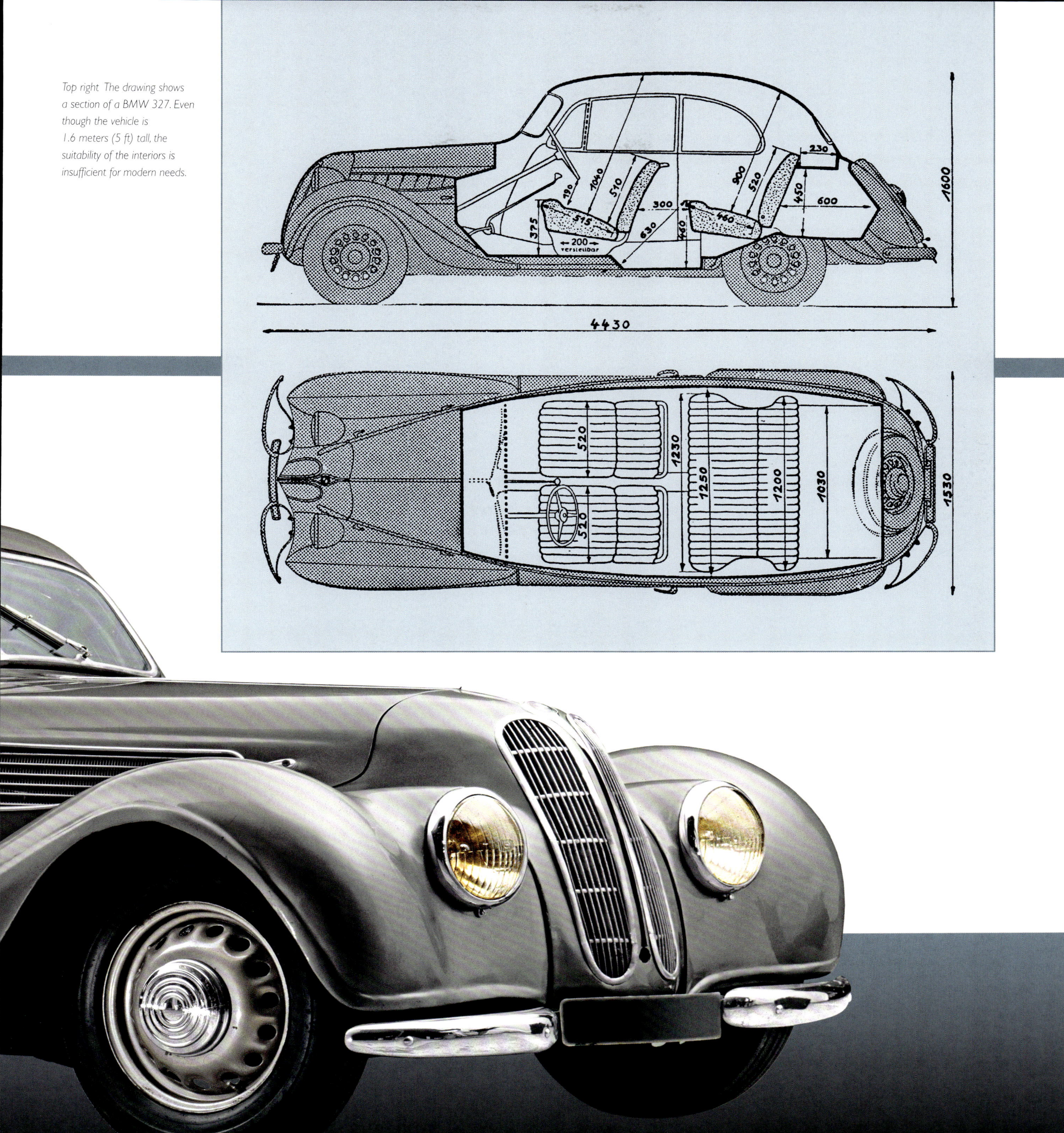

Top right The drawing shows a section of a BMW 327. Even though the vehicle is 1.6 meters (5 ft) tall, the suitability of the interiors is insufficient for modern needs.

The situation was becoming grim in Germany, and people no longer invested their money in luxury cars or powerful sports cars. Even the ambitious project for the KdF model (which became the VW Beetle after the war) was put aside. Instead, Ferdinand Porsche was commissioned in 1938 to continue to work on the KdF for military purposes. The plan was quite clear. It was to weigh 550 kg (1212 lbs.), have a 400 kg (882 lbs.) load, low production costs and the possibility of large-scale production. At the end of 1939 the first prototypes were ready. The typical angular body design and the reclining windshield were features that arrived with later prototypes, which were named Type 62. After the ground clearance and the engine torque were increased, the commanders of the Wehrmacht ordered the production of the vehicle, which in the early 1940s was called Type 82.

But why was the Type 82 called Kübelwagen? The lightweight off-road vehicle used for military purposes often did without doors to limit the weight to the utmost. So, in order to prevent the passengers from falling during the ride, the designers created very low bucket seats. In German, *Kübel* means bucket, hence the name. The famous VW field vehicle had only one small aesthetic drawback. It had doors, and the seats were not bucket-shaped but rather stuffed over a spring frame.

The Type 82 was powered by an air-cooled engine with 985 cc displacement that had an output of 23.5 hp. It was also lightweight, and the power was exploited to the full. The Kübelwagen met all the requirements of an off-road vehicle even without a four-wheel drive. Yet, during the war a 4x4 version was produced, the Type 87. In 1943 the Kübelwagen was equipped with a slightly more powerful motor (1.131 cc displacement, 24.5 hp). From 1940 to 1945 about 52,000 Kübelwagens were manufactured.

The Second World War was just around the corner, and in the late 1930s many automobile companies felt the impact of the difficult situation. One of these firms was Wanderer. In 1885 Johann Baptist Winklhofer and Richard Adolf Jaenicke had established a bicycle repair shop in Chemnitz. Two years later they began to make bicycles on their own, in 1902 they started producing motorcycles and the following year they began production of typewriters (Continental), while in 1905 they presented their first prototype of an automobile, the Wanderermobil. Actual automobile manufacturing had to wait until 1913, but the car was an immediate and great success. The Wanderer 5/12 PS W1 rapidly became extremely popular with the public, which fondly called it the *Puppchen* (little doll) as a tribute to an operetta by Jean Gilbert that was the rage at the time. The Puppchen was only 1.5 m (5 ft) wide and three meters (10 ft) long. Over the years the small Wanderer was constantly improved and continued to be produced until 1930. At that time it was known as the W8 5/20 PS. Naturally, Ferdinand Porsche was called upon to design the next model. Wanderer was very ambitious, so that Porsche decided to build one six-cylinder and two eight-cylinder engines, but only the former, which was entirely made of light metal, was actually produced with the name W14. Then came the Great Depression and Wanderer was bought by the Auto-Union AG, which was established in 1932 as an amalgamation of Audi, DKW, Horch and, of course, Wanderer. In this combination of firms, Wanderer was responsible for the mid-price sector. In 1935 the W21, a direct competitor of the highly appreciated Mercedes V170, arrived on the market. Up to the W24 (and many other models, since the names of the Wanderer cars caused quite a lot of confusion), the elegant automobiles had a 2.6-liter engine with six cylinders in line and a power output of 60 hp and more. The most attractive and longed-for model was a two-seater Cabriolet known as W52k, a name that is difficult to define and classify.

Wanderer also produced racing cars that performed rather well in the long Liege-Rome-Liege race, one of the most important in the period just before World War Two. Wanderer participated in this race with its roadster, the Stromlinie Spezial Sportwagen, and in 1939 won the coveted team qualification. For years this remained one of the last important victories of the German automotive manufacturers.

The Wanderer, here at the 1931 International Motor Show in Berlin (in the forefront, a W11 Cabriolet with a six cylinder 2.5 liter), was one the many auto brands that never survived World War II.

WANDERER
14
14 WANDERER 14
ADLER
16
16 ADLER 16
PEUGEOT
SEEGERS
GLASER
CONTINENTAL RECORD

CHAPTER 4

The Beginning of a Miracle

The Speedster version of the 356 (here from 1957), was designed for the American market where it was incredibly successful. Today these 1500's are the most expensive collection of vehicles of the 356 series.

Germany had lost the Second World War: in 1945, at the end of the conflict, the country was completely devastated by bombs. The production capacity of the German industry in 1946 was only 30 percent compared to that in 1938. In addition, after the war, all production facilities in the east were lost: Opel had to give up its plant in Berlin, BMW that in Eisenach and DKW lost the one in Zschopau. In 1945 the annual production of the automobile industry amounted to just 1,293 units.

It took a few more years before the country could get back on its feet. Help came from the United States in 1947, when a secure ally was needed against the newly formed Eastern bloc: Germany availed itself of the best of the Marshall Plan, namely the aid earmarked for the reconstruction of European countries destroyed by war. The production embargo was lifted only in 1949 and by 1951 Germany had already produced 276,622 automobiles.

Between 1950 and 1964, industrial production in Germany actually increased by 185 per cent, thanks largely to the automobile industry. In 1953, production surpassed one million cars for the first time. The millionth VW Beetle saw light of day as early as 1955, just 10 years after the end of the war. It was a special version with a gold color. The year before Germany won the football world championship in Switzerland, the German people thought "we are back to being someone." It was the signal for new German awareness. It also highlighted another issue: in 1952 only 9.6 percent of newly manufactured cars were bought by private German customers, and in 1960 this percentage had risen to 49.9 percent. In the same year the German automobile industry produced 2,052,881 vehicles. Not only did "Made in Germany" vehicles have a good reputation worldwide, they were also very competitive at an international level because the manufacturing plants built after the war were decidedly modern and had highly motivated staff. In Germany, in the early sixties, almost one job in ten was related in some way to the automobile industry. In the fifties the German

automobile industry also obtained great results in terms of export.

In any event having a car was no longer enough. Driving was not as important as what was being driven. Those who achieved success wanted to show it, to differentiate themelves from those who, maybe after a lifetime of savings, had been able to afford a VW Beetle. During the fifties, German manufacturers were at the point of modifying vehicles every year, even if just a little. The true connoisseur would have been able to understand if a model was a new car or a used vehicle. The pressure to purchase a new vehicle each year became the need of a particular primary social stratum: a "social model" already very popular in the thirties.

In 1950, the German automobile industry was known abroad mainly thanks to the VW Beetle and other inexpensive products, certainly very distant from the initial car models or from the thirties, when the "Made in Germany" car was considered to be the most precious and sought-after vehicle. Even in sports it took many years before the German manufacturers were able to enjoy success. At the end of the fifties however, Germany was once again a leader in the automotive field. Vehicles such as the Mercedes 300 SL or the BMW 507 were amongst the most sought-after products among connoisseurs and enthusiasts, and the Porsche brand quickly realized that success in sports could be a great advertising vehicle for a small company.

In 1953, Mercedes finally launched a vehicle with Ponton chassis, the 180 (W120/W121), which initially received a cold welcome from the still conservative clientele.

The vehicle now known as the VW Beetle has had a long history. In 1925 the Hungarian engineer Béla Barényi had a detailed plan in mind to build a common car. A certain Josef Ganz also made an important contribution to this effort in the twenties, but, it has never been possible to ascertain the true extent of his contribution. The real father of the German "Volkswagen" (the people's car) is certainly Ferdinand Porsche, who was not only behind it, but was personally charged by Adolf Hitler with the task of designing this vehicle and putting it into production.

Porsche had thought for a long time about manufacturing a compact economy car. In 1931 he designed one for Zündapp, but the car was never produced. In 1933 NSU united with Porsche in an effort to work towards the same objective. The Neckarshulm company was not as demanding towards the Austrian engineer as Zündapp, and thus Porsche once again had the opportunity to devote himself to the idea of an air-cooled rear engine. Three prototypes were built and tests were performed in 1934 with very encouraging results.

In 1933 Porsche was charged personally by Adolf Hitler with the task of building a "Volkswagen." On 17 January 1934, a detailed plan was presented, and on 22 June 1934, a contract was signed with the association of the automobile industry, for the construction of a prototype which had to be completed within 10 months. Porsche failed to comply fully with the terms, but at the end of February 1936, the people of Berlin were presented with two models: a sedan (V1) and a convertible (V2), in a commercial area of Daimler-Benz.

These vehicles (plus three other cars - the so-called VW Series 3 - built in the body shop in the private quarters of Porsche) were inspired by the prototypes that Porsche had built for NSU and already revealed the appearance of the future Beetle. They were equipped with boxer engines. The VW series 3 was subjected to detailed testing. The results were positive and so Daimler-Benz went on to build pre-series vehicles (29 sedans and a convertible), which successfully travelled a total distance of 2.4 million kilometers (1,5 million mi.)!

Then at the beginning of 1938, Karosseriewerk Reutler produced the pre-series VW 38 with a body made entirely in steel, with front door stop seals, front and rear bumpers and the famous "Pretzel" shaped window ("two piece"). This vehicle had a central tubular chassis with a sheet steel base torsion beam suspension, and was propelled by a four-cylinder, four-stroke, air-cooled boxer engine, which went up to 24 hp with a capacity of 985 cubic cm. (60 cubic in.) The tare was about 750 kg (1653 lbs.).

On 26 May 1938, Adolf Hitler laid the inaugural stone at the Volkswagen plant in what is today Wolfsburg. It was not possible however, to mass produce the Beetle anymore at the time, since the plant had to dedicate itself to producing materials for war. In its place, cross-country and amphibious vehicles were being built. Production resumed immediately at the end of the war. Despite the massive damage caused by war, the first "Bretzelkafer" (standard sedan, model 11) was delivered in 1946 and in 1948 production was in full swing. In 1955 it had already been possible to deliver the millionth Volkswagen. But where had the name Beetle come from? It was the *New York Times* which wrote in 1938 of "millions and millions of small shiny Beetles, which were soon to populate the German highways." The nickname had been borrowed from the U.S. (Beetle or Bug) in the fifties. In Italy, VW used the name "Maggiolino" from 1961, while in Germany it was named Kafer when another model, the VW 1500 (Type 3) was introduced to the market.

Bottom left Starting in 1931, Porsche put himself as chief of the design department in Stuttgart. A few years went by before a Porsche vehicle was launched in the market. This picture portrays him working on the Beetle.

Right This VW Beetle, which only existed as the Type 1 back then, was born as early as 1938-1939. World War II blocked any possibility of producing this incredible vehicle in series.

Left Adolf Hitler and Ferdinand Porsche at Hitler's fiftieth birthday celebrations, in April 1939. Porsche was already at the service of Hitler to design an "automobile for the people."

Right On 26 May 1938, in Fallersleben, after a 15-minute inaugural speech, Adolf Hitler laid the first brick of the "KdF" automobile city. The site was rechristened Wolfsburg only after the war.

Hauptamt

Top left Despite the destruction brought on by the war, production in Wolfsburg was back on track as early as 1946 and in 1948 it was in full production. This picture is from 1954.

Bottom right This 1952 Beetle, Deluxe edition was destined to be exported. Between 1946 and 2003 (end of production in Mexico) a whopping total of 21.529.646 Type 1 models were built.

Top center The picture shows the Norwegian cargo "Havfalk" in August 1950. Beetles being exported to the US are about to be loaded on a ship in the Hamburg harbor. The Beetle was a huge success in the United States.

Top right Many companies happily adopted the Beetle, as shown in this ad by the radio equipment producer Telefunken in 1951. The VW was the perfect symbol of the German economic miracle.

TELEFUNKEN
Autosuper
lassen jede Autofahrt zur Freude und Erholung werden
Auto-Spitzensuper mit 6 Röhren 6 Kreisen und 1 Z
Saugkreis und Auto-Mittelklassensuper mit 5 Röhren
6 Kreisen sind mit und ohne Drucktastenabstimmung liefer
bar und haben Einbaumöglichkeiten in viele Wagen
typen. Ihre hohe Empfangsempfindlichkeit, ihre Trenn
schärfe und naturgetreue Wiedergabe, die einem Heim
super in nichts nachstehen, werden auch Sie begeistern
TELE FUN KEN
Halle
Stand 21

In addition to the Type 1 model, VW also produced the Type 2 model "the Bulli" starting from 1950 which became almost as popular as the Beetle. It was already called by this name in 1949 when the first model was celebrated behind the closed doors of the plant. Today nobody remembers where this nickname originated from. We know, however, who the spiritual father of this model was and the story goes like this: Ben Pon, a Dutch importer of VW was walking through the Wolfsburg factory one day in April 1947 when he saw a strange vehicle, assembled by workers to transport heavy pieces. Pon immediately drew a couple of sketches and it took little to convince the then chairman of VW, Heinrich Nordhoff, to build a vehicle of the type. The "Bulli" was a remake of the Beetle in the sense that instead of the central support platform, a lateral steel structure had been used. The engine reached 24.5 hp just like that of the Beetle, but the payload reached a good 750 pounds. Production began on 8 March 1950, initially with ten units a day. The vehicle was available only in blue and grey. Demand grew so quickly that soon VW realized that it had hit the jackpot. In 1951, the Samba bus was introduced, intended exclusively for the transportation of passengers (it soon became a cult object in California). Then in 1952, the pick-up was presented (also with double cab from 1958). In 1956, the Transporter, the official name of the "Bulli", began to be produced in a new factory in Hanover. 1.8 million units of the "Bulli" were produced up until 1967.

It was much more than a vehicle intended for transportation. In the fifties it became the symbol of German revival and economic miracle, perhaps even more so than the Beetle. It was not fast but extremely safe and reliable. It was used by many; the post office, the police, firefighters, hospitals, even railroads (there were even some transporters with a frame built specifically for the train track).

The VW minibus, called Type 2 within the company, reached the market in 1950 and obviously recalled the Beetle. The shape of its unmistakable design was the work of the Dutch VW importer, Ben Pon.

Top left Starting in 1957 the Rekord lost the Olympia name. In the beginning, it was the P1 (until 1960), then the P2 (until 1963), and then, quite illogically, the A, shown here in an ad poster.

Bottom left During World War II the production facility of Opel in Rüsselsheim was destroyed almost to its foundations. In any case, as a General Motors affiliate, Opel enjoyed special treatment during the post-war period.

Bottom center The Opel Olympia Rekord was presented for the first time in 1953 at the International Motor Show in Frankfurt. Compared to its predecessors, the new Opel, thanks to its modern Ponton chassis, was a veritable revelation. Sales were good.

Right In December 1947, a new edition was born, based on the Olympia which was already presented in 1935, and was produced until 1953 with no significant modifications. Even its successor was called Olympia, to which the tag "Rekord" was added.

The intention was to show off what they had, and nothing suited this purpose better than a car. In 1953 the German "economic miracle" began to blossom and the automobile industry managed to make the biggest profit ever. In 1950, Opel was able to reopen its factories in Rüsselsheim and the concept of "social market economy" was understood by families seeking comfortable and possibly more spacious vehicles.

Inspired by the Olympia and already presented as early as 1935, the Opel Rekord Olympia was introduced to the market in 1953. The nose which resembled a shark, immediately caught the eye. In summer, when work was resumed after the holidays, a slightly modified model was presented. Some American techniques had also made their way to the German automobile industry, and it was no wonder that Opel was the first to embrace them. The brand had already belonged to General Motors since 1929 and in 1931 the company was entirely absorbed by the Americans. The Opel family had earned 33.3 million dollars from the transaction.

In 1957, it was the turn of the Rekord P1. Hans Mersheimer, the chief designer at the time (which back then was still known as a "craftsman"). He had a European, and thus smaller version in mind, of the Chevrolet Bel Air, and the results turned out to be great. The car had a slightly unusual appearance because of the negative inclination of the wheels. And there was not much under the hood: 45 hp with a 1.5 liter engine had to suffice.

The Rekord was also produced in a kombi (station wagon) version in 1958. This model was called Caravan, once again thanks to the American influence. "It is a car and a van." Obviously the Caravan was much loved by artisans who could use it for private and business purposes. The P1 was produced only until 1960 and then quickly transformed to the P2 because GM imposed very tight deadlines. This turned out to be a success, too. After the VW Beetle, the Rekord was the second best-selling car in Germany in the fifties.

OPEL

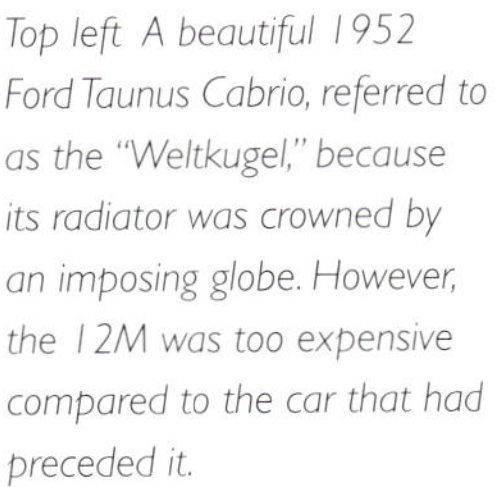

Top left A beautiful 1952 Ford Taunus Cabrio, referred to as the "Weltkugel," because its radiator was crowned by an imposing globe. However, the 12M was too expensive compared to the car that had preceded it.

Top center A photo from 1958 shows the final controls on a Ford Taunus 12M in Köln-Niehl. In eight years 250,000 Taunus 12M were produced – certainly not a huge amount when compared to its competitor, the Beetle.

Bottom center Köln-Niehl again, the Ford plant, and once again the Taunus 12M but this time we are in the paintwork unit. The "M" in the name stands for "Meisterstück" (masterpiece); Ford initially wanted to call this Ford, the "Hunsrück."

Ford Europe, a subsidiary of the American company favored at the political level, was able to resume production as early as 1948. At the beginning there was the "Buckeltaunus", a model which had already been produced between 1939 and 1942. In 1952, however, the "Weltkugeltaunus" was introduced to the market, which with its innovative pontoon body caused a great sensation. The Taunus 12 M was so called because the front was decorated with a stylized map of the world. Initially it was equipped with a 1.2- liter four-cylinder 38 hp engine. Later a 1.5- liter 55 hp version was added, called 15 M. The Weltkugeltaunus was available as a two-door sedan, a three-door station wagon and as a convertible with Deutsch bodywork (Borgward and Opel also built the convertible version). The letter M stood for "Meisterstück" (masterpiece). In 1959 the world map was taken away but new rear headlights were added.

The successor, P4, was hardly a masterpiece. The vehicle was designed in America to compete with the VW Beetle. But the first front wheel drive Ford did not have particularly good luck: the transversal arms were mounted directly on the engine; which therefore had to take on a function for which the design was not appropriate. Ford was not so fortunate with the two-door coupe version of the Taunus P4 produced between 1962 and 1966 either. The roof of this two-door which was unsightly in proportion, had been ordered from France and was 15 mm (0,59 in.) shorter. The launch of the vehicle was delayed by several months.

Inspired by the Taunus, a van called Transit was produced in 1953. It was designed by Albert Haesner, who had already taken part in the design of the VW Bulli. Unlike the VW Transporter it had a front engine, which had a much larger loading area than that of the German competitor. The first Transit however had a reputation for being unreliable, noisy, and badly cushioned. The Transit was far more successful in England than in Germany, where it was certainly overshadowed by the Transporter.

Isabella is a unique name for a car. It is said that

Right Ford models were known as Taunus as early as in 1939. Here we see an ad from 1958, when Ford was the rage with the so-called "Streifen-Taunus." The 15M was finally equipped with a more powerful engine.

8 P 002

K-EH 390

TAUNUS 17 M DM 6650.– a.W., DM 7090.– a.W. viertürig

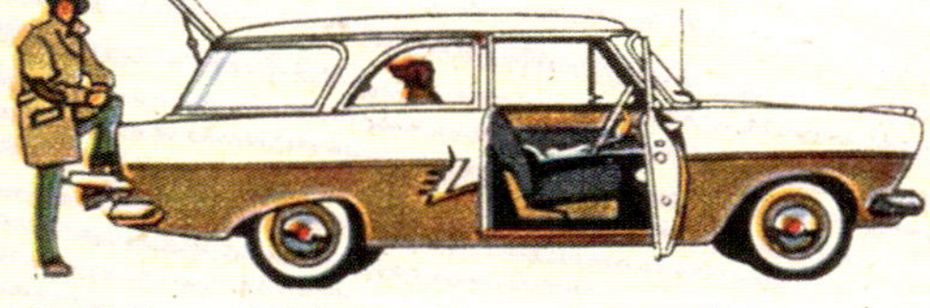

TAUNUS 17 M KOMBI – Dieser elegante Mehrzweckwagen bietet Komfort und Bequemlichkeit für fünf Personen oder - immer wie Sie es brauchen - eine Ladefläche von 1,8 qm. Er beweist zugleich, daß auch ein Kombi die Eleganz eines Personenwagens bieten kann.

TAUNUS 12 M · TAUNUS 12 M KOMBI ● TAUNUS 15 M · TAUNUS 15 M KOMBI ● TAUNUS 17 M · TAUNUS 17 M (4 türig) · TAUNUS 17 M KOMBI TAUNUS 17 M de Luxe · TAUNUS 17 M de Luxe (4 türig) · TAUNUS 17 M de Luxe KOMBI

Das Automobil Ihrer Wünsche - gebaut von **FORD**

Bottom center "It doesn't matter to me, you can even call it Isabella," is what the chief of the company, C.F.W. Borgward is believed to have said to whoever asked for a name for his new creation. And that's how this beautiful car got a beautiful name.

when the owner of CFW Borgward was asked what name to use, to keep the prototypes still a secret, he replied, "for me it is the same, put down Isabella." However in 1954 the car was introduced to the market with the name Hansa 1500. It was christened Isabella Borgward only later, in 1957. This was also the beginning of a revival in 1954 because when the car came on the market after a design phase of only 10 months, some children's diseases broke out and quickly spoilt the appetite of potential customers.

The reason for the enthusiastic reception of Isabella was primarily its design and some technical goodies. The front suspension was equipped with double transversal arms with helical springs and stabilizers, which at the time were installed only in race cars. The four speed transmission was fully synchronized, and the clutch was operated by a hydraulic system. And the price was DM 7,265 which was certainly more than that of an Opel Rekord or a Ford Taunus, but this was altogether a different experience with its elegant and free-standing body. The Mercedes 180, which, unlike the Borgward, was not particularly beautiful or technically advanced, cost much more at the time.

In 1955 Borgward added a station wagon and a very beautiful convertible to the product line. Then the TS model was added with 75 hp instead of the original 60 hp. The convertible was not a particularly successful vehicle.; It was certainly beautiful, but the car was not rigid enough. It therefore had to be modified, which lead to an increase in the price and weight. In 1957 a wonderful coupe was introduced to the market that the Germans also turned into a convertible, but at DM 17,000, the price was outrageous for the time! In 1961 the Borgward group declared bankruptcy. A couple of other models of the Isabella were built up to 1962. In all, a total of 202,862 units were produced, now in great demand by fans.

Top left The Opel Kapitän, on the market since 1958, was a good example of how German manufacturers were getting closer to American standards of greatness, tailfins included.

The economic miracle, however, called for other bigger, more impressive, more prestigious cars. In the fifties many had made a fortune. From the moment that families living in the suburbs were not able to afford cars, a certain clientele wanted to show off the fact that well-being could be obtained by using automobiles.One of the vehicles already targeted to the highest social classes shortly after the war was the Opel Kapitän. The first post-war model, offered from autumn 1948, was again inspired by the Kapitän and presented in 1939 at a world premiere at the Geneva Motor Show. The design was slightly adapted to the trends of the time. This was followed by continual changes with chrome parts being continually added and the engine becoming inreasingly powerful. The Kapitän 51 was a much loved status symbol, and was for a time in third place in terms of sales after the Beetle and the Opel Rekord in Germany. The Kapitän underwent a total restyling for the first time in autumn 1953, when it received a pontoon body and a unique radiator grill resembling shark teeth. From November 1953 to July 1955, 61,543 models of the 68 hp version had been produced.

Beginning in 1958, the American dream was identified by the Opel Kapitän P 2.5, which, like the Cadillac and Chevrolet, featured a wide panoramic windscreen. The car was then driven by a 2.5 liter 80 hp engine. However, the "Schlüsselloch-Kapitän" was already replaced in 1959 by the P 2.6, which had a markedly flatter design and European style. The power was increased to 90 hp, which allowed the Opel to reach 150 km/h (93 mph). In just over three years, almost 146,000 models had been sold.

In 1964, a tier above the Kapitan, Opel's upper segment was enriched by the Admiral and the Diplomat which shared the body design and partly the engines as well. The Kapitän had represented entry into the upper segment and the Diplomat, with its 4.6-liter 90 hp V8 engine (a Chevrolet production) was the right model. The Diplomat was also produced in a coupe version, manufactured by Karmann in Osnabrück. This variation was even equipped with a 5.4- liter V8 engine. However, only 347 models were manufactured. With this car, Opel had made its entry to the major segment.

Top In the 50s the product range that BMW offered for its upper segment was amazing, ranging from the 501 to 507. However, BMW did not get rich with these vehicles, it was actually on the brink of failure.

Bottom center The BMW 501 (two liters, six cylinder, 65 hp), presented in 1952, had a rather weak motorization, therefore the Bavarian manufacturer added the 502 in 1952, that pumped out 100 hp with its 2.6 liter V8.

In 1952, BMW also made an attempt in the upper class, with the 501 model, whose 6-cylinder in-line engine with a capacity of 2 liters reached 65 hp. It was not much for the propulsion of a modern sedan, and was christened by people as the "baroque angel." The 4.73 meter (15 feet) long car could barely reach 130 km/h (81 mph) after a very long acceleration time. It was for this reason that in 1954 the 502 was introduced, whose 2.6- liter V8 engine going up to 100 hp pushed the BMW to 160 km/h (99 mph). This version was also used by police and firefighters, and one unit was even transformed into an ambulance.

However, the BMW 501/502, with its subsequent variations in coupe and convertible versions, did not record big sales success for the brand from Monaco. In the twelve years of production, only 23,000 models were manufactered, perhaps because the BMWs, with their prices between DM 11,500 and DM 22,000, were too expensive even for the upwardly-mobile Germans. Inspired by the 501/502, the legendary 507 (Roadster), the underrated 503 (convertible), and the rather odd Bertone CS 3200 were produced. Another variation, the 505, never even arrived at the assembly line. This 5.1m long limousine was conceived as a competitor of the Mercedes 300. It is said that the then Federal Chancellor, Konrad Adenauer, had lost his hat getting into the BMW and after that had remained faithful to Mercedes. The bar, the intercom and folding desk for writing served no purpose. Two models of the 505 were produced and that was the end of it.

The "Baroque angel" almost ruined BMW. In 1959, BMW was about to be taken over by Mercedes, but the small shareholders and the Quandt family prevented this from happening. As a gesture of gratitude, Quandt received a unique piece, a Bertone CS 3200 convertible, certainly not a big loss for BMW because the 8-cylinder Bertones were certainly not meant for sale.

Bottom right The design of the BMW 503 clearly shows its American influence (as well as the desire to comply to overseas markets). It was a large, delegation car. Its engine system, with its modern V8, was more than enough.

In those difficult years, the brand from Monaco was able to survive on its economy cars. After the failure of the 501/502, BMW did not have any more liquidity, but knew that their best chance was increasing production of vehicles of very contained dimensions, such as that of the Messerschmitt or the Goggomobil. A design of their own was just out of the question because of the lack of funds, however, BMW had had good experiences in the past with manufacturing under license. The solution came from Italy. Renzo Rivolta, the head of the motorcycle factory Iso Rivolta (which would later produce interesting automobiles also) had built an unusual car with front door stop seals. The Iso-Isetta had the appearance of a refrigerator on wheels - which was not by pure chance. Before Rivolta, the company had actually produced refrigerators. BMW bought the license and optimized the Isetta by mounting among other things, a single-cylinder engine of their own design (the company had experience, produced motorcycles). On 5 March, the BMW Isetta was presented to the public. The price was about DM 2,580. The company from Monaco did not stabilize, but managed to gain time. Between 1955 and 1962 the "Motorcoupé" sold a good 162,000 units.

In 1957 a version with four seats, the BMW 600, came on the market which, in addition to the front door, also had a side door and a rear bench. This version was propelled by a 19.5 hp engine with two cylinders.

In terms of sales of these cabin scooters, only one company was more successful, Glas with its Goggomobil. The Goggo was not a cabin scooter like the Isetta or Messerschmitt, but it was a very small sized sedan with four seats and a two-stroke two cylinder engine. It was introduced to the market a few weeks before the BMW Isetta, and was slightly more expensive (DM 3,500). Up to 1969 a total of 284,491 units were produced.

The first cabin scooter was the Messerschmitt which arrived on the market as early as January 1953 in the KR 175 version. The manufacturer of the vehicle was Fritz M. Fend, who had planned the vehicle for a single seat. The Messerschmitt still wanted to build only two seaters, thus leading to the birth of these cabin scooters - technically quite complicated - with their aerodynamic shape, the two front wheels and only a single wheel and the engine in the rear. One could get into it by raising a Plexiglas dome. The KR 175 cost only DM 2,100. Twelve thousand pieces were produced in 1955; not enough to prevent failure. In the postwar years, there were many other small German cars on the scene. One of them was the Lloyd LP300, with the body initially in plywood covered with artificial leather. Its nickname was "flash of scotch tape." The public said, "He who is not afraid to die drives a Lloyd." Between 1950 and 1963, 170,000 units of the small Lloyd were produced, in the most disparate variations (LP 300, LP 400, LP 600, and Alexander).

The Kleinschnittger, a far less fortunate model but with a similar design, was introduced to the market in 1950. It looked like a toy car. The car was propelled by a 125 cm3 engine with just 6 hp. One oddity was that the Kleinschnittger had no reverse gear. The vehicle was extremely light, it could be turned by raising it.

Top left *At the 1956 Earls Court Motor Show in the London the Goggomobil had the honor of being visited by the actress and future writer Jackie Collins, posing here in a leopard guise on a T300.*

Top center *The 600, like the small Isetta, was propelled by an elaborate motorcycle engine (from a R60) which produced 19.5 hp. Once again the ad plays with the 'dream-car' concept.*

Right The Isetta, produced from 1955 on, was immediately called the "Knutschkugel" (love nest) by the people, and rarely has a nickname been so appropriate. The Isetta was propelled by a 0.25 l motorcycle engine.

The most famous car before the advent of direct injection was certainly the Mercedes 300 SL. Let's go back to 1951. In that year, Mercedes-Benz decided to participate in competitive sports again. First, of course, it had to construct the car. The engine, a six-cylinder in-line 3-liter one, was already available – it came from W186. The power was increased, and the engine was mounted horizontally tilted to the left to an angle of fifty degrees. The four-speed transmission connected to it came from the 300 model. It was robust but for an engine, not exactly light.

Nothing could be done about the weight of the engine and transmission of the W194. Even the axles, borrowed from the 300, were made of steel, and so, to optimize the weight, other factors had to be looked at. The only possible interventions could be on the body and the chassis. Mercedes resurrected the idea of a light tubular frame. Thus a lightweight tubular lattice frame was created, composed of very thin tubes joined in a triangular formation. It was resistant to torsion and subjected to stress testing of thrust and traction only. It weighed only fifty kilograms and became a distinct sign of not only the W194 and the mass-produced version made in 1954 (W198), but also of the luckiest race cars of 1954-55. For a tubular lattice frame to be very stable, it must be designed to provide the greatest room possible in the passenger area. This need led to the birth of the famous doors like the wings of a gull. In 1952 the W194 participated for the first time in a race coming second to the Mille Miglia. In the 24 hour Le Mans, it won a legendary victory. The SL 300, its sporty version, also won the Carrera Panamericana, the most difficult competition at the time.

Mass production of the 300 SL was not anticipated but Maximilian "Maxi" Hoffman, the American importer of Mercedes-Benz, had long sought a sporty car for its customers. The sporty coupe race car obviously made for a good start. After very careful evaluation, the decision for mass production was made in favor of the street version of the 300 SL (W198). At the same time, it was announced that a smaller roadster, the 190 SL (R121), would be produced. Not even six months had passed after the decision of the Board of Directors that the two sports cars were already celebrating their "premiere" at the International Motor Sports Show, held in New York from 6 to14 February in 1954. In August 1954, production of a "car with wings" began in Sindelfingen.

Mercedes never imagined a series production of the W194. Yet Maxi Hoffmann, the American importer, kept insisting on a sports car to contrast the stern conservative image of Mercedes. The Mercedes 300 SL with its gull-wing doors (W194) was probably the last European dream car of the 50s. It wasn't just the gull-wing doors that were out of the ordinary, but even its direct injection engine, and besides, it was one of the first race cars to be used on regular roads.

300 SL
Überlegener Sieg
im Großen Jubiläumspreis vom Nürburgring
für Sportwagen
1. Hermann Lang, 2. Karl Kling, 3. Fritz Riess, 4. Theo Helfrich
alle auf Mercedes-Benz Typ 300 SL
Hermann Lang fährt die schnellste Runde mit 131,5 km/std und
MERCEDES-BENZ
722

Top left The German postwar audience had to wait many years after the war before German cars would be successful in racing. The ad celebrates the victory of four 300 SL drivers on the Nürburgring in 1952.

Right The last Grand Prix of the 1955 season took place on 11 September on the new track in Monza. Manuel Fangio won after a tough battle against Stirling Moss (who then retired), both on Mercedes W196.

Bottom left The 1955 Mercedes-Benz 300 SLR is one of the most legendary race cars of all times. With this car Stirling Moss won the Mille Miglia in 1955; the staring number 722 corresponds to the starting number in Brescia.

The BMW 507 came more than a year after the Mercedes 300, and was not quite as lucky as the car with wings from Stuttgart. Indeed, in those years it contributed to serious financial difficulties for BMW. Between 1956 and 1959 only 251 units were produced. But the Bavarian company was still considered by experts and enthusiasts to be an authentic icon in the history of the automobile. This was partly because at the time there were many celebrities such as Elvis Presley, Alain Delon, the pilot John Surtess and the "bond-girl" Ursula Andress, who owned this DM 26,500car. More importantly it was for the glory of the name and the creator of the unique design of the 507, Albrecht Grad von Goertz (to be more precise, Albrecht Graf von Schlitz gen Von Görtz and von Wrisberg, from 1914 to 2006). Goertz was not a designer by profession. After arriving in the United States in 1936 he had begun to work on washing machines, but his talent emerged quickly. After the Second World War, he got to know Raymond Loewy who hired him for Studebaker. The two did not agree on much, so Goertz started on his own and in 1953 BMW gave him the responsibility for designing the 503 and 507 models inspired by the 501/502. The second masterpiece of Goertz was the Nissan 240Z, which came on the market in 1969. To remember the great achievement of Goertz, he worked on the top M5 and M6 models and enabled them to reach 507 hp.

The 507 Roadster had a 3.2 liter V8 engine that delivered 150 hp. It was not a bad engine. The weight of the vehicle with an aluminum body only amounted to 1,250 kilograms, much less than that of its competitor, the Merceded 300 SL. Today the 507s have become the most sought after BMWs by collectors. There was also another famous designer who worked on the BMW with the 3.2 liter V8 engine: Giovanni Michelotti. His BMW 3200 Vignale Michelotti, which was the first made in 1959, remains a unique piece.

Another vehicle came on the market in 1955 whose design; even when there was talk of a prototype, was so compelling that the then head of VW, Heinrich Nordhoff, only took a few hours to decide to produce the car without making any changes. We are talking about the VW Karmann Ghia. The car, known in the company as a Type 14 model, was the idea of Wilhelm Karmann. In 1951 he spoke for the first time to Nordhoff about the possibility of producing a sporty coupe inspired by the VW Beetle. But the first designs were not exciting, the model 14, especially the front, strongly resembled the Type 11 model. Then Luigi Segre entered the picture (at that time Segre worked at the Ghia bodyshop of Turin) and his designs convinced Karmann immediately and, as already mentioned, even Nordhoff. Karmann set up an assembly line in Osnabrück and on July 14,

1955 the vehicle was presented to the press. The reception was not encouraging though; "the parody of a race car," wrote the important magazine 'Auto, Motor und Sport'. This whim was not exactly cheap. The coupe featuring an air-cooled, four-cylinder 30 hp engine cost DM 7,500, a lot of money for those times. But the public loved the Karmann Ghia, which in some sense embodied the dream of the sports car for the average man. Starting from 1957, a light convertible version also saw the light of day.

At the same time as the plant in Osnabrueck, Karmann opened a second plant in Brazil in 1960, where along with the Type 14 model, production began on the bigger Type 34 model which however never had the same luck as that of the smaller version. Production was to cease a little after 42,000 units were made. Instead, Model 14 was built in Brazil and Osnabrück until 31 July 1974, after a total of 443,478 units (between coupe and convertible) left the assembly line.

The Karmann Ghia represents, more than any other German car, that shining symbol of rebirth in Germany. People dreamed of owning a Mercedes 300 SL or a BMW 507, but then bought a Karmann Ghia which was more accessible financially.

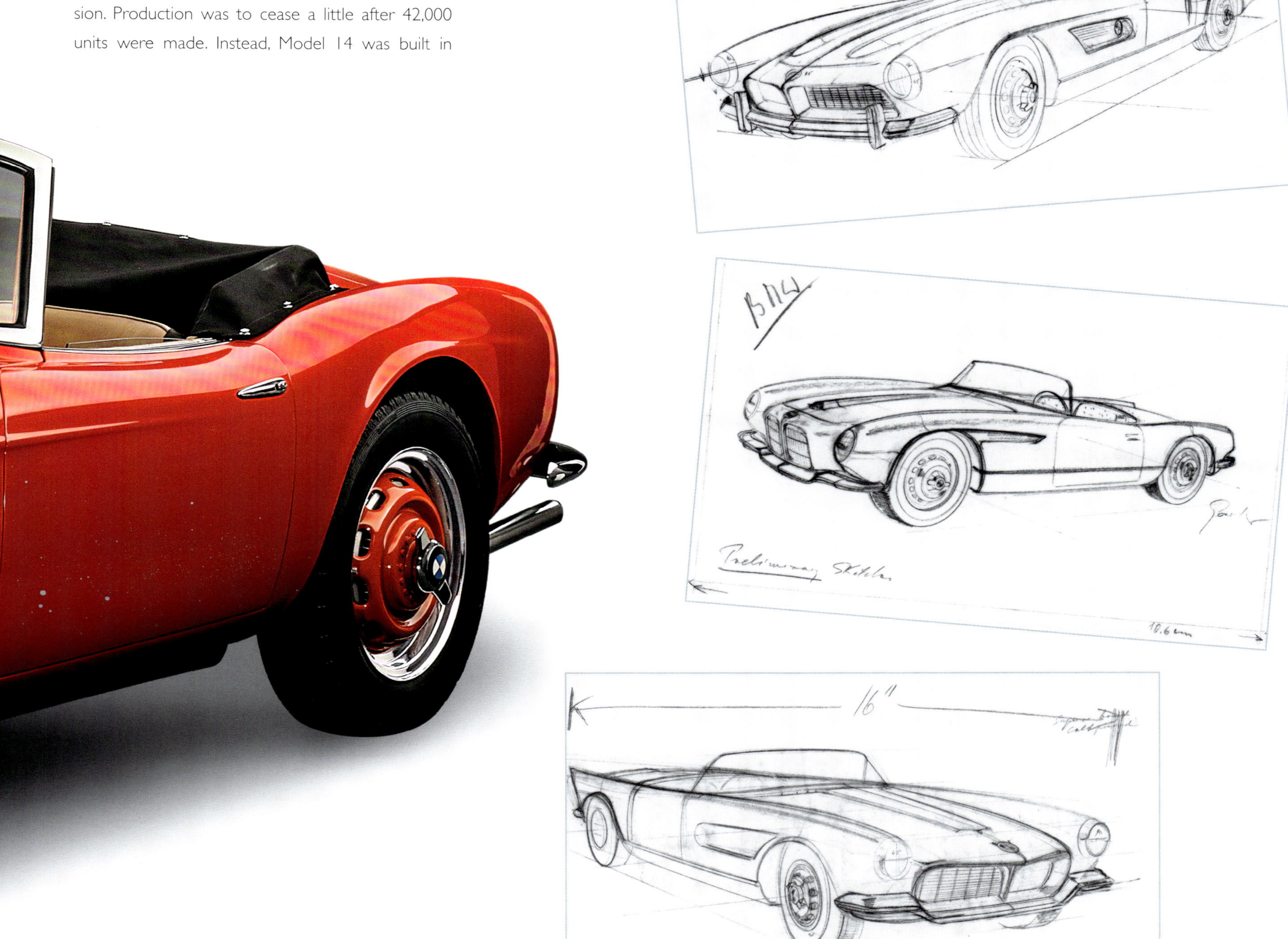

Bottom center With the BMW 507 Albrecht Graf von Goertz created one of history's most beautiful automobiles, recognized today as a masterpiece. Between 1956 and 1959 only 251 models of the 507 were produced, and almost ruined BMW.

Right Albrecht Graf von Goertz was also schooled by Raymond Loewy. The impulse to create this sports model came from the US. The so-called 'gills' that Albrecht Graf von Goertz wanted on the 507 are integrated today in BMW's sportier models (M3, M5, M6).

The fifties also saw the rise of a brand that for years remained the symbol of the "made in Germany" sports car, the Porsche. Ferdinand Porsche was one of the dominant figures of the German automobile history in the years before the war, and certainly influenced significantly more than a car. After the war it was his son Ferry who brought Porsche back on track. His father Ferdinand, worked in the company until shortly before his death in 1951. On 15 June 1948, Porsche introduced Porsche nr. 1, for use on the road. The first true Porsche was the roadster with a central motor, with a more powerful engine of about 35 CV, borrowed from the VW Beetle. The car was built in Gmünd in Austria, where Porsche had retired during the Second World War to continue manufacturing without being impeded by allied bombings.

The Porsche was mass produced with the name 356, but with a rear engine. The first 50 units were built by hand in Gmünd in aluminium. From the beginning, there was a coupe and a convertible version. The 1.1-liter, air-cooled engine derived from the engine group of the VW Beetle, produced an output of 40 hp and enabled the vehicle (weighing less than 800 kg, 1764 lbs.) to reach a speed of 140 km/h (87 mph). The design of the first Porsche was the work of Erwin Komenda, who had already designed the VW Beetle. In principle, these first Porsche models had much in common with the first Volkswagen. The front axle assembly was used with longitudinal arms patented by Porsche, just like the rear oscillating axle integrated with torsion bar suspension, connected to longitudinal struts. Even the engines of the 356 were a reminder of the original VW, but of course they were constantly modified. Starting from 1953 an engine with a countershaft built by Ernst Fuhrmann, with 4 camshafts placed in the front, was available by paying a premium. In its basic version it already had the potency of 110 hp and in race car versions, such as the beautiful 904 GTS, it could go up to 155 hp.

The first model was manufactured until 1955. It was identifiable by its windshield split in two, which from 1952 however no longer had dividers, but continued to be folded (the famous glass inflection). From 1955 to 1959 the spotlight was on the 356 A model, whose body was always produced in three versions and the engine in five versions. Then the 356 B was produced until 1963, and from 1963 to 1965, it was the turn of the 356 C. The variations and special versions were so numerous, including that of the engines, that their classification becomes very complex. In all, 76,302 units of the 356 were produced. Not only was it the first sports car in post-war German production, but it was also the beginning of a new passion for racing.

Bottom left Ferry Porsche (right) portrayed with Karl Rabe (left) and Erwin Komenda. Rabe was an important collaborator of the family, and had been working with Ferdinand Porsche since 1913.

Bottom right In the 50s, the 356 was much appreciated by the public, and still are. In competitions with vintage cars, classic Porsches are among the fastest.

Top right In this picture we see Ferdinand Porsche (right), his son Ferry, who built the 'first' Porsche with the 356, and Erwin Komenda (left) the author of the Porsche design (who had previously designed the Beetle). The early Porsche 356, which was still made of aluminum, was hand-crafted in Austria, in Gmünd. Then, Porsche in Stuttgart built more modern production facilities.

PORSCHE

Left The 356 was constantly improved. Don't forget that in 1948 it was built almost entirely out of parts from the Beetle. It was called the 356 because it was the 356th project by Porsche.

Top right Ferry Porsche was the driving force for the first years of the Porsche brand. Here he is in 1958, proudly showing a production warehouse full of 356 A models in Stuttgart-Zuffenhausen.

Bottom right From the beginning, Porsche put great value to constant research on quality, so it is no surprise that even today many of the 76,302 356 that were built are still in circulation.

CHAPTER 5

Big Dreams and Unbridled Times

The coupes of the W108/109 series (here, a 280 SE), class 1971, so-called 'Flachkühler' (flat radiator) today, are vintage cars that are much requested. A mere 29,000 models were created, to which 7000 convertibles were added.

The sixties were troubled times. The construction of the Berlin Wall, the Vietnam War, revolutions of 1968, landing on the moon–just to mention the most important events. In 1964, Germany still had an unemployment rate of 0.08% and in 1966/1967 the "economic miracle" ended abruptly. This was a country that only five years earlier, had needed foreign workers because the workforce was not sufficient to meet the huge demand.

But faith in progress was unshakable in Germany. The political situation was very confusing and a strong coalition between the CDU/CSU and the SPD was needed to restore tranquility in the country. As a result, the recession was quickly defeated, and soon the "all clear" was given, even for the automotive industry.

In 1960, 1,816 million automobiles were produced in Germany, approximately 21% more than in 1959. In 1967, 2.3 million were manufactured, as much as 19% less than in 1966, but in 1968 the figure was up to 2.86 million, approximately 25% more than the previous year. In 1969 it easily reached the threshold of 3 million units, going up to 3.3 million at the end of the decade. No one would have believed this to be possible. Germany became the largest European manufacturer of cars, ahead of France and Italy. More than 30% of production was exported (1970) and only 11% of cars sold in Germany were imported. However, things were not going well for all the classic brands. Borgward had to leave the scene, BMW was on the borderline and for a while was not acknowledged by Mercedes, the productive forces of DKW/NSU/Auto Union were fused together. Instead, things went really well for Mercedes, VW could still rely on the Beetle, and Ford and Opel had powerful American companies behind them. The cars became bigger, more powerful, and the German car industry was able to assert itself more and more. In Germany they were also producing cars that the whole world dreamed of, such as the Porsche 911, which in subsequent decades became a symbol of everything that was sporty. The German car manufacturers, in the wake of Mercedes, succeeded in earning an image that would be decisive in the decades ahead; the "made in Germany" quality would be synonymous with excellence all over the world.

The already mentioned Mercedes 300 SL had a 'younger brother' from 1955. Or perhaps it would be more correct to say a sister. The 190 SL was actually perceived as a 'car for men'. This was also because a scandal that shook Germany in 1957, was closely connected to this car. A young prostitute from Frankfurt, Rosmarie Nitribitt, was found dead in her home on 1 November 1957 with a wound to the head and signs of strangulation on the neck. At that time she was a person of public interest and the images of the young woman in her black Mercedes 190 SL, with red leather seats, were well known.

The 190 SL was not based on the 300 SL, but was rather a sporty version based on the 180/190 models of the time, better known as 'pontoon'. This Mercedes 'pontoon' did not stand for its elegance and performance, and the 190 SL (with the internal code W121 BII) with its 105 hp certainly did not have a particularly powerful engine either. The model was available in three versions, to keep up with the Roadster. There was also a sporty version in which it was possible to remove the load bearing and the roof for use on the racetrack, but this version was sold in very few units. In total a good 26,000 units of the 190 SL were sold by 1963, a good example of the "we are somebody again" mentality prevailing in Germany at the time.

Like its big brother, the 190 SL was developed on the impulse of 'Maxi' Hoffman, the American importer of Mercedes. Hoffman wanted cars which would oppose the conservative image of the brand in the United States. In a space of just five months, two prototypes were developed, which in the case of the 300 SL, already based on race cars since 1952, was considerably easier. To the SL 190, in comparison to the prototypes, several improvements still had to be made before Walter Häcker and Hermann Ahrens came up with a really harmonious design.

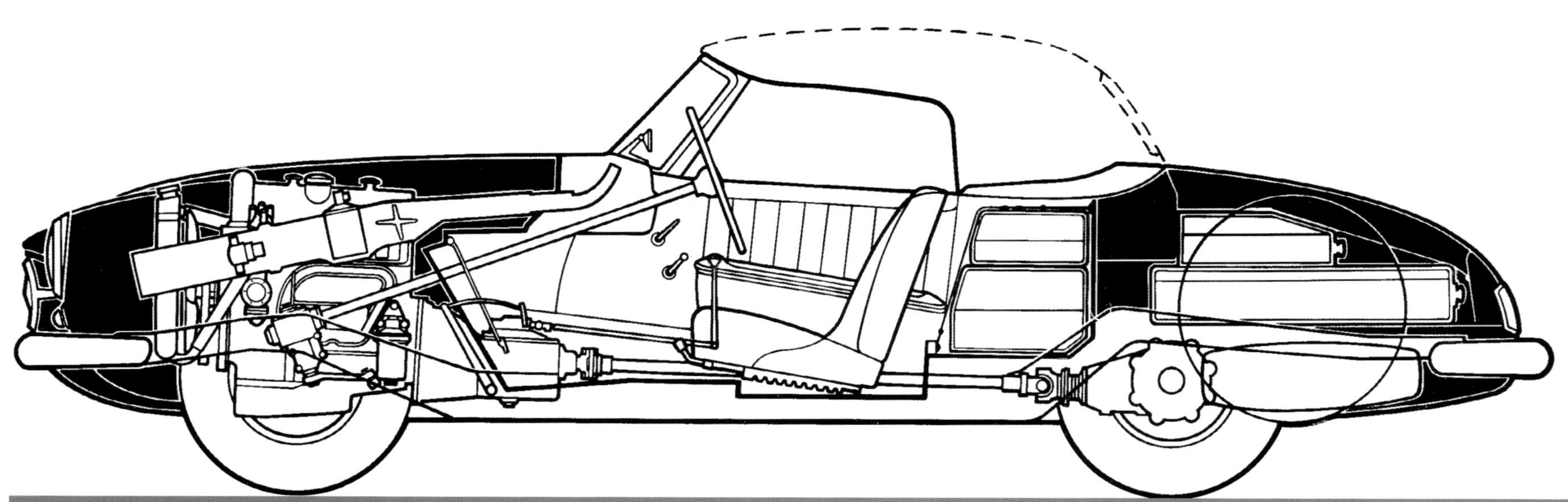

Bottom left The look of the 190 SL wasn't cooked up by a famous designer, but by two drafters; Walter Häcker and Hermann Ahrens. The car was developed from the very conservative 180 (W120).

Right The price of the 190 SL (16,500 DM) remained unchanged during the entire production period. In Germany it was a nice way of expressing the concept 'we have gone back to being someone' of the economic miracle. The 190 SL, produced from 1955 to 1963 (W121 BII) was the little sister (it truly was a 'sister', as it was loved by female customers) of the 300 SL. However, with its 105 hp, it was no sports car. Like the 300 SL, even the 190 SL was designed in just six months. More than 25,000 models were sold, despite the fact it wasn't really cheap initially.

Left The successor of the 190 SL was a very successful model. The 230 SL (W113), was presented in 1963. The 2.3 liter, six cylinder, produced 150 CV but it needed to be revved up. The Mercedes 230 SL was soon nicknamed 'pagoda', a nod to its removable roof. Over the years, the W113 became more powerful, first as the 250 SL (1966), then as the 280 SL (from 1967 to 1971).

Right In the 1979 Bandama Rally, which covered 5,600 kilometers (3,480 mi.) through the savannas of Cote d'Avoire, Mercedes surprisingly won four times with the 450 SLC 5.0 (W107).

In 1963, at the Auto Show of Geneva, the heir to the 190 SL, the W113, was presented. This car became known as the "pagoda" because of its vaulted concave hardtop, and was sold at a premium. The levels of performance were gradually strengthened, starting with the 230 SL (1963-1967), then moving on to the 250 SL (1967) and finally ending with the 280 SL (1968-1971), making for a total of 48,912 units produced. The most common W113 models were the two-seater convertibles with folding roofs, but a hardtop version and a four-seater hardtop version were also available at a premium.

This car was a milestone for Mercedes-Benz. The 'pagoda' was based on the 'tail fin' (internal code W111), and was the first car in the world with safety features. The 'pagoda' took advantage of this attention to safety and had an area with impact-absorbing elements and slightly deformable front and rear elements, but the seat belts were available only with a special set up. However, the W113 consolidated the image of Mercedes as a particularly advanced manufacturer.

The 230 SL delivered 150 hp, so the 250 SL was no longer powerful. Moving on, the 280 SL reached 170 hp. The 'pagoda' still enjoys great popularity today, especially in Germany and USA, as more than half the W113s produced were exported.

But the story of Mercedes SL continues till this day. It has one of the most extensive series of products in the history of the automobile. In 1971 the successor to the W113 came on the market, with the internal code of W107. The rather angular design was once again the work of Friederich Geiger, who had already designed the 'wings of the gull' doors. Over the years the SL became increasingly powerful. The standard engine was a three-liter, six-cylinder in-line, with dual-head camshaft, but beyond that 3.5 and 4.5 liters V8 engines were also mounted (1972). The subsequent 5.5-liter V8 engine was the largest since 1985, but with its 231 hp it did not have the same success as the 5-liter V8 of the 450 SLC 5.0 (1978), which generated 240 hp.

The W107 was also the model that brought Mercedes back in the motor racing spotlight. In the London-Sydney marathon rally, the SL occupied the first, second, sixth and eighth places. This was a great success, for the first time, for the automobile company from Stuttgart. In 1978 Mercedes came up with the 'ship', the 450 SLC 5.0 and in the difficult race in Bandama it won two important victories in 1979 and 1980.

The W107 was produced for 18 years up until 1989. It was followed by the R129, which 'only' reached its thirteenth year, until it was replaced by the R230 in 2001.

Porsche 911 has a history as long as that of the Mercedes SL, but unlike Benz, which from time to time continually developed a completely new design namely the 911 models including the most recent ones, Porsche always refers to the original designs of Ferdinand Alexander 'Butz' Porsche, the son of Ferry Porsche. However, the influence of the Director of Porsche-Karosseriekonstruktionsabteilung (yes, so called at the time), Erwin Komenda, who had already designed the VW Beetle and Porsche 356, is not irrelevant but will probably never be clear. It is true, however, that 'Butz' Porsche had a great career as a designer.

The fact that the 356 needed a successor was already clear to Porsche in the late fifties. This was because the four-cylinder 2-liter boxer engine had been taken to the maximum power threshold. The new model was presented worldwide to the public in 1963. It had an air-cooled boxer engine, but this time with six cylinders and dry cup lubrication. The first version released delivered 130 hp, but had an unmistakable sound, which still distinguishes the 911. The new Porsche was introduced with the name 901, but since the French car manufacturer owned the rights to all numbers with a zero in the middle, the car made its entry with the name 911. Beginning in 1965, when production of the 356

Bottom left The 912 was a lightened 911, not only as far as the engine is concerned. The cockpit only featured three instruments instead of five, but the 911's interiors were available to buy as an optional feature.

finally ceased, the 912 was produced which featured a four-cylinder rear (90 hp) boxer engine, and production continued until 1969.

In 1967, for the first time the power was increased, and the 911 S started to deliver 160 hp. In 1969 the engine capacity was increased to 2.2 liters, and by 1971 to 2.4 liters officially (though it was 2,341 ccm). The more powerful S version delivering 190 hp was already the fastest mass produced car in Germany.

Right *The 911 was quite expensive, so from 1965 to 1969 a direct successor to the 356 was built, the 912. It was initially propelled by a 1.6 liter four-cylinder engine. In 1976 a 912 showed up again in the US.*

The Carrerra RS was even faster. It was introduced in 1972 and was originally intended to be produced in only a limited number of 500 units in order to be approved as a race car. From its capacity of 2.7 liters, this sports car delivered 210 hp and weighing just 975 kilograms, it was perfect for sports. In light of such success 1,590 units were produced in total (and to think that today about 3,000 are in circulation...).

Over the years, the 911 was continually improved. In 1974 the "Model G" was introduced to the market and was easily recognizable by the so-called 'accordion' bumper to meet the requirements of American crash testing. Over the next few years the engine capacity and power increased steadily. But according to the plan at the time, production of the 911 was to stop in 1981. Fortunately, at the end of 1980, the American Peter Schutz took over the reins of Porsche, and instead of halting production, expanded the 911 range by adding a coupe and the Targa model (in 1965) and later a convertible (in 1983). In 1974 the Turbo version was also added (which will be dealt with separately in a later chapter).

The 911 was completely revamped yet again in 1988. The car was officially called 964, but was still marketed under the name 911, for the simple reason that in those days, the 911 was the only Porsche model to have some success. The six-cylinder air-cooled boxer engine in the meantime had moved up to a capacity of 3.6 liters, and the standard version delivered 250 hp. Besides ABS, airbags and power steering (all series), the time had also come for a four-wheel drive version, the Carrera 4. In 1993 the 964 was replaced by the 993, the last 911 with an air-cooled engine. Its career ended in 1997 with the introduction of the 996 model. But in the meantime the 997 model had already arrived (2004).

Bottom center The 1973 Carrera RS 2.7 was recognizable for its unmistakable rear spoiler and its 'war colors'. However, red was not a typical color for the RS, it was much better in white. The Porsche 911 Carrera RS 2.7 (here from 1973) was one of the most evolved sports cars from the 70s. It had a 21 horsepower, and only weighed 975 kg (2149 lbs.), guaranteeing quite a bit of fun at the wheel!

Right Beginning in 1965, the Porsche 911 was available in the Targa version as well. The name comes from the Italian 'targa', meaning plate or crest, and Porsche had no problem recalling the Targa Florio race in the name.

Bottom left On land, the Amphicar wasn't really a beauty, but when it was running and it turned waterproof (and it really was), the ride became a very special one.

Right The movie producer Kevin McClory, with his wife Bobo Segrist and their children are portrayed here on an Amphicar in Nassau, the Bahamas.

Unlike the Mercedes SL and Porsche 911, another project called the Amphicar which aroused great excitement in Germany in the early sixties, did not meet with success. This unique car was developed by Hans Trippel who was hired by the Amphicar Corporation. The car was produced from 1961 to 1964.

Its peculiarity was that it was able to float. With the underframe reinforced by a load bearing body, this vehicle was also airtight in some parts. It was propelled by a 1.2-liter 38 hp engine of the Triumph Herald, a motor unit not known for its reliability. But in any case, the chassis with independent wheel suspension on the front axle, McPherson shock absorbers and longitudinal arms on the back axle, were quite advanced for the time, and the four-seater convertible was even fun on the road. For the gear in water, it was possible to lower two rear propellers, handled by the front wheels. But in Germany, anyone who wanted to drive the Amphicar needed to have a nautical license in addition to the driving license. And a lot of patience. Trippel's creation was as ingenious as unreliable. It was necessary to furnish it with 32 lubrication nipples - and it all had to go in water every five hours. In addition, the Amphicar rusted quickly.

The intention was for at least 25,000 units to be made, even with the support of the Quandt family, one of many others engaged by BMW. 3,878 units were produced and then the company had to declare bankruptcy. What discouraged buyers, in addition to technical problems, was also the high price of DM 12,000 – an insurmountable obstacle for many. For the same sum in the early sixties, you could buy a discrete sports car. The new cars were still available for three years after the bankruptcy, so the provision of spare parts remained efficient for many years.

A much more important invention than the Amphicar, in the history of the automobile, was the Wankel engine, or the rotary piston engine. Just like the amphibian car, interesting in itself, the rotary-piston engine still had to await its moment of glory.

Rotary piston cars had already existed in the sixteenth century. The principle that the motion of the moving parts is only around one center of gravity, had already been used for the construction of hydraulic pumps. But a couple of centuries had yet to pass before the first engine worked. From 1932 it entered the scene with the name Felix Wankel (1902-1988). Wankel was a self-taught person and not a mathematician. Because of his extreme myopia, he did not even have the experience of driving a car. But he had a lively imagination – and after the first attempts with conventional combustion engines, he soon dedicated himself to rotary piston engines. In 1933 he obtained a patent for the first eccentric rotor engine.

The principle was relatively simple and logical. Instead of pistons that in a traditional piston engine move up and down, in a Wankel engine the wheel disc moves around a shaft intermittently. In this way the motor unit has a significantly lower number of moving parts and requires less space. Also no valves are needed, and there are less related parts such as the camshaft, tappets and rockers. There are further advantages as well. A Wankel engine is perfectly balanced, which creates a smooth ride and uniform torque because the cycle is longer by 50%.

Wankel was able to resume his research on automobiles only after 1951, after NSU assigned him the responsibility of developing rotary piston cars, which after a short time was extended to rotary piston engines. At the NSU Wankel worked with Hanns Dieter Paschke. The two did not always get along, but Paschke contributed decisively to the development of the engine which took the name Felix Wankel. At one point, Paschke began to develop their concepts but Wankel did not know anything about it. Finally in 1957, after some technical changes, NSU-Mann, the first eccentric rotor engine was actually put into action.

About this engine called KKM57 Wankel had this to say; "They made my racing horse into a horse for plowing."

To this the director of NSU, von Heydekampf, replied "At least it was only a horse for plowing."

They invested yet another six years and many millions in development before the first cars with the Wankel engine could be presented to the public in the autumn of 1963; the NSU Wankel Spider and a Mazda with a bi-rotor engine.

In the autumn of 1964, the NSU started to be mass produced, but this happened too soon because the evolution of the Wankel engine was still far from complete. Mazda had much more success with its Cosmo Sport, and this also stimulated the NSU. Even the significantly advanced NSU Ro80 was placed on the market very hastily, without thorough testing. The first cars suffered from a design error, the sealing strips of the Wankel engine had not been designed properly. The Ro80, which with a purchase price of DM 14,500 (1967) cost as much as a Mercedes, actually became marketable only from 1970, but soon the oil crisis was to erupt. The high fuel consumption became a crucial point and in 1977 the production of Ro80 stopped. Only 37,500 units of this extraordinary car were produced.

20 years had already passed since Volkswagen had put the Beetle into circulation. For all this time the company had Model 1 or the Beetle, and Model 2 or the Bulli. In the late fifties it became clear to the automobile company from Wolfsburg that they could not continue forever. From the outset it was clear that the Model 3 was not exactly the greatest, presented to the International Automobil-Ausstellung (IAA) in 1961.

Left In 1961 Volkswagen finally managed to add a third model to the Beetle and the Bulli. The Type 3 was built on the Beetle but it offered more space. The 1500 was available in a combo version from the very beginning. It was the first VW to be called 'Variant'. However its trunk was quite small due to the rear engine.

The VW 1500, so named because of its large engine (in addition to the radial fan flanged on top of the crankshaft, which allowed it to make for a longer and flatter engine), was certainly a beauty. It was not a great success, although the space offered was significantly better and there was also a combined version called 'Variant'. The Type 3 model cost DM 6,300, about DM 1,000 more than the Beetle, which Model 3 was obviously largely based on.

In 1968 Model 3 had a successor, logically named Type 4. The official name was VW 411 (412 from 1972), but the car was known by the suitable nickname of 'Nasua'. The badmouthers said, "4 doors, 11 years late." The 411 was still based on the concept of the Beetle, the air-cooled boxer engine was mounted in the rear. At least these cars, with an engine capacity of 1.7 and 1.8 liters this time around, were much more powerful than the Model 1, going up to 85 hp. The 80 hp version was interesting from a technical standpoint, with electronic fuel injection developed by Bosch. In the six years of production, only 367,728 units of Model 4 were produced, a painfully small number for Volkswagen.

But VW was not done with experimentation yet. In 1970 the company introduced a completely new car, the K 70. It was the first Volkswagen with an in-line, water-cooled engine, and front-wheel drive. The car was developed by NSU, which had worked on a successor to Ro80 since 1965. In 1969 the presentation was postponed because of the imminent takeover of NSU by VW; they did not want to give room to any direct competitor of the new Audi 100. However, since the public had already been informed, and loud protests were heard from potential customers, VW introduced the 70K to the market in autumn 1970; only the combined version, even if already designed, was abandoned.

The 70 K liked for its considerable spaciousness, was bigger than the other cars in the group. The 585 liter trunk was huge. NSU had designed the K70 again with a Wankel engine, but the angular VW arrived on the market only with the conventional gasoline engine (with a capacity of 1.6 or 1.8 liters, going from 75 to 100 hp). Between 1970 and 1975 more than 211,000 units were produced, but since the interchangeability of parts compared to other VW products was weak, or totally absent, production did not prove fruitful. At least the construction of the 70 K paved the way for new generations of Volkswagen, the Passat and especially the Golf.

Right *NSU was the first true pioneer of the Wankel engine, a revolutionary engine that was mounted as standard series on this beautiful 1963 Spider for the first time. However it was riddled with too many problems for the NSU.*

In the early sixties Opel also wanted to create their own sports car. It would, to some extent, renew the extremely conservative image of the brand. In the winter of 1963 this project started to develop, primarily with studies in plasticine. In the 1965 edition of the International Motor Show, the prototype was displayed called 'Experimental Opel GT' which had the shape of a bottle of Coca Cola, which in those years also characterized the Chevrolet Corvette. The audience was enthusiastic, and even the strategists of GM, who would have gladly included a sports car in the group at a price lower than that of the Corvette, encouraged the project.

Three years passed before the Opel GT finally arrived on the market; Opel happened to lack production capacity. The car could not be produced on the same assembly line used for the Kadett B, on which it was based. Thus the chassis was ordered from the French company Chausson, and the varnishing of the interior was French, specifically of Brissoneau & Lotz (which later proved to be a boomerang, when Renault took over Brissoneau & Lotz) . The chassises, once ready, were delivered to the plant in Bochum, where the engine, gearbox and the axles were mounted. The GT was available in two versions, the smaller with a 1.1 liter engine and 60 hp, and the 1900 GT with the engine of the Rekord with1.9 liters and 90 hp, which propelled the Opel to185 km/h (115 mph). The purchase price was about DM 10,000, which made the GT a great deal of money. The small version had no trunk, the luggage had to be stowed behind the seats, so adjustable headlights had been provided and the GT 1900 had a bulge on the hood.

The response was huge, not only in Germany but also in the United States. More than 60% of the 103,463 units produced were exported to the US. But the end came in 1973 when GT was not able to pass the stringent crash-testing in United States. Not to mention the huge bumper, later introduced as a compulsory feature, which was not expected from the timeless shape of the 'German Corvette'.

Opel was already prepared with a perfectly legitimate successor in 1970, or at least a stopgap: the Manta. This car was Rüsselsheimer's answer to the Ford Capri, which had sold very well since 1968. Yet the Manta, with its low line, the long hood and the jaunty tail looked more sporty than it actually was. The first Manta went up to 90 hp, powered by the same engine as that of the Rekord and GT. But the stylish Opel, which was initially aimed at young customers, quickly became an initial product loved by makers of cars, which in those years had just begun to take its first steps.

The Manta A was built until 1975, followed by B, which was the coupe version of the Ascona B, introduced simultaneously. But it had far from the charm of the initial version, the engines were not significantly enhanced (110 hp in the 2.0 E). This situation changed over the years, but the Manta B was produced for at least 13 years. The largest variations (i300) were equipped with a six-cylinder 3 liter engines from the Senator/Monza. In total, over 1 million Manta were sold. And in Germany endless jokes were told about the owners of this car and their little blond passengers.

In US, in the mid sixties the so-called 'Pony Cars' had great success. Positioned one notch below the real sports cars such as the Corvette, the Ford Mustang was the first (and also the most successful) representative of this new category. The Detroit automobile company was of the view that it could take this concept to Europe, and developed a dis-

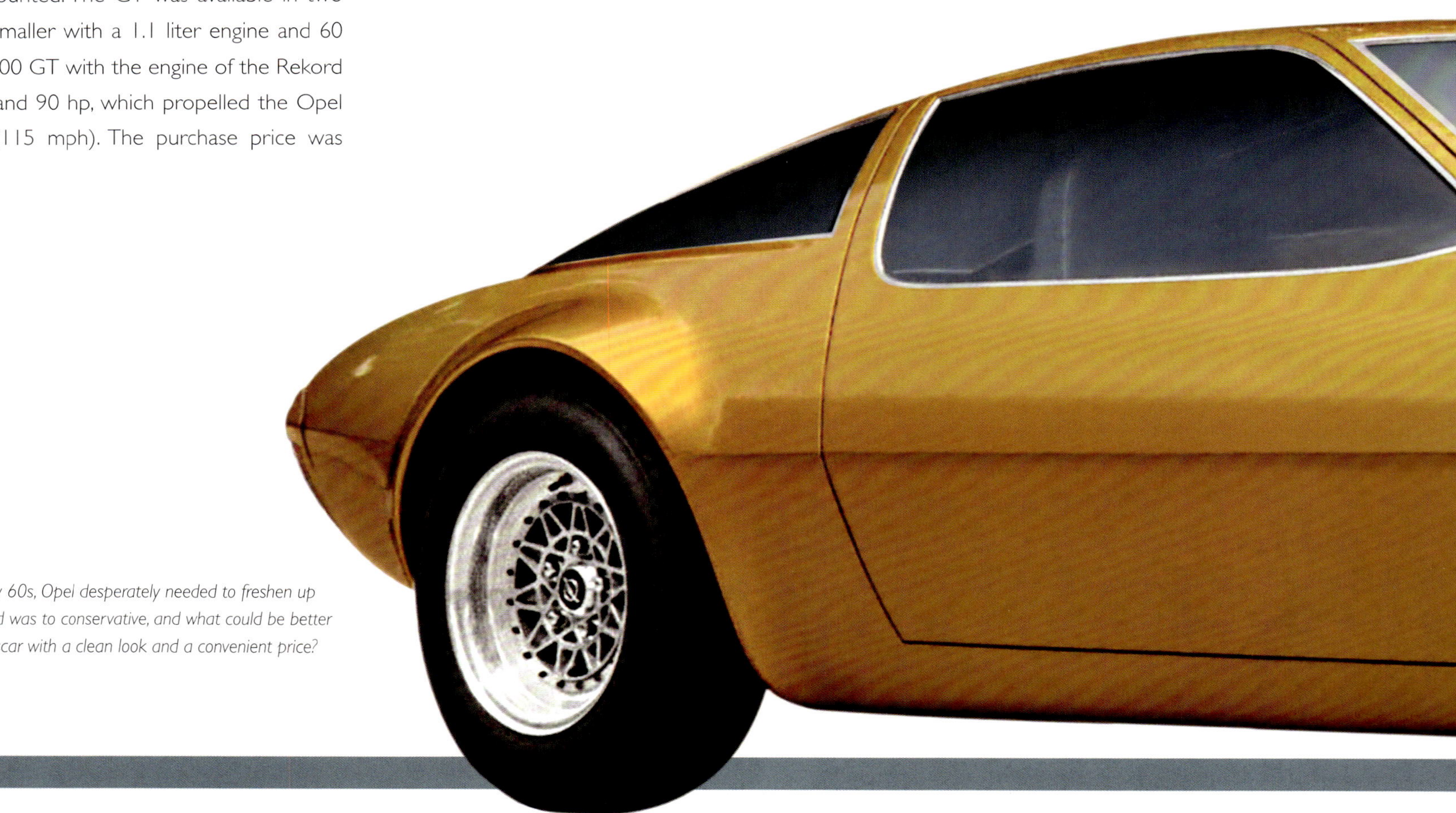

Center In the early 60s, Opel desperately needed to freshen up its image; the brand was to conservative, and what could be better than a small sportscar with a clean look and a convenient price?

tinctly sporty car code-named the 'Colt'. But the Colt name was already owned by Mitsubishi and the first Ford was introduced in Europe in January 1969 in Brussels under the name Capri.

The technique of the Capri was based on the Cortina, or more precisely on the Taunus. This fast Ford was built in England, Belgium and Germany. The British and German Capri initially differed a little because of the engines. The main engine installed in the German Capri was the first generation of the first two-liter V6 engine. Starting from 1969 a 2.3-liter V6 engine with dual carburetor that delivered 125 CV was used, and from 1970 a 2.6-liter 150 hp engine with Kugelfischer injection system was used in the the Capri RS 2600. These cars quickly reached the status symbol of cult objects. There was also a racing version, the 2.6 hp, which was almost unbeatable in its class.

With the 1973 model, the Capri underwent a little restyling and then was significantly modified in 1978. The primary model was the 3.0 S, which in 1981 was replaced by the 2.8i with160 hp. Even more powerful was the 2.8-liter V6 Turbo188 hp, marketed from 1981. The Capri was produced (in England) until 1986 and a total of 1.89 million cars were built in different countries.

The Capri had great success as a race car. Its peak was in the early seventies, and then once again in 1978 in the DRM Championship (Deutschen Rennsport-Meisterschaft) with the Ford Zakspeed Capri Turbo1.4. This car went up to 600 hp, but at the beginning failed to impose itself against BMW. Klaus Ludwig won the championship only in 1981, surrounded by a flock of Porsche of around 200 hp.

An year before the Capri, Ford had introduced the Escort to the market. This was supposed to be the 'anti-Beetle', but in Germany where this Ford was popularly called the 'dog bone' (because of the shape of its radiator grill), it never became very popular. This was an entirely different situation compared to Great Britain, where the Escort was a real champion in terms of sales. Various versions of the Escort were produced until 2000 – and and enjoyed great success especially on the race tracks.

Right *An ad from 1975 for the special 'Black Magic' series of the Opel Manta GT/E A. The car definitely looked wilder and sportier than it actually was, but customers loved it anyway.*

Top left The 60s saw BMW's rebirth: the brand managed to impose itself, garnering victories in sports too, without reaching the class and the name of Mercedes however.

Bottom center From 1961 on the BMW was the Bavarian brand's 'new class'. The design was the work of Giovanni Michelotti. Finally BMW managed to close the gaps that were made with the Borgward Isabella.

Bottom right In a matter of two years BMW managed to sell almost 24,000 models, which was true medicine for the financial woes of the Bavarians: the 'new class', opened the doors to new hope.

In the early sixties, BMW continued to have bad luck. Liquidity was very low, sales were rare. *Der Spiegel*, already one of the most important publications in Germany, wrote in 1959 that BMW only built cars for "laborers and bank managers." Shortly afterwards, the 'new class' was introduced, presented to the International Motor Show in 1961 and financed by the Quandt family. The first model to be introduced to the market was the BMW 1500. Its exterior was designed by the Italian Giovanni Michelotti, who was then a kind of interior designer for BMW, and was operated by a completely new four-cylinder engine, built by Alexander von Falkenhausen. The 1.5 liters generated 80 hp. In 1963 the series was expanded with the 1800, which already went up to 90 hp, folloed by a 120 hp TI and a TI/SA (SA stood for 'Sonderausstattung' meaning space set up), which reached at least 130 hp. This car was also the first in the long and prestigious career of BMW in the area of sports cars: in 1966 Hubert Hahn was the first race car driver to drive twice around the notorious curve north of the Nürburgring circuit in less than 10 minutes. He was driving an 1800.

The 'new class' starting from 1964 was also available in convertible versions, and from 1965 as a coupe with a Karmann chassis (2000 C, CA, CS). But the most important thing for the further evolution of BMW was certainly the two-door, which in 1966, made its debut with the name 1600-2. From this the 02 series was born.

The BMW called 114, was originally designed as a low end addition to the product range, but despite having only two doors, soon surpassed the 'new class' in terms of sales. The more powerful versions had a 2-liter four-cylinder engine, while the more sporty versions were named TI and TII. The TI was equipped with a double Solex carburetor, while the TII had Kugelfischer engineering which enabled it to go up to130 hp. In 1971 a sloping tail verson called 'touring' was added. Baur created two convertibles and starting from 1974, the 'turbo' was the maximum that one could aspire to. The 02 had great success as sports cars and strengthened the image of BMW as a sports brand throughout the world.

A 'Made in Germany' product of excellence from the sixties was the Mercedes 600, with the internal code of W100. Already the number one designer of Mercedes in the mid fifties, Fritz Nallinger had started the preliminary work. He had in mind a car that included all the possible technical craftiness of the time. So his 'great travel car and company car' had to have air suspension, automatic transmission, air conditioning, windows and seats with hydraulic control (note, not electrical, it would have been too cheap!), power steering and power brakes. Moreover, Nallinger had naturally also looked overseas, at Detroit, where more refined models of the Cadillac already possessed all these accessories (excluding seats with hydraulic control).

In 1960 the first prototypes were ready and in 1963 the car came on the market. It was propelled by a completely new 6.3-liter V8 engine which delivered 250 hp. This engine pushed the great 600 (373 mph) to 200 km/h (124 mph), which gave it the title of 'the greatest sports car of all time'. It went from 0 to 100 km/h (62 mph) in 10 seconds flat, at least in the short (5.54 meters, 18 ft), lighter (2.5 tons) version. The 600 was also available in a coach version (6.24 meters, 20ft, up to 3.3 tons) and as Landaulet (limousine in the front and convertible in the back). Two less beautiful coupes with a wheelbase of less than 22 cm (9 in.) were also constructed, but they never went beyond the experimental phase.

Left *The W100 series, better known as the Mercedes 600 was state of the art in every aspect. Mercedes wanted (and was capable of) proving that Stuttgart could build the world's best cars.*

Top right *Inner shot of a very particular Mercedes 600. This Pullman Landaulet was built in 1965 for Pope Paul VI. One can safely assume that the pope never actually drove the car himself.*

Mercedes expected to produce up to 30,000 units of the 600 a year. But up to1981 only 2,677 units had been produced – this was a terrible loss for Daimler. In particular this was due to the fact that in 1963 just the development costs per car amounted to DM 37,000 – against a purchase price of DM 56,500 (but between 1963 and 1979 it was already more than DM 175,000 for the coach which was nearly DM 100,000 more than the price of a 450 SEL 6.9 and was not less representative). The 600 was important for its image. It gave quality and refinement to the brand with the star, so much so that over the course of ten years, tens of heads of state, sports personalities and other distinguished people were seen in the largest of all Mercedes. Among others, famous owners of the 600 were John Lennon, Coco Chanel, Elvis Presley, as also Idi Amin, Leonid Breschnew, and Mao Tse-tung.

Bottom right *The Mercedes 600 was a powerful vehicle, even in its 'short', version. Obviously, thanks to its eight cylinders, 6.3 liters, which produced 250 hp, the car was also an exceptional cruising limousine.*

At the other extreme of the Mercedes 600, there was the automobile production in the former DDR. Although after the Second World War there were still manufacturing plants in the east, it was difficult to continue the manufacturing of automobiles in the fifties. While in West Germany millions of Beetles were already circulating, the scarcity of materials still continued to plague the DDR. In 1954 the policy makers decided to build another 'popular car', following the example of the Lloyd built in Bremen in 1950. But there was a problem; the shell had to be made of plastic, because the sheet metal drawing of the right quality used in the automobile industry was not available in the Eastern Bloc.

The first prototype named P50 was already built in 1954 at the research and development center of Karl-Marx-Stadt. The chassis consisted of Duroplast, a mixture of phenolic resin and cotton. But it had no success, so, Automobilwerke Zwickau (AWZ, formerly Audi) became involved in its evolution. In 1957 there were 50 pre-series units known as P50 'Trabant'. The small car with its two-stroke 18 hp eccentric rotor engine met great favor, such that AWZ and Werk Sachsenring (formerly Horch) merged to form Automobilwerke VEB Sachsenring Zwickau.

Top left A busy gas station in Bad Doberan, East Germany in 1978. In the DDR almost all cars that circulated were DDR-built. In addition to the Trabant we also see two Wartburgs.

Top center East Germany was not immune from American influence. Obviously there were wash stations: like this 'PGH Waschbär'; the picture is from 1972.

In 1963 the 'Trabi' was completely reworked and equipped with a larger engine (23 hp) and the name 600, derived from the latter. In 1964 a new version was already produced, the 601, more than 18 cm (7 in.) long, with the aesthetic that was kept almost unchanged until 1991. Starting from 1965 a combined version was also produced, the Trabant 601 Universal, which had a trunk capacity of 1400 liters. A total of more than 3 million units were produced.

But there was also a second brand in the DDR which manufactured cars. Wartburg. In this case the former BMW plant in Eisenach was used – and the DKW F9 developed in 1940 was used as a basis for the first model, the 311. In 1956 the first models

were introduced to the market, with a two-stroke engine like that of the Trabant. There were widely varying versions of the chassis of the 311, 312, 313 and 314, including the 'Campinglimousine', a 'Sportwagen' and a 'Kabriolett'. In 1963 Wartburg launched the 353, which was produced until 1988 with minimal changes (1.2 million units).

Bottom center Auto production in East Germany certainly could not satisfy market demand, so cars, even the most damaged ones, were always being repaired. A picture of a Trabant being worked on.

Right Naysayers might say that this 1972 picture shows a typical image: a Trabant at a mechanic. The 'scotch-tape race-car' from the DDR certainly did not want to be known.

The 'Trabbi', which was built with almost no modifications from 1958 to 1991, was ultimately, the 'Volkswagen' of East Germany.

CHAPTER 6

Golf Eclipses Every Other Car

The first Porsche Turbo (correctly: turbo) from 1974 (pictured here, a model from 1977) was very much a 911 but was named 930. With its 260 hp it could reach over 250 km/h (155 mph).

The decade-defining automotive theme of the '70s was the oil crisis, or rather crises: those of 1973 and 1979-80. The most serious one was that of fall 1973, when the Organization of Petroleum Exporting Countries (OPEC) deliberately cut oil production quotas and the price per barrel (159 liters) rose from three to five dollars. In 1974 the price went up to as much as 12 dollars. Suddenly, industrialized nations could see just how deeply dependent they were on fossil fuels, and Germany went so far as to implement Sunday driving bans four times between November and December 1973.

Clearly even the German automobile industry suffered. Whereas 3,649 cars were produced in 1973, this figure plummeted by 22.2% to 2,839 in 1974. This was the greatest setback since production resumed after the Second World War. And customers, whose wallets were hit directly by the OPEC embargo, for the first time, looked primarily at the automobile's consumption. All of a sudden, more was no longer better.

But there were other problems. As early as 1965, a lawyer named Ralph Nader, who was involved in consumer protection, had published *Unsafe at Any Speed,* a book in which he was able to prove that many American automobiles had construction defects. The direct consequence of this was that, from 1976 onwards, in the USA, there was a halt in the sale of convertible vehicles. Undoubtedly, the direct effect on the German automobile industry was marginal, though increased consumer awareness regarding these problems, in turn, forced it to invest billions to improve safety.

Mercedes was the first automobile manufacturer in 1980 to produce a car fitted with an airbag (even if in the early '70s in America, Ford had installed the first airbag with the Mercury brand).

For Volkswagen on the other hand, these difficult times turned out to be a blessing. In 1974, the Wolfsburg Company launched the Golf, which was precisely the right answer to daily problems. It was a small, compact vehicle that, with its front-wheel drive, transverse engine and, most importantly, hatchback design, was completely different not only from the Beetle, but also from the traditional rear wheel drive "three-box" notch back sedan, which, in the past, had dominated this important sector. The compact category became the Golf category with next to nothing left for the competition. It is important to point out, however, that the Golf was not ahead of its time and certainly was not revolutionary. Indeed, as early as 1967, VW had launched its 1100, with a similar structure and dimension, and hatchbacks had been around for some time (such as the Renault 16, issued in 1965). But VW had outstanding success with the Golf and the German automobile industry had created, once again, at the right moment, the vehicle which would change the lives of whole generations. Proving to be long-lived, the Golf celebrated its 50th anniversary in 2024.

Art for a work of art: the first VW Golf of 1974, with its clean e essential logic, was an absolute masterpiece. Giugiaro managed to create much more than an immortal design. It was definitely angular, yet beautiful.

The invention of the turbo compressor dates back to 1905, when a Swiss engineer filed a patent for fuel intake at constant pressure and volume. Several years passed, however, before the first automobiles with a turbo-compressor-charged engine were produced – the early '60s to be precise, with some American models like the Chevrolet Corvari. But the turbo theme was only addressed seriously in the '70s by the German automobile industry, starting with a minor BMW series (1973) and then, more significantly, from 1974 onwards by Porsche.

To increase the power of a naturally aspirated engine by means of turbo compression is, in reality, a simple and efficient solution. A turbo compressor consists of an exhaust gas turbine positioned in the flow of the exhaust gases and connected to a compressor in the air intake manifold by a shaft. The turbine is activated by the engine exhaust gases thereby activating the compressor. The latter in turn increases pressure in the air intake manifold, so that more oxygen is made available for the combustion of a greater amount of fuel. This determines a higher average pressure and torque, which increases power.

When BMW presented the 2002 "turbo" at the Frankfurt Motor Show in 1973, on the one hand, there was great enthusiasm, while on the other hand the vehicle came onto the market at a bad time. The oil crisis was at its height and the German economy was in a recession. As one might expect given the context, the BMW turbo was not a success and only 1,672 vehicles were produced.

But the 170 CV BMW, with its distinctive original white, red and blue colorway and the "turbo" mirror image writing on the front spoiler (so that it could be also read in rear view mirrors) still had several weak points. The turbo compressor activated only at 3,000 revs/min; at lower revolution speeds, due to very low engine compression, the difference was considerable. For this reason, performance was not as lively as BMW expected it to be.

Porsche did not fare much better with the 911 Turbo, launched in 1974.

Once again, the turbo charger was only activated at 3,000 revs/min, and it happened with such brutal force that many a vehicle was destroyed at the hands of inexperienced drivers. As there were many changes made to the 911 (including aesthetic, with widened wheels and mudguards, and the impressive airfoil), an internal code, 930, was assigned to the Porsche turbo. The turbo compressed 260 PS, reached speeds over 250 km/h (155 mph) with incredible acceleration – Porsche was at the same level as the outstanding Lamborghinis and Ferraris.

Bottom center The 1974 Porsche 911 Carrera RSR Turbo 2.1 is among the most legendary race cars of all times: it symbolizes the beginning of the turbo era in racing. This beautiful motorized machine produced 500 hp.

Top right In the early 70s very few knew how a turbo engine worked. Even the BMW 2002 turbo was not only available in its very aggressive 'battle colors'. The first models also had the words '2002 Turbo' written backwards so that it could be read from the rearview mirrors of the cars in front.

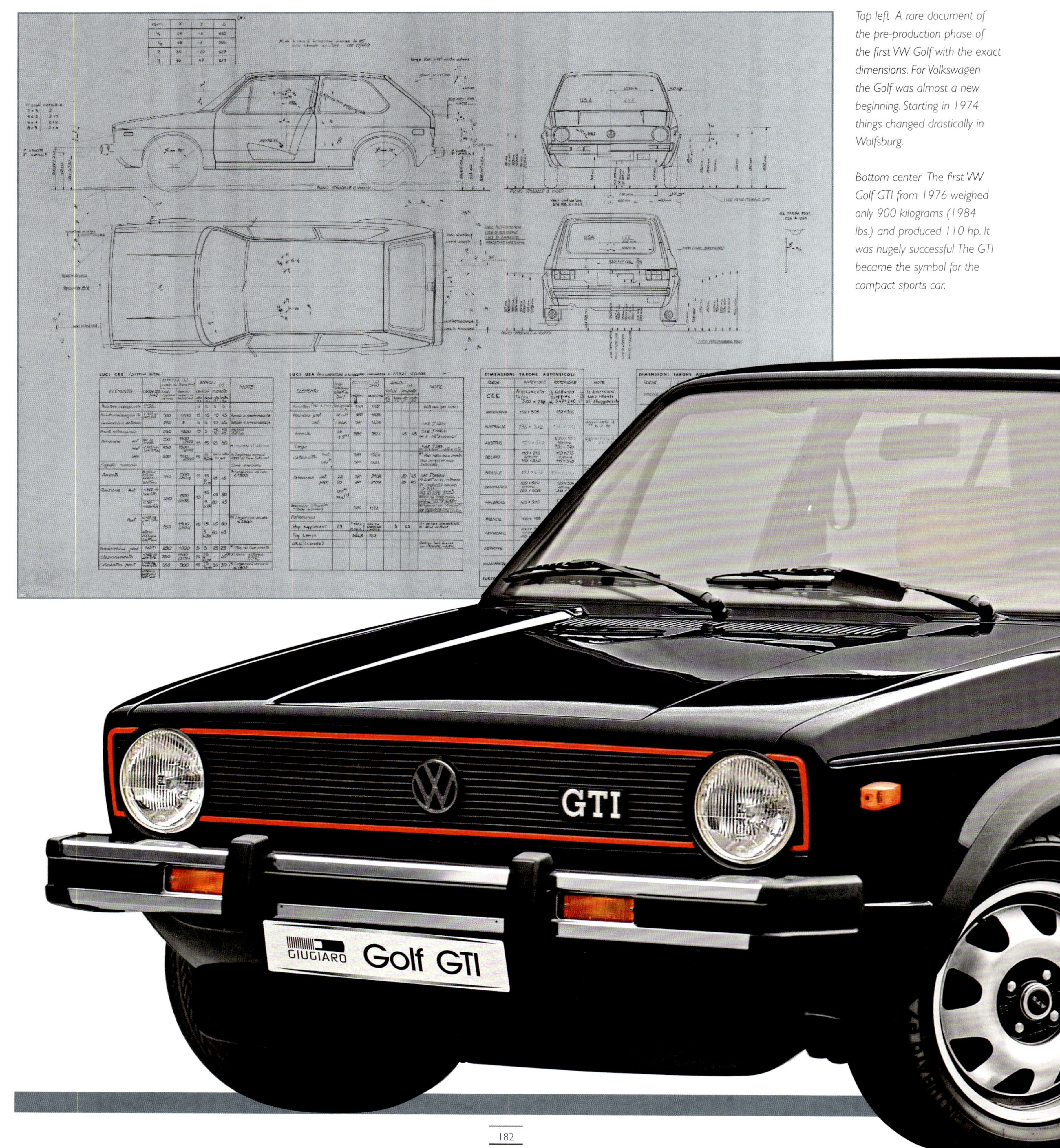

Top left A rare document of the pre-production phase of the first VW Golf with the exact dimensions. For Volkswagen the Golf was almost a new beginning. Starting in 1974 things changed drastically in Wolfsburg.

Bottom center The first VW Golf GTI from 1976 weighed only 900 kilograms (1984 lbs.) and produced 110 hp. It was hugely successful. The GTI became the symbol for the compact sports car.

The VW Golf however, far more than the turbos, symbolizes a whole generation (Florian Illies, *Generation Golf*, 2000) and is a metaphor of a balanced company. It is also more Teutonic than a Mercedes S Class, the proclamation of the German character with all its defects and virtues; German-made quality, practical, boxy, excellent to the point of perfection and totally boring. If cars were people, it would be a charmless class geek who not only knows everything but can do everything too. The half measure of everything – though well over 26 million of them have been sold worldwide.

In reality it is extremely simple; whoever does nothing wrong, by definition does everything right.

Excitement: zero. Fantastic design: zero. Original technical solutions: none. So, why?

The market sector, the specialists, everybody laughed at the first Golf in 1974, with its square edges, designed by the great Italian master Giorgio Giugiaro, the total opposite of the rotund, and for this reason immortal, VW Beetle. But the public seemed to have been waiting for this break with the past, being before appearing to be, a reasonable space, a reasonable (at the time) price. At its peak, more than 400,000 models were sold in Germany.

Even though the Golf gave its name to a whole market sector and, over three decades, all of its competitors imitated Volkswagen (mediocrity is everybody's worst adversary, as Goethe said), the Wolfsburg-based company, with its bestseller, had not invented anything new. Cars with a hatchback and foldable back seats already existed before 1974, and the "space-saving" front-wheel drive had already been known for some time. The GTI alone – launched in 1976, 110 horse power, weighing less than 900 kg (1,984 lbs.) – was a novelty that nobody had been bold enough to produce. At the time, VW intended to crank out only 5,000 units; to date more than 1.3 million have been made.

If we want everything to stay the same, then everything must change, wrote Lampedusa in 1958 in *The Leopard*. In the Golf, everything and nothing has changed; it has grown up into an adult car. In the meantime, we've come to the eighth-generation restyling. The best times are over now, and as you get into a new Golf, you can feel the effect of time. It does not roar and it is not as hungry as a beast. There are competitors with more space, a better sense of space, plastic everywhere, even if there are more attractive alternatives. Even so, everything is fine, everything is in its right place, multimedia features carry the day and things are exactly as you expect them to be.

In these changing times, driving purely for pleasure hardly exists any more. The transportation of goods and passengers in their free time is what individual mobility is all about today. And few, almost none, are as successful as the Golf. An advertising campaign like that of the Chevrolet some time ago, which boasted that half of Americans had been conceived in a Chevy, would not be suitable for the Golf, regardless of the generation. It would be better to describe it with Baudrillard's words: "Its splendor floods the grayness of everything else with light."

But for decades VW did not manage to establish itself as a trend-setter, having remained anchored for far too long exclusively to the Beetle/Transporter, and after having produced a few flops. But in the challenging early '70s, the oil crisis was still to come and the Germans (among others) knew how great their dependence was on the producing countries, and therefore VW was able to launch a second winning product, alongside the Golf. However, it was Audi that took the first steps towards a smaller and more refined car. The Audi 50 was presented in 1974 (it had been developed in just 21 months, a record at the time in the automobile industry) and VW's economy version, the VW Polo, only came onto the market in 1975. But unlike the little Audi model, which ceased production in 1978, the Polo has had a long life so far; it still exists, and today has reached its sixth generation (the last restyling, in 2021, updated its aesthetics and technology).

The first Polo was indeed a basic vehicle. From an aesthetic point of view, it was certainly identical to the Golf designed by Giugiaro but it was minuscule at 3.5 meters (11.5 ft) long. The interior door panels were made out of cardboard, on the driver's side, there was no lock or sun visor. One of the reasons that vehicles weighed only around 700 kilograms (1,543 lbs.), was that engine capacity was available in either 0.9 or 1.3 liters. It was only in 1978 that a GLS version with improved finishing was produced, and in 1979 the GT with 60 PS made its debut. From 1977 onwards, a "three-box" notchback sedan called the Volkswagen Derby was also available. But VW was not very successful in the first few years with the Polo. It was produced using particularly cheap sheet metal which was very prone to corrosion.

The competition answered only a year later; in 1976. Ford launched the Fiesta. Even though it was only 3.5 meters (11.5 ft) long, Ford did not economize on the production of the vehicle which was codenamed Bobcat. Furthermore, in England, where the Fiesta was much more successful than in Germany, more powerful models were soon made available, such as the Fiesta S, in 1980 which went up to 84 PS. For the first time, lateral decorations became a part of standard production. In 2023, Ford announced it would stop production of the Fiesta in Europe and replace it with a fully electric version of the compact Puma SUV.

At a considerable distance behind VW and Ford, Opel struggled along, presenting its first utility vehicle only in 1982, called Corsa. This was also due to the fact that the car manufacturer from Rüsselsheim had no experience in front-wheel drives and the 1979 Kadett was its first front-wheel drive model. The Corsa is still on the market, also sold in an electric version.

In the '70s, Volkswagen was also quicker than the competition in another sector. In 1979, the Golf Cabriolet appeared on the market, and years passed before Ford with the Escort, Opel with the Kadett and Peugeot with the 205 followed VW's example (in the case of Peugeot, to rather disappointing sales numbers too). Not only was the Golf Cabriolet one of the first vehicles with a fixed roll bar, it was also a resounding success for Volkswagen. It added a touch of eternity to the top of the sales lists of convertible cars. It was produced in two editions, the first from 1979 to 1993 and the second from 1993 to 1998 based on the Golf III. From 1998 to 2002, minor stylistic modifications were made, officially redubbed the Golf IV Cabriolet, though the changes were marginal. Following the end of Karmann production, surprisingly no more Golf-based convertibles were produced and neither the new Beetle Cabriolet (launched in 2003) nor the Eos (launched in 2006) can be considered a direct descendant. This is especially clear if we observe the sales figures.

The '70s-era Cabriolet was extremely heavy. For the first time in automotive history, above all in the USA – by far the largest market in the world as far as the Cabriolet was concerned – the safety of cars was discussed. For convertibles, there was particular worry over what would happen in the case of overturning and lateral collisions. Together with Karmann of Osnabrück, VW therefore developed the strong fixed roll-bar (not aesthetically elegant), which caused the first model of Golf Cabriolet to be nicknamed the "strawberry basket."

With this roll bar and some other reinforcements, the Golf Cabriolet could easily comply with rigid American regulatory requirements. The transition to a convertible with the first Golf Cabriolet was not equally efficient, however. Its soft top had to be made out of vinyl, because at high speeds, it tended to inflate to such an extent that it lifted up like a sail. With the Golf III/IV Cabriolet however, VW managed to keep these problems under control.

Notwithstanding the great successes, the convertible Golf never managed to completely win over true VW aficionados, many of whom missed the undeniable charm of the Beetle Cabriolet.

The convertible version of the VW Golf reached the market in 1979. Once again, Volkswagen showed its business sense: years would go by before the competition would reach them. People called it the 'Erdbeerkörbchen' (little basket of strawberries). When the speed increased, the folded top tended to move of its own accord. Years went by before the problem was solved.

Left Some legendary Quattro models pictured together: in the forefront the S1 'Pikes Peak' from 1987, right back is a S1 'Rally' from 1985 and further back is another rally version from 1984.

Right The 1980 Quattro was propelled by a 2.2 liter, five cylinder engine, 200 hp turbo. With constant improvements, more than 11,000 units were produced. In March 1980, at the Genf Motor Show, the first Audi Quattro was introduced. Four-wheel drive became an important characteristic for the Ingolstadt manufacturer.

At the end of the '70s, the VW/Audi alliance began working towards a technical evolution, which today is adopted as an obvious component by numerous manufacturers, and not just in Germany: four-wheel drive. Undoubtedly, as early as the '60s, various car manufacturers launched four-wheel drive vehicles (the first one that comes to mind is the Jensen FF, of which at least 320 units were produced, and Ford provided the British Police Force with 22 Zephyrs with four-wheel drive), but only Audi with its "quattro" four-wheel drive was truly successful. The company chose the Italian word *quattro*, which is a registered trademark, and therefore must be written in lower case. The decisive impetus in the evolution of the quattro four-wheel drive came in 1977 from Audi's Director of Research, Jörg Bensinger, who, during some tests carried out in Scandinavia, noticed that a VW Iltis – 75 PS, maximum speed 100 km/h (62 mph), from 0 to 100 km/h (62 mph) in 21 seconds – used as a courtesy car became faster and easier to drive on snow. He referred this discovery to the head of Audi automotive development at the time, Ferdinand Piëch, and requested the authorization to develop a prototype based on the Audi 80 with a five-cylinder (160 PS) turbo engine and four-wheel drive. This vehicle and other prototypes impressed the VW Board of Directors so much that they gave the green light immediately to develop a four-wheel drive Audi.

The quattro was presented at the Audi stand at the Geneva Automobile Fair in March 1980. Even the quattro was based on the Audi 80 and from the coupé derived from the latter, and it was enhanced aesthetically with wider mud guards, bigger bumpers, and a rear spoiler. The vehicle, which over the years became famous as the "Ur-quattro" had permanent four-wheel drive with a central and a rear differential block. In the initial years, the Ur-quattro was in production for ten years with a total of 11,452 units – it was possible to manually engage or disengage both blocks or just the rear one. Over time, the quattro transmission was constantly improved, the Torsen differential being the most representative example.

From 1984 onwards, a more powerful version of the Ur-quattro was produced, the Audi Sport quattro. The wheel base was 32 mm (1.25 in.) shorter but the length was still 416 centimeters (164 in.). The engine delivered 306 PS. The Sport quattro also represented the base vehicle for group B rally cars. In 1984, Audi won the World Rally Championships in both the manufacturers as well as the drivers (Stig Blomquist) categories with the short quattro.

When BMW was thinking of producing a super sporty car in 1976, the objective was not exactly a model for mass production. But when the M1 saw the light in the autumn of 1978 at the Paris Fair, the resonance was so great that the Munich automobile manufacturer could reasonably make a decision in that direction. It had succeeded in a sensational achievement and the M1 was the most admired debutante in Paris. An M1, with its central 277 PS engine, at the time, cost exactly 100,000 Deutschmarks – the price of four BMW 323i's, which had equally distinguished origins.

The BMW Turbo (E25), launched in 1972, had pointed towards M1. Designed by Paul Bracq, it was an experiment with the new turbo technology, but its design had a decisive effect on Giorgio Giugiaro and his designs for the M1. Initially the M1 should have been produced at the Lamborghini plant at Sant'Agata Bolognese, but the deal was not closed and Baur of Stuttgart won the contract. Only 460 units of the M1 were produced.

A decisive step in the evolution of BMW was the creation of BMW Motorsport GmbH which, for the Bavarian manufacturer, had the same effect as the quattro for Audi. All of BMW's M models are developed and produced by this company, which boasts some great success stories, like the M3, the "Granturismo" vehicle which had the greatest success of all time, or the M5, the symbol of a very fast family sedan.

But Motorsport GmbH had deep roots which went back to the beginning of the 70s. At that time, in 1971 some light coupes of the 3.0 CS model, called CSL, had been produced jointly by BMW and Alpina. These served as a testing for car racing. 169 units of this first CSL series were produced, each weighing only 1,165 kg (2,568 lbs.). Between August 1972 and the same month of 1973, 939 units of a second CSL series was produced but with a 200 PS engine rather than the previous 180. However, it was the third step in the evolution of the 3.0 CSL (from July 1973 to November 1975, the 3.2 liter, 206 PS) which had the greatest success of all. The "Batmobile," distinguished by its enormous back wing, was the first BMW to enjoy the future colors of M GmbH.

Bottom right *Unfortunately, the BMW Turbo (E25) designed by Paul Bracq and presented in 1972 was only a guinea pig. Yet, in those years the central turbo engine was unusual for BMW.*

Top right The author of the BMW M1 design is Giorgetto Giugiaro. Initially the vehicle was supposed to be built by Lamborghini but the idea soon lost steam. The BMW M1 is one of the milestones of the Bayrische Motoren-Werke's history. Between 1978 e 1981 only 460 units of the M1 were built. Obviously BMW used the M1 in races as well – the most admired was the unusual Procar Series, which, in 1979/80 accompanied several Formula 1 races as a sideshow.

Commissioned by VW, at the beginning of the 70s, Porsche had built a sports car which, because it had parts in common with the VW/Audi program, should have been very economical to produce. But although the VW dealers asked repeatedly for a successor to the VW-Porsche of the past, the 914, the vehicle was not built. Wolfsburg was still feeling the effects of the oil crisis, and it still had to digest the huge investment made for the Golf. Porsche re-acquired its construction rights to produce the vehicle with its trademark and the 924 name. But the 'Volks-Porsche' was produced from 1976 onwards mainly at the Audi plant in Neckarsulm. It was indeed for this reason that many parts came from the VW/Audi storerooms.

Initially the 924 was not well received by the Porsche family. This was not only due to the cheap parts but also the fact that the small Porsche was produced exclusively with a four-cylinder engine. However, in the mid-80s the 924 and its direct descendants, the 944 and the 968, had a significantly greater success than the legendary 911, and in 1986, 30,784 units were sold whereas the 911 only just reached a third of this figure. Strangely, the "transaxle" design (with the engine in front and a rear gear box on the rear transmission axle) was applied to the 924 (and also to the 944, 968 and 928). This guaranteed a balanced weight distribution and a rather sporty transmission, but it proved to be more expensive to produce. It was precisely these costs which brought about the end of Porsches with a front engine: in 1994 the 968, with the most powerful model exceeding 300 PS, was abandoned.

Only a year after the 924, Porsche launched the 928. This vehicle, like the 924, was built with the 'transaxle' construction design. Originally, it should have replaced the 911 and was therefore fitted with an extremely powerful engine for the time, a V8 4.5 liter with 240 PS. But Porsche customers did not accept the 928 as a sports car; they still only saw in it a "Granturismo" car, which was true. At the end of the '70s, the 928 was, from a technical point of view, certainly a better car than the 911. Nevertheless, the customers with their continuous protests succeeded in having the "nine eleven" made more powerful and improved, to such an extent that the trend changed again and the "classic" Porsche once again became the trademark, flagship product.

The fact that it was rarely used in car races was a problem for the 928. The expensive structure of the rear axle which went down in history as the Weissach axle was certainly a case of pioneering evolution but it was not suitable for the racing circuits. Over the years, the 928 was fitted with great care. The most powerful model, the GTS produced between 1992 and 1995 developed 350 PS with a 5.4-liter engine.

Bottom center In the mid-seventies, Porsche built an affordable sports car on behalf of Volkswagen. VW then halted the project. Porsche bought the rights and in 1976 the 924 was born.

Top right Section drawings of a 1976 Porsche 924. In the early years of production many components came from VW/Audi, which turned off Porsche enthusiasts, who were loyal traditionalists.

924

The Mercedes G Class has been in production without almost any modifications since 1979, and is rightfully considered one of the world's best off-road vehicles. It was designed upon request of the Shah of Persia, who needed a hunting vehicle.

With the G (which stood for *Geländewagen*, the German word for cross-country vehicle), Mercedes-Benz created a true classic, that has remained almost unchanged from 1979 until today. Development began in cooperation with the Austrian Steyr-Daimler-Puch in 1972, it seems upon the insistence of the Shah of Iran, who at that time owned 18% of Daimler shares and wanted a vehicle for hunting but also for his border police. The suits at Daimler hoped that the German army would be a possible customer, but due to costs, the latter chose the VW Iltis. In 1975, mass production had already started and Graz was selected as the production location where even today the G continues to be made.

The Mercedes G-Wagen is a classic off-road vehicle, with a sectioned chassis similar to that used for the Land Rover Defender (which is two decades older than the G). Rigid axles, springs with long spring travel, high ground clearance, and locking differentials are a few of its peculiar characteristics. Even today, the G is still a valid cross-country vehicle in terms of its design. But in the meantime, it has evolved from being an untiring work vehicle to a trendy status symbol. Whereas it is increasingly difficult to find it on dirt tracks, it is frequently seen in city parking lots, in front of fashionable clubs and expensive shopping malls. From being one of the most spartan cross-country vehicles, it has become more akin to a covetable SUV. There is no more demand for sober and reliable diesel vehicles (the first G had a 2.4 liter 72 PS which reached 117 km/h, 72 mph) but for opulent 8 cylinders. The present top-of-the-range version, the G55 AMG, develops 500 PS, thanks to which it also moves with great agility on a light terrain. Currently there are three models of the basic bodywork available, a short wheelbase cabrio and two station wagon models, a short and a long wheelbase.

CHAPTER 7

Hard Times for Automobiles

The 959 was the ultimate 'super car' of the 80s. 450 hp, twin turbo, all wheel drive, top speeds of over 300 km/h (186 mph), and went from zero to 100 km/h (62 mph) in only 3.7 seconds.

The 80s also saw, among other things, the end of Communism. This was significant for the German automotive sector because the main market, the domestic one, became bigger overnight. But, previously it was not doing well. In 1980 German automotive production fell from 3.93 to 3.52 million units. The industry went through a very slow revival and two figure growth rates were a thing of the past. In 1989 production reached 4.56 models in Germany, a result which was well above expectations.

But, another matter became increasingly important. In 1989 the 'Green' Party was founded, the environment movement finally had a political voice. Initially the latter was rather weak but after the Russian nuclear disaster at Chernobyl (1986) it gained considerable importance. Even mass motorization, in constant growth, the increasing number of accidents, the traffic problem et cetera, caused also by the limited use of non-profitable rail transport, were increasingly the subject of criticism. This is also why, in the 80s, designers repeatedly affirmed that design was now of secondary importance. However, it was not a glorious decade for the automotive industry, vehicles were increasingly alike, technical features were far more important than aesthetics and for this reason, in those years, few vehicles were worthy of going down in history as outstanding products.

The sales of Japanese car manufacturers were not yet a cause for concern. But many managers were already somewhat worried by the Far East because the Japanese had already overtaken German producers in the 80s in terms of efficiency. *Lean Management* was the password and production was *'just in time'*.

One of the principal players in this context was Jose Ignacio Lopez de Arriortua. At the beginning of the 80s he had set up an Opel plant in Spain which became a model for efficiency. His concept was based on the fundamental principle of production growth without investments because this should be made (and financed) by the suppliers. In 1987 Opel put him in charge of production and purchasing and a year later he was given the same position in GM Europe in Zurich. Lopez's influence was long lasting; he became synonymous with cheap and often faulty parts which the customer then had to pay for with high repair costs. Lopez was subsequently responsible for a huge scandal in the 90s when he moved to VW, for taking to Wolfsburg, with him, the designs of the new Opel Corsa.

Left Design models from the late 80s during the rafting phase for the C140 (the coupe of the S Class W140, 1992-1999). Note the more disparate intakes, especially the American ones.

Right Scenes from a long project: in the late 80s the Mercedes design studio is working on the new S Class (then known as the W140). Computers are still not widespread to all sectors.

Once again BMW had good intuition. Very soon the Bavarians understood that customers were after was more powerful vehicles. Now this field could either be left to the specialists (an activity that was also carried out by BMW thanks to its tight links with Alpina or Schnitzer) or BMW could address this field in a more dedicated way. In the mid 80s, BMW, through its M GmbH, took an important and decisive step which had long term effects. In 1986 the BMW M3 appeared on the market. The M3 was not exactly the first M GmbH vehicle; in the early 70s there had already been the light version of the 3.0 CSL. In 1978 there was the M1, and at the beginning of the 80s the letter M featured on some models of the 5 series of the time. But the M3 represented a step forward. BMW marketed at a reasonable price, a vehicle which represented a basic platform product that was also perfect for racing –and which rendered the work of third party 'tuning' specialists obsolete.

The first M3 (E30) had a four cylinder 2.3 liter engine which was developed with 194 bhp. Initially, it was only available in the two-door saloon version, but from 1989 onwards it could also be ordered in the Cabrio version. There were obvious differences with respect to the 'normal' E30. The wider mud guards, spoilers, and the side skirts made it stand out. But the modifications went much further. The rear window was flattened for reasons of aerodynamics, and the boot door was lighter and 4 cm (1 in.) higher. This considerably improved straight line stability – and the results were clear, since the first M3s reached a speed of 245 km/h (152 mph) and went from 0 to 100 km/h (62 mph) in 6.9 seconds. Between 1986 and 1992 about 18,000 units were produced: a sensational success for BMW.

But the first M3 was not only a success in terms of sales, it also showed its strength on the racing circuits. It was the most successful 'Granturismo' vehicle in the world. It has won more than 1,500 races, 60 championships, 7 European Mountain championships and, the 24 hours of Spa and Nürburgring 8 times. In 1987 Roberto Ravaglia became first Granturismo world champion driving an M3.

Naturally the M3's career did not end in 1992 when the E30 was replaced by the E36. A new version of the M3 was born with a six cylinder, 3 liter engine and 286 bhp. Initially there was only the coupe, version, but from 1993 there was also the four-door saloon, and from 1994 there was the Cabrio. From 1996 onwards the six cylinder 321 bhp 3.2 liter engine was used and from 1997 the M3 with the SMG (Sequential Manual Gearbox) available as an optional was the first mass production vehicle in the world to have a sequential gearbox. By the end of 1999 exactly 71,242 units of the M3 (E36) had been produced. The subsequent model E46 had a completely new six cylinder 3.2 liter engine based on the high-rev principle. The car developed 343 bhp and went from 0 to 100 km/h (62 mph) in only 5.2 seconds. Of particular interest was a rather limited edition (however, over the years 1,383 units were produced) of a special model called the CSL which was significantly lighter and had a much more powerful engine (360 bhp). The CSL has already become a much sought after collector's item.

Finally, in 2007 the youngest variation of the M3 (E92) appeared on the market. Under its hood it had an eight cylinder 420 bhp 4 liter engine. But for many M3 fans, the E92 which weighed around 1.7 tons, betrayed the original ideal. It is too difficult to handle and aesthetically too showy.

Top right The BMW E30 series was produced between 1982 and 1994, consolidating BMW's fame as a sports sedan producer. The 3 was available with refined six cylinder engines too.*

Bottom right From 1990 onwards, the E30's successor was the E36 (until 2000). Even this model was built in many versions, including the powerful M3. The only thing missing was the all-wheel drive, which was no longer available.*

Überlassen Sie ihm doch mal das Steuer Ihres 6-Zylinders.

Wenn Sie einen BMW 320i fahren, ist es durchaus möglich, daß Ihr Begleiter zum Kavalier der alten Schule wird. Obwohl er voll emanzipiert ist.

Er weiß zu schätzen, daß Sie im Beruf und Privatleben Ihren Mann stehen. Genauso wie er weiß, daß Sie sich für die Fahrkultur eines 6-Zylinders entschieden haben.

Für starke Durchzugskraft in allen Drehzahlbereichen.

Für schnelle Beschleunigung (von 0 auf 100 km/h in 10,2 s) und ein sportliches Fahrwerk, das die 129 PS sicher auf die Straße bringt.

Dafür sorgen auch die serienmäßigen Niederquerschnittsreifen.

Dazu kommt die umfangreiche Ausstattung: 5-Gang-Getriebe, elektronische Einspritzung, Check-Control und Energie-Control. Das Interieur vermittelt durch Funktionalität und Design das Gefühl von Perfektion.

Daß der BMW 320i auch ein Juwel für's Auge ist, bleibt Ihrem Begleiter sicher ebenfalls nicht verborgen.

Bei den Metallic-Grundfarben schwarz, polaris und delphin können Sie die individuelle Ausstattung 'Shadow' wählen. Mit schwarzen Fensterrahmungen und Seitenleisten. Stoßstangen und Außenspiegel in Wagenfarbe.

Daß er Sie fragen wird, ob Sie ihm einmal das Steuer überlassen könnten, ist sicher. Und seien Sie dann so souverän, es auch zu tun.

BMW 320i Kauf, Finanzierung oder Leasing – Ihr BMW Händler ist der richtige Partner.

Freude am Fahren

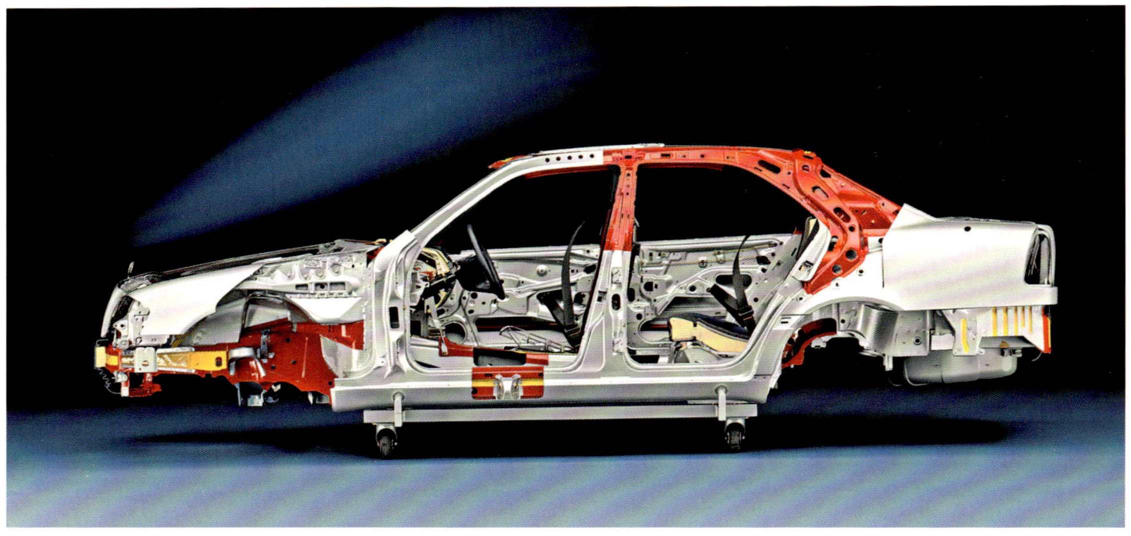

The success of the BMW 3 series (E21 since 1975) gave Mercedes-Benz food for thought. To go against the 3 series, meant moving away from its traditional market sector of the sought after middle class to a lower range for the noble Stuttgart manufacturer. Initially this was very difficult for the Daimler management. However, on the 8 December 1982, the Mercedes W201 was launched. The model which was denominated 190, was also known as 'Babybenz'. Mercedes themselves had designated it as a 'compact class' but of course the W201 was not at all 'compact' because it certainly did not compete with the VW Golf which, at that time was extremely successful. But even the model denomination itself indicated, on broad lines, the esteem initially enjoyed by the 'Babybenz' within the company. But the critics were soon silenced, the 190 was extremely popular and, in a little more than 10 years, around 1.9 million units were sold which made the W201 one of the most successful models in the entire Mercedes history.

Mercedes had dared to make a break from the rather conservative design of the past. A short, high, thinner tail section, streamlined towards the rear became a distinguishing feature of the W210 (and also of its successors) and the 'Babybenz' was the first Mercedes without chrome finishing, with the exception of the radiator grid.

The W201 had some extraordinary technical innovations. It was the first Mercedes with a back 'tridimensional' axle, and it was the first vehicle of modern times to have a single arm windscreen wiper. Its engines however, were more conventional and in this field Mercedes was not on the same level as its competitor in Munich. This was also the case with the 190E 2.5-16 which was produced to compete with the M3 and which was noted more for its showy rear wing than for its engine power. But in 1992 Mercedes won its most important race with this vehicle, the DTM (Deutschen Tourenwagen-Meisterschaft), the German 'Granturismo' championship; the four valve cylinder head of this vehicle was made by Cosworth.

In June 1993, the W201 was replaced by the W202. The new Mercedes medium class was christened C Class – and caused some problems for the trademark, because of significant quality problems and above all rust.

Top left Beginning in the 70s, American laws in particular, prescribed strict guidelines to manufacturers for passenger safety. Here, a C Class in a controller crash-test.

Bottom left Mercedes constantly increased its efforts to enhance safety (as early as in the 60s). Beginning in 1997, Mercedes installed airbags and brake guards as standard on the W202.

Top right Klaus Ludwig in a Mercedes 190 E 2.5 16 at the DTM in Mainz-Finthen, 14 May 1989. It was the 'world premiere' for the Mercedes AMG and the driver, Klaus Ludwig (No. 1), left the race during the first lap.

Bottom right The fortunate Baby-Benz (W201) was available in many engine versions (four, five, six cylinders, always in-line). The build was always the same: front longitudinal engine.

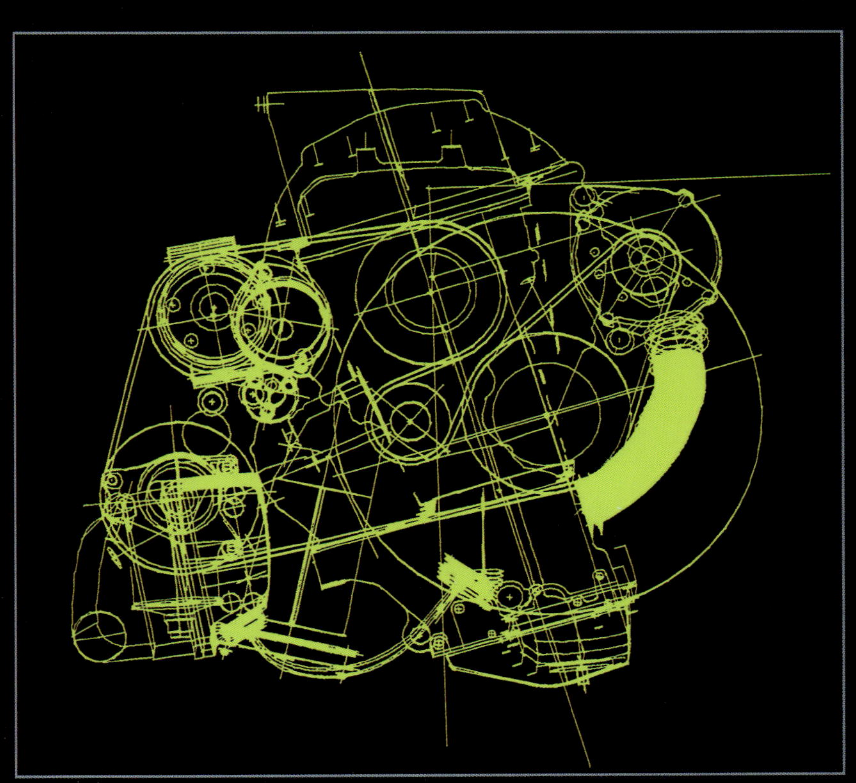

MASSKONZEPTION C126
SIFI. 12.03.77 SCHEURING

ÜBERHANG 870

These problems never occurred with the Mercedes flagship model, the S Class. In the past there had already been other Mercedes models denominated 'S', the W108/109 (1965–1972) was known to the public as the 'S class' but only the W116 series which came to the market in 1972 was officially denominated the 'S class'. For those who are amazed at how demanding Mercedes is of itself, 'S' stands for 'Special'.

The W116 was an extraordinary vehicle. With this vehicle, Mercedes not only claimed leadership in the top range but was also able to affirm it. However, the Stuttgart manufacturer also exploited the competition's weak points, with the Americans who were suffering the effects of the oil crisis and Rolls Royce/Bentley struggling with a massive decline. For these reasons the 450 SEL 6.9, presented in 1975, was considered the best car in the world and not only by the German press. In 1978 the W116 was the first vehicle in the world to be fitted with a completely electronically controlled ABS. By 1980 more than 470,000 W116 units had been produced.

From 1979, Mercedes was able to increase its advantage even further with the W126. With around 900,000 units sold, the W126 is the most success-

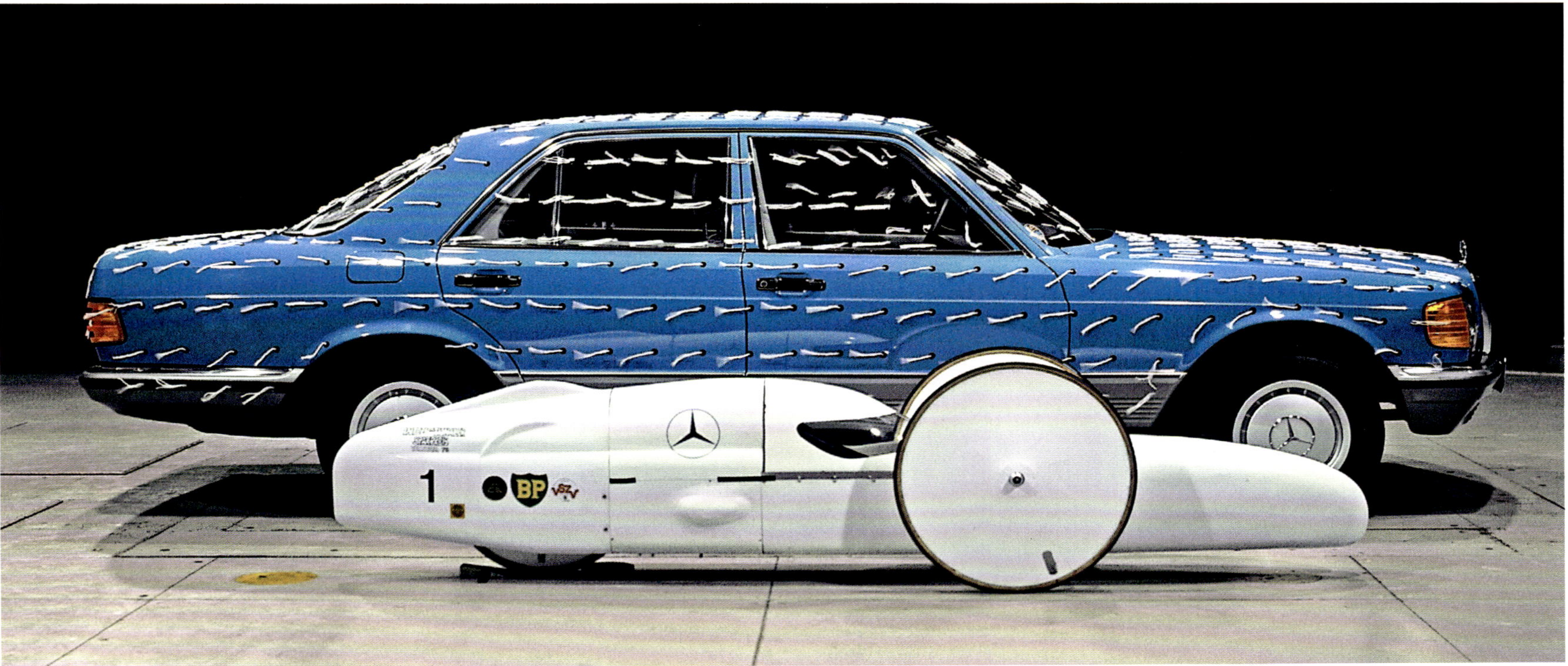

ful S class, as well as the top end vehicle with the highest number of units sold in automobile history. One must consider nonetheless, that this model was produced over 12 years, an unusually long period of time.. The success of the W126 was not surprising. Bruno Sacco had created an outstanding timeless design and Werner Breitschwerdt, as technical manager managed to include many touches of finesse. American and British competition remained way behind; only BMW with its 7 series (E23 from 1977, E32 from 1986) could compete. Audi, with its A8 only arrived on the market in 1988.

In 1981 the S class was the first European automobile to boast an airbag as an optional. In the brochures of the time it was called an 'air cushion'. The passenger's airbag appeared for the first time with the 1988 model.

As early as 1987 there was a first Acceleration Slip Regulation system (ASR), the 300 SD produced from 1985 to 1987 was the first diesel vehicle with a diesel particulate filter. Even today the W126 is a classic example of a high quality top end saloon. This is why this S class is still so popular almost 20 years after going out of production.

Top left A marvelous drawing from March 1977. It represents the S-Class coupe (W126, unofficially known as C126), which was presented in the fall of 1981. Notice how long production times were.

Bottom left A 1:5 scale model of a Mercedes S-Class (W116, 1972-1980) is automatically analyzed on a longitudinal, transversal and vertical section. This procedure was important to understand the implements that were to be used in production.

Top right The W126, built from 1979 to 1991, is the all-time best-selling high-end vehicle. Almost 900,000 units were built. This S-Class helped the Mercedes brand gain worldwide fame.

Bottom right An S-Class (W126) in the wind tunnel during an aerodynamics test. In the foreground, a 'Sparmobil', the car that on 8 July 1979, covered a distance of 967 km (601 mi.) with only two gallons (one liter) of diesel.

Top left and right *Even today, although computer technique is very advanced and almost all phases of design are done in front of a screen, much care is put into realizing the first 3D models of a new car.*

It could also be due to the fact that its direct successor, the W140, produced between July 1990 and September 1998, was a real flop. It did not even reach half the sales of the W126. On the one hand, it was due to the fact that the design was not particularly elegant or outstanding. Furthermore, the W140 was just too big (5.11 meters long, 17 ft). With the first vehicles produced it was demonstrated that the total allowed weight was reached with only four people on board. Mercedes was forced to react with costly technical changes.

Meanwhile there had already been two generations of S class, the W220 (1998 – 2005) and the W221 (from 2005). Whereas the W220 still represented a well contemplated and elegant return to the old virtues of the S class, the current model was once again rather pompous and showy, and like the unfortunate W140 turned out to be rather difficult to sell.

Bottom left A design study for the 1987 W140. The impression is that the designers of the day had exhausted their lucky streak. The W140s were a flop (406,717 units).

BMW

Left The BMW 8 Series, chassis code E31, was sold starting in 1989. The cars did not achieve the success they were supposed to: in ten years only 30,000 were sold.

Top center Alpina is known as an auto manufacturer since 1983. The small and refined company from Buchloe has gained excellent fame with cars that are based on BMWs.

Even though BMW, thanks to the M3 which was mass produced starting from 1986, made a great (or should we say the greatest?) business deal, some other well-known names managed to keep abreast. The pragmatic example is certainly Alpina from Buchloe in the Eastern Allgäu district. In the 70s. Burkard Bovensiepen and his men were part of the team, when BMW entered the world of granturismo racing with the 3.0 CSL. Since 1963 Alpina was already known as a capable and reliable racing car engine tuning outfit. At the time Alpina already had a racing team, with drivers like Niki Lauda and Derek Bell, among others. In 1978 Alpina officially became an automobile manufacturer, producing vehicles based on BMW products; since 1983 the company has been registered as an automobile manufacturer at the federal bureau of transport in Flensburg. At Buchloe they were very proud to be the 'smallest automobile manufacturer in the world'.

The first vehicles to be produced by Alpina, as an automobile manufacturer, were the B6, the C1 and the B7 Turbo. The latter with its 300 bhp was, for a certain period, by far the fastest standard product saloon in the world, a title which the B10 Biturbo (360 bhp since 1989) claimed back. While in the initial years Alpina was happy to contribute to the decisive power boosting of BMW models, today it limits itself to perfecting them. The B3 Biturbo for example with its 360 bhp is much less powerful than the current M3 with 420 bhp, but the Alpina version goes from 0 to 100 km/h (62 mph) in only 4.8 seconds and offers gear characteristics which are much better than the standard M3.

In addition to automobile production, over the past decades Alpina has established itself as one of the best ecological traders in Germany.

Erich Bitter's is a very different story from that of Burkard Bovensiepen with Alpina. Bitter was a rather good racing driver and, from 1964, imported Abarth vehicles into Germany. In 1971 he founded Bitter GmbH & Co. K.G. and soon after, in 1973, he presented Bitter CD. This large coupe was based technically on the Opel Diplomat of the time and therefore had a V8 5.4 liter 230 bhp engine. The design was exactly what Opel at that time never managed: elegant. In total, by 1979, 395 units of the Bitter CD Gebaut were made by hand. The successor was given the name SC and was based on the Opel Senator A. Its six cylinders developed 180 bhp and 210 bhp in a subsequent version. There was also a Cabrio version of the SC and, in total, 495 units were produced up to 1989. Then there was a long silence from Erich Bitter. Only recently has he reappeared on the automobile scene, this time with the Vero. It is a variation, with slightly different bodywork, of the Holden Statesman (Australian GM) powered by a Chevrolet 6 liter V8 (378 bhp). Not even the Vero will bring success to Bitter.

Eberhald Schulz also has an interesting career behind him. Initially, at the end of the 60s, he drew attention to himself with the Erator GT, which was aesthetically like a Ford GT40. It had a 5 liter Mercedes engine and was only 96 cm (38 in.) high and extraordinarily fast for the time, reaching 315 km/h (196 mph). Subsequently, he created the Mercedes CW311, probably the only vehicle which was not produced in a Mercedes factory, which however boasted the famous star. In 1981 Schulz founded his own company, ISDERA ('*Ingenieurbüro für Styling, Design und Racing*'). Little by little ISDERA produced an increasing number of cars, first a small roadster, which still exists today, in 1984 the Imperator which aesthetically speaking, was very similar to the CW311, in 1993 the Commendatore, also available in the 620 bhp version and lastly, the 'Autobahnkurier 116i', which with its two eight cylinder Mercedes engines joined together and the baroque design (it was modeled on the Mercedes 540K 'Autobahnkurier' of the late 30s) will perhaps always remain a unique model.

Top left The Porsche 956/962 were among the world's most successful sports cars of all times. In the 1986 IMSA, Al Holbert won six races out of eighteen; the first ten places were taken by eight Porsche 962.

Bottom center In order to build the 959, Porsche relied on space technicians: bumpers and rear end were in Kevlar, the front hood and the doors were in aluminum.

But far more than Alpina, Bitter, and Isdera, which were undoubtedly all refined hand made cars, the 'state of the art' of the of the 80s was symbolized by the Porsche 959. This evolution derived from the rally 959 designs with which Porsche intended to demonstrate what it was worth in long distance rallies which were so fashionable at the time. Indeed, a Porsche-Prodrive team won the Paris-Dakar rally in 1984, but it was really by accident and it happened with the wrong car, a 911, at the time still called 953, with four-wheel drive. In fact in the Fall 1983 Porsche had already presented the 959 at the International Motor Show.

Another four years went by before the first vehicles were on the road. In all, 292 models were produced, 113 in 1987 and 178 in 1988; another eight vehicles of a special series were added in 1992.

What made the 959 so unusual was that to produce it, Porsche used only the best and most expensive components. The roof, mud guards and part of the tail were made out of Kevlar, the front was in polyurethane, the front hood and the doors in aluminum. For the first time in a standard production engine fuel injection with two turbo compressors and an intercooler was deployed. The air cooled 2.85 liter, six cylinder boxster engine was made out of an aluminum alloy (it had four valves per cylinder, two over head camshafts on each side and digital fuel injection) developed up to 450 bhp. The maximum torque was 500 Nm. It had a manual six speed gearbox and, of course, four wheel drive.

Officially the 959 weighed only 1,450 kg (3 lbs.), but measurements indicated an empty weight as high as 1566 kg (3.452 lbs.), around 300 kg (661 lbs.) higher than the Ferrari F40, its rival at the time. Notwithstanding this, the 959 went from 0 to 100 km/h (62 mph) in only 3.7 seconds and it reached a maximum speed of 317 km/h (197 mph). But with regard to handling, this Porsche proved to be surprisingly awkward – and only truly expert drivers managed to control its power which was quite extraordinary at the time. There is still some doubt as to whether all the famous owners of a 959 such as Herbert von Karajan, the comedian Jerry Seinfeld or Martina Navratilova, succeeded in doing so.

There was also political unrest behind the Porsche 959. The two founders of Microsoft, Bill Gates and Paul Allen each bought a second hand USA version of the 959 in 1998. But they could not drive the vehicles because of the very high emissions levels, until the then president of the United States, Bill Clinton personally signed a federal law which authorized millionaires to use their toys.

In 1982, the regulations for automobile racing were changed once again and the A, B and C groups were re-introduced. In the sports prototypes group there were practically no limits regarding the engine. This was good for Porsche because they had a powerful and resistant 2.65 liter twin turbo boxster which, besides being powerful (620 bhp), was also very reliable. Around this engine, which in 1981 had already claimed success at the 24 hours Le Mans (Ickx/Bell won with a Porsche 936), Porche built the 956.

The racing car had another great success. In 1982 Porsche, with the 956 at Le Mans won a triple victory (Ickx/Bell won again), in 1983 Schuppan/Holbert/Haywood reached the top of the podium, in 1984 and in 1985 the private Joest team won this legendary race with a Porsche 956, in 1986 and in 1987 the undisputed leader was the direct successor of the 956, the 962 (2.9 liters biturbo, approx 680 bhp).

The 956 engine had been converted in 1983 from mechanical to electronic injection. In this way not only was consumption reduced, but the engine power was increased (640 bhp). The sports car was available in two versions, with a short and long tail; the shorter vehicle was used on the narrower circuits, while the longer model was used on circuits such as Le Mans, where often the maximum speed was reached thanks to its special aerodynamics. At Le Mans the maximum speed was around 350 km/h (217 mph), lower than the legendary Porsche 917, one of the most successful sports cars of the 70s.

In 1982 and 1983 Jacky Ickx won the world driver's title in a Porsche 956, while at the end of the 1984 season it was Stefan Bellof who won the world title. Bellof, the first to go round the notorious north curve in Nürburgring at an average speed of more than 200 km/h (124 mph) in a 956 died in 1985, in a 956 in an unfortunate overtaking maneuver at Francorschanps. The Porsche 956/962 is among the most successful racing cars of all time.

New Horizons

The characteristic front view of a 1999 BMW Z3 M Roadster. The 3.2 liter six cylinder at the time produced 321 hp, enough for a breath-taking ride.

CHAPTER 8

It was a decade of madness. Everything seemed possible, the economic situation was favorable, all the stock market indexes were sky rocketing and the German car manufacturers thought that the world was their oyster. In 1994, BMW purchased the English Rover brand, in 1998 Daimler-Benz merged with Chrysler and in the same year the Volkswagen Group extended its own empire with Bentley, Bugatti and Lamborghini.

But this great madness cost the German automobile industry a great deal of money and energy. The Volkswagen Group was exhausted by a dispute with BMW over rights to the Rolls-Royce name which ended with BMW retaining the name 'Emily' and an enormous price for Volkswagen to pay for Bentley. The Manager of VW, Ferdinand Piëch, dissipated other resources with Bugatti; he wanted to get involved in the field of super sports cars but the project for a 1001 bhp vehicle with speeds of more than 400 km/h (248 mph) was postponed for years to come.

Even BMW had only problems with Rover. No synergy was achieved, the English were most uncooperative, their factories and their cars were completely obsolete and by the time the Bavarians decided to admit defeat on 16 March 2000, the English adventure had cost them 9 billion German Marks. The Chairman of the Board of Directors, Bernd Pischetsrieder, was forced to leave and the technical director Wolfgang Reitzle thought it wise to follow suit. The only thing left to BMW of the English automobile adventure was a bad after taste and the Mini trademark which however, could be brought back to life in a very short time and promised to be very successful.

Even the so-called merger between Daimler-Benz and the American car manufacturer Chrysler

turned out to be a disaster. Although it should have been a 'Merger of Equals', the Germans immediately took control. According to the vision of the Managing Director at the time, CdA Jürgen Schrempp, a 'Welt AG' (which also owned the Japanese automobile company Mitsubishi), should have been created. The only outcome however was chaos and Schrempp was forced to leave. The co-ownership of Mitsubishi was once again abandoned at great loss, and in May 2007 came the separation from Chrysler.

The public will probably never know how so many billions were wasted in the senseless 'Welt AG' affair; the loss of nine billion suffered by BMW with Rover seemed insignificant in comparison. Mercedes in this decade had more problems with the Elk Test which the A class did not pass, and quality issues seriously damaged the star which had shone so brightly in the past.

From 1993 onwards, in Germany, only cars with a three-way catalytic converter were allowed. It was a clear sign that the times of uncontrolled and above all senseless consumption, were over. The environmental theme was there to stay, even in the automobile industry. Unlimited individual mobility was still a measure of everything, the '*Golf Generation*' wanted to, and could, enjoy the prosperity and well being associated with selecting an automobile; but now in addition to the problems of safety which were brought to the fore in the '70s, there was also the issue of protecting the environment.

But in actual fact, the outlook for the German automobile industry was even better. In 1990 in Germany 4.66 million automobiles were produced. After a decline in 1993 (3.794 million automobiles, 22% less than the year before), the production figures rose constantly, reaching a staggering 5.348 million units in 1998.

Lamborghini belongs to Audi since 1998, and therefore belongs to the Volkswagen group. The Germans saved the brand from total failure, no wonder, when one thinks about vehicles such as the Reventon.

Top left A brief history of the most famous BMW Roadster, in Dutch. And that's how it truly is, although BMW does not have Mercedes tradition, Munich still churns out perfection after perfection.

Bottom center Built from 1989 to 1991, The BMW Z1 was the first work by BMW Technik GmbH, founded in 1985; the authors of the project were Ulrich Bez (currently at Aston Martin) and Harm Lagaay (who then moved to Porsche).

BMW had presented its Roadster Z1 to the International Motor Show as an image and technology vehicle in 1987. Officially, it was said that it was to test the reactions of the public but the production of a limited series, in reality, had already been decided. BMW Technik GmbH, a BMW subsidiary, founded in 1985, just like M GmbH which had been so successful, was to take charge of design and production. The chief Porsche designer, Harm Lagaay, was in charge of design and Ulrich Bez, now manager of Aston Martin, was in charge of construction.

The Z1 was really an extraordinary vehicle. From the exterior, the hidden doors were clearly visible in the side paneling, and the Z1 could also be driven with the doors open. From the exterior, one could not see that the engine had been moved back. Indeed, it was almost a front-central engine which guaranteed a balanced distribution of weight. This engine was the only part which came from the great series, the six cylinder 2.5 liter 170 bhp engine, gave the Z1 outstanding performance.

The Z1 did not have any additional options, and customers could choose only the color and internal finishing. Between 1989 and 1991 exactly 8000 units of the Z1 were produced.

Surprisingly, five years passed before BMW launched another roadster, the Z3, produced in the USA. It was surprising because the Z1 had exceeded all expectations, and because Mazda with its MX-5 in 1989 enjoyed great success not only on the sales front but also in terms of image.

The BMW Roadster did not owe its success to a car show room but to the James Bond film, Golden Eye. Initially the Z3 was available with a choice of only two four cylinder engines but a year later, the six cylinder 2.8 liter engine was added and this made the BMW a rather neat sports car. The 'Shooting Brake', a two-seater produced in 1998 and officially called Coupe, was interesting, but not particularly loved by customers. Only 17,815 Coupes (E36/8) were produced, whereas 279,273 units of the (E36/7) Roadster were produced.

After a restyling in 1999, the top of the range models were the M-Roadster and the M-Coupe, fitted with the six cylinder 3.2 liter engine known as M3. In the Z3 however, the engine developed 'only' 325 bhp instead of 343 because the exhaust pipe was considerably shorter than that of the 3 series.

The Z3 was replaced in the Fall of 2002 by the Z4 (E85). Even today, the design that was created by the former chief BMW designer Chris Bangle arouses a certain degree of skepticism. This is evident even due to the fact that in 2006 BMW decided on a complete restyling, but the sales figures did not improve significantly. There is also a Coupe version of the Z4 but it does not have an original style like that of the Z3 Coupe.

Left For the Z3, BMW ventured out to America, in Spartanburg, South Carolina. Out of nothing, a new, modern factory was born, where currently X5s and all the Z4 variants are produced.

Right The BMW Z3 built between 1996 and 2002 in the US in Spartanburg, was a perfectly compact Roadster produced by BMW as an answer to the Mazda MX-5, a car that was strangely very successful.

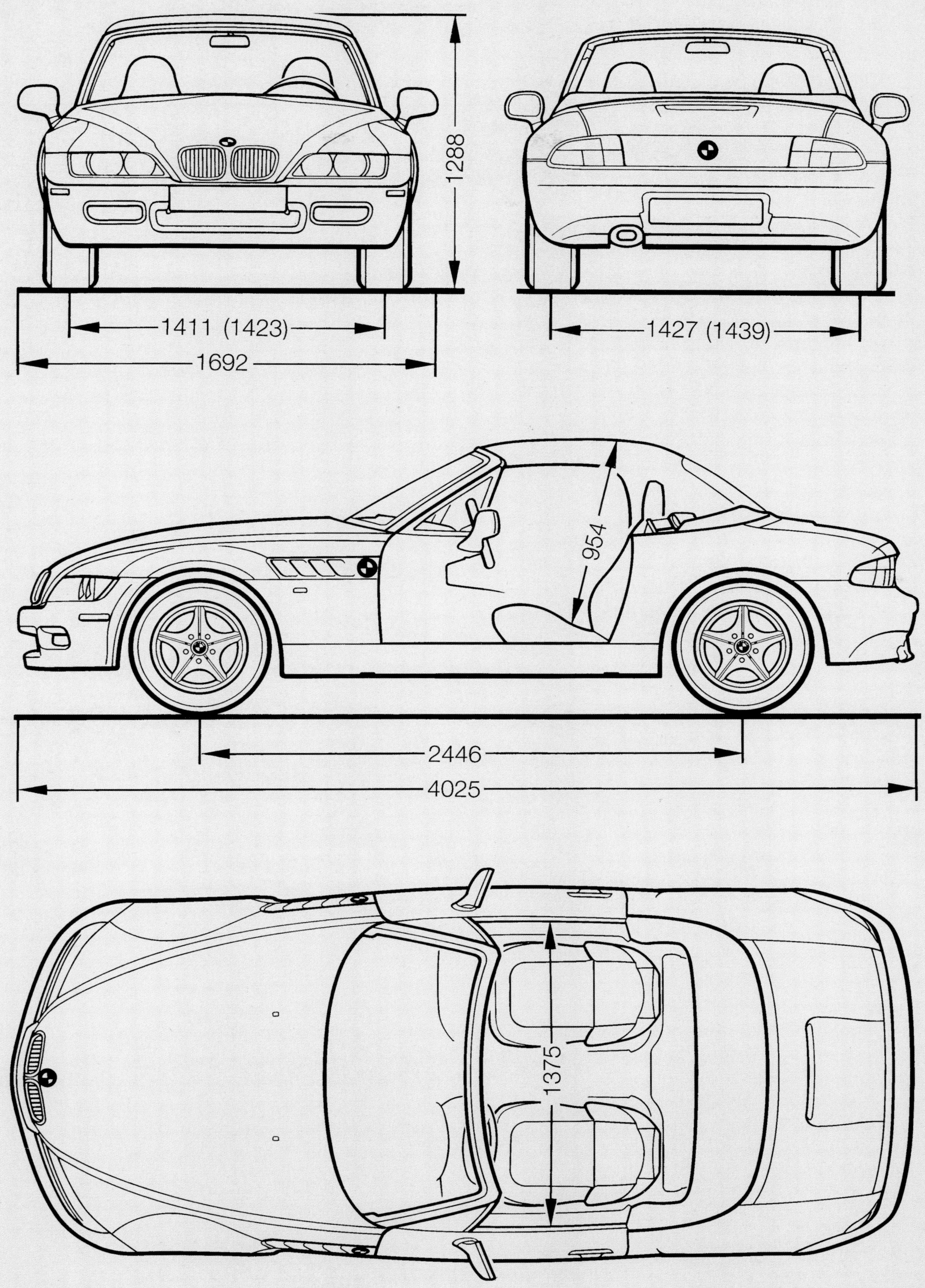
1288
1411 (1423)
1692
1427 (1439)
954
2446
4025
1375

The Z3 made a triumphant entrance with the James Bond flick 'Golden Eye' (1995). In six years, 279,273 units of this Roadster were built, to which another 17,815 units of the extraordinary coupe were added.

Top left and right The American Chris Bangle (born in 1956) was the chief designer for BMW from 1992 to 2009. His work has been the subject of many controversies. Some of his projects were never accepted (see the 7 series, 7, E65/66, from 2001).

Top center Chris Bangle with his team of designers.
As much as Chris Bangle was criticized, let us not forget that the Board of Directors has the ultimate say as far as the design of new products is concerned.

Bottom center History will deem whether Chris Bangle, the chief designer of the Z4 presented in 2002, got it right or not. An early sign is the fact that it underwent a facelift in 2004.

5,703 units of the BMW Z8 were built from March 2000 to July 2003, of which 555 'Alpina' (with automatic shift). The engine was a 5 liter, 400 hp V8 (drawn from the M5), the design is of timeless beauty. The designers went back to the legendary BMW 507 even when designing the interiors of the Z8. Out of this concept came a clean, aesthetic, and easy on the eye interpretation. The design of the Z8 is attributed to Henrik Fisker but it was the Greek Andreas Zapatinas (who then moved to Alfa and Subaru) who designed the Roadster's shape, drawing inspiration from the 507.

Bottom left The Scirocco was presented three months before the Golf, most likely because the manufacturer Karman was more flexible than the Wolfsburg. The GLI had the GTI's 110 hp engine.

Top right The VW Scirocco was born form on a hunch by Giorgetto Giugiaro, the author of the Golf design: he had formulated the concept of a two door sports coupe while working on the Golf. The project was sponsored by Karman because VW was not interested at the time.

Bottom right The Opel Calibra with front-wheel drive, for the first time on the market in 1990, cannot be considered the direct successor of the Manta. In fact, it was too expensive and a commercial flop.

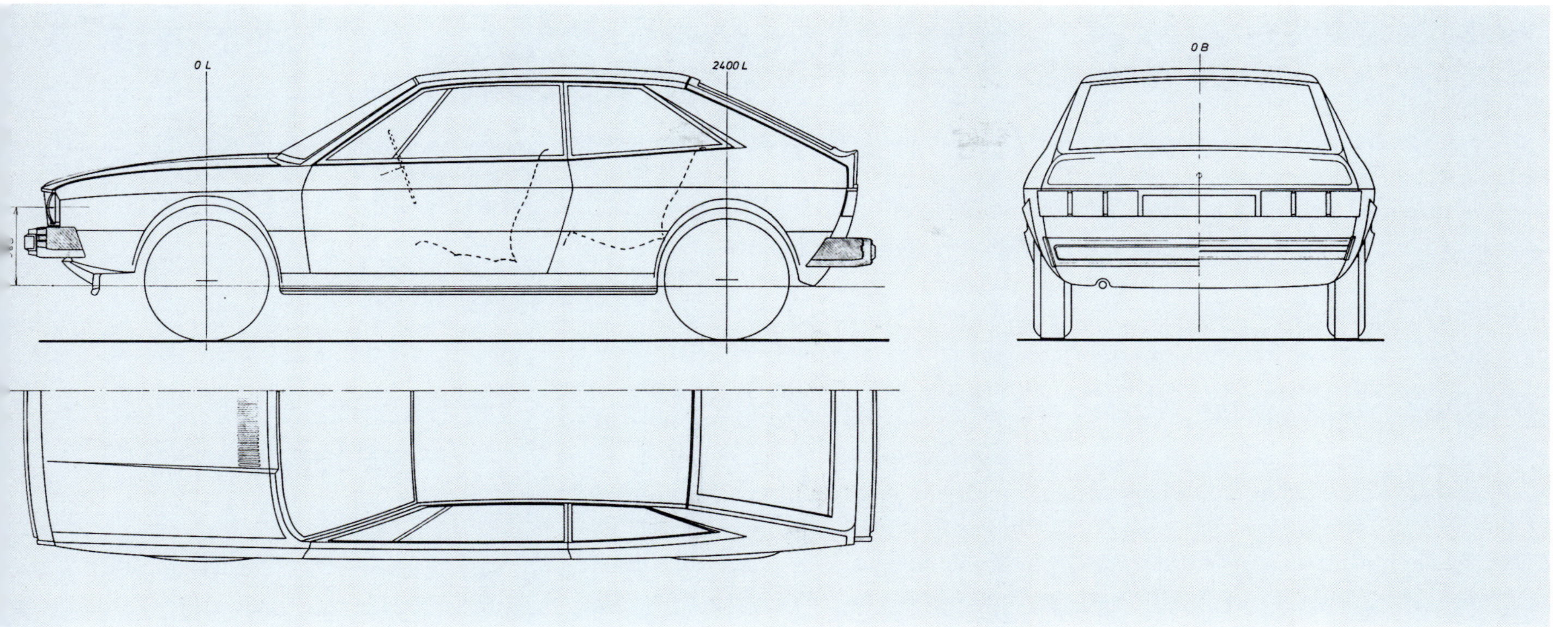

With the Scirocco, in 1974 Volkswagen had introduced, together with the Golf, a Coupe which brought a breath of fresh air into that sector of sports cars. Moreover the Scirocco was designed by Giugiaro, for whom it represented success; half a million units were sold by 1981. In the Scirocco's long series it never equaled such aesthetic beauty, and as a result was vastly less successful. In eleven years production 291.000 units were sold.

It was also for this reason, that from 1988 onwards, Volkswagen began the production of the Corrado. In actual fact, this vehicle should have been called 'Typhoon' because all VW models got their name from a type of wind, but a Typhoon had an excessively negative connotations, and therefore the Spanish sounding name Corrado was chosen (from 'correr' to run). But like the second generation Scirocco, even the sports coupe was a huge flop. After seven years and only 97.521 units, production was terminated. There was no direct successor and for the time being VW had had enough of sports coupes; only in 2008 a new Scirocco was launched.

The Corrado was, nevertheless, an extremely interesting vehicle. The only version initially available was the G60 which refers to a so-called 'Scroll Compressor', a sort of supercharger (the compressor was invented in 1905 by Léon Creux). The Corrado even had a speed-activated rear spoiler which came out automatically at 120 km/h (74 mph) and which, as indeed measured, reduced the force on the rear axle by 64%. Since 1991 the Corrado was available even with a six cylinder engine.

At Opel, production of the legendary Manta was stopped in 1988. Officially there were no direct successors, but the Calibra sports coupe, presented as a study in 1989 to the International Motor Show, was considered a ray of hope, and not only by Opel fans. The Calibra based on the Vectra, with 2 + 2 seats, was already at the dealers' sale rooms by the 9 June 1990. However, unlike the Manta, the Calibra was a front-wheel drive.

But the engines available had not changed much; there were two different two-liter four cylinders engines, one developed 115 bhp, while the other developed 150 bhp. The more powerful version had been developed by the king of engines, Fritz Indra and was the first Opel to integrate the four-valve and double overhead camshaft technology. In 1990 the Calibra 4x4 was launched, and from 1992 onwards the Calibra Turbo 4x4 with 204 bhp was added as the flagship product. This Calibra reached a speed of 245 km/h (152 mph) and went, at least on paper, from 0 to 100 km/h (62 mph) in only 6.8 seconds.

Production of the Calibra ended in 1997 after 239,639 units. This means that it was much more successful than the VW Corrado, but it never came anywhere near the sales figures of the Manta. Perhaps for this reason, nobody was contemplating a successor to the Calibra.

While the coupes seemed to have gone past their peak in the 80s and in the 90s, they declined definitively towards the end of series models, in this period another category of vehicles came into the limelight: estate cars. It is perhaps Audi, with its Avant models, which had the honor of making these practical vehicles attractive once again in the customers' eyes.

The first Avant came onto the market in 1977, the Audi 100 C2. However, it was not a real estate car but it had an obliquely cut tail and a hatchback. The name Avant was only used again in 1991 for the Audi 100, and from 1992 onwards the Audi 80 was also available in the Avant version. But the Avant estates only really came to life in the A4 and A6 models. They had finally and permanently become 'lifestyle' cars. The trunk volume was not exceptional and for this reason Audis could be attractive from an aesthetic point of view. A couple of years went by before BMW and Mercedes caught up with Audi in this sector.

The excellent image was undoubtedly due to the very sporty RS2, RS4 and RS6 models. The RS2 was the first of these models and 2,891 were produced between 1994 and 1996 which was the result of a joint exercise with Porsche. The RS2 was officially available only in the Avant estate version but it is probable that there are at least 3 RS2 saloons which never featured on sales brochures. The RS2 had a five cylinder turbo engine which developed 315 bhp and which, thanks to its performance, took Audi to the top of the sports car category. However, the brakes did not match its extraordinary power.

Audi only re-started production of an RS model in the year 2000 for its A4 series, now called RS4. This time it was produced in league with Porsche but by its subsidiary Quattro GmbH, that from the end of the 90s produced Audi sports models (like M GmbH for BMW). The RS4 had a 2.7 liter V6 engine, revised by Cosworth which developed 381 bhp. In two years 6,030 units were produced.

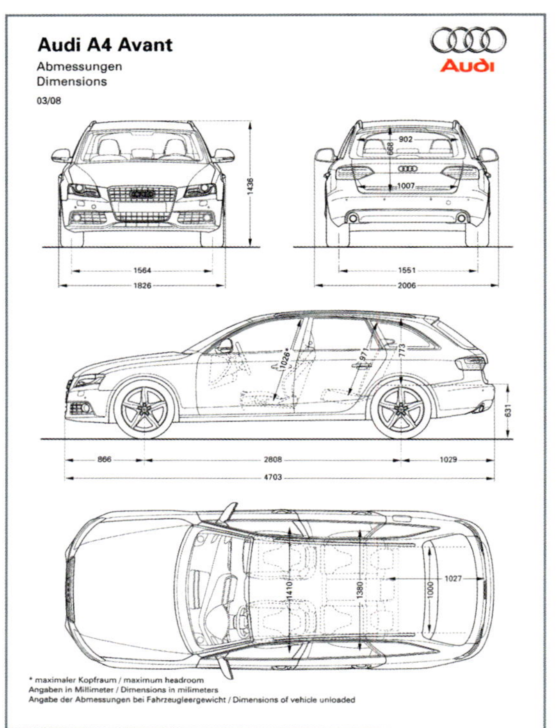

Top center The 2.81 meters (9 ft) wheelbase of the new Audi A4 is really long for a mid-size category, but the available space is sub-par, even for the combis.

Bottom left. The most recent A4 (pictured here, an Avant) is definitely more advanced than its predecessor and surpasses its traditional competitors by a long shot (BMW 3 Series, Mercedes C-Class).

Right. The youngest version of the Audi A4 – the fourth since 1994 – reached the market in late 2007. These drawing were slightly optimistic: in reality the A4 B8 is not that elegant.

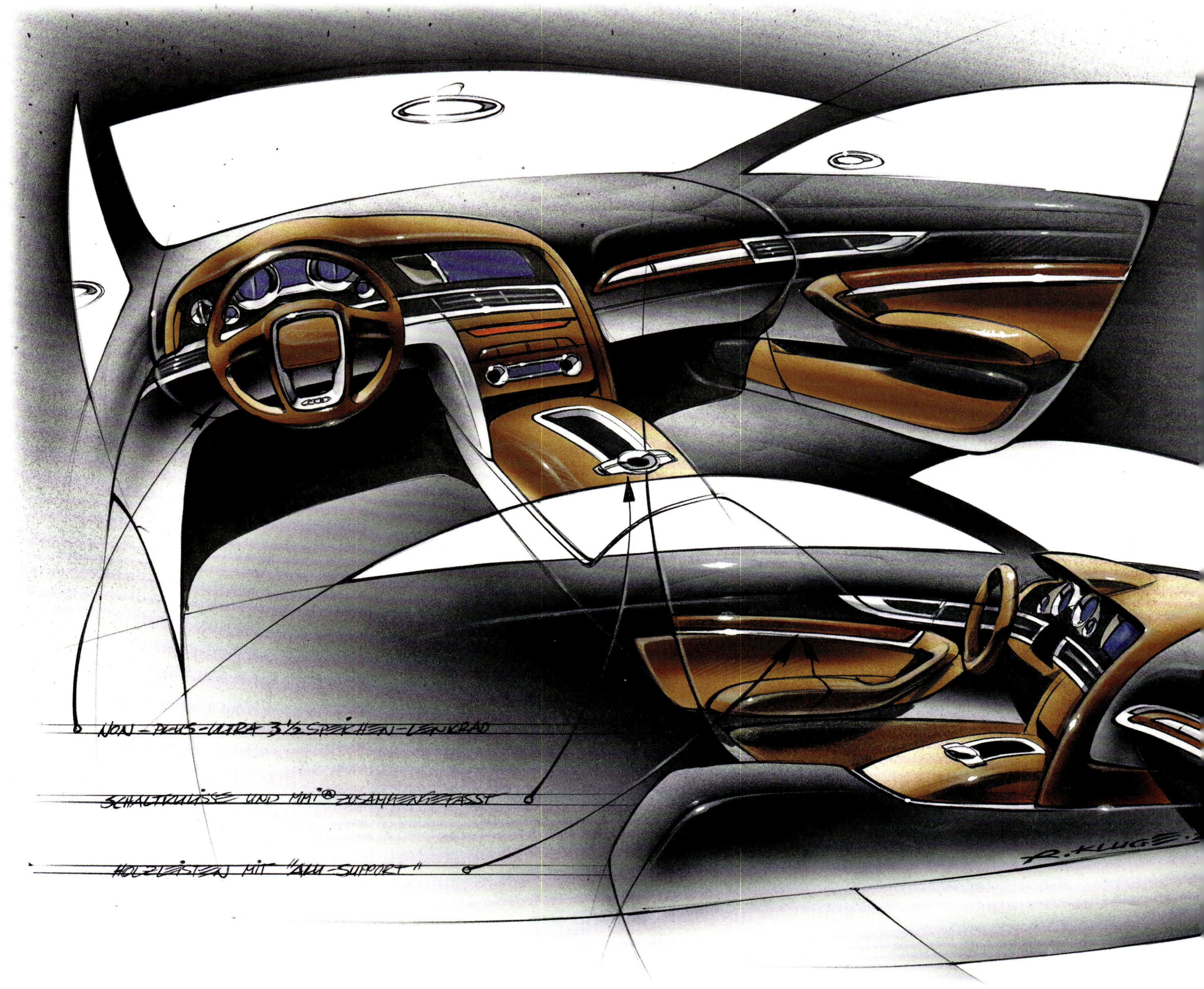

Left Let's not forget that Audi belongs to the Volkswagen Group, where synergy plays an important role, even though the sketch of this A6 interior does not really give that impression.

Right The most recent version of the Audi A6, internal code C6, has been on the market since 2004. These drawings clearly show the direction taken by Audi in terms of design.

S.WADA 03
Audi MODERN x Sporty
LOW x WIDE
Dynamic
MOVEMENT
S.Wada 03
STRONG FACE
ONE FRAME
GRILLE DIRECTION
DYNAMIC MOVEMENT
EMOTIONAL DIRECTION
S.WADA 03

Top left and top right The concave-convex lateral lines that are easily recognizable became reality thanks to modern production methods. Back in the day, it was not possible to mold steel this way.

Bottom center The first among the Audis, the A6 was equipped with the Single-Frame-Grill, starting a trend that never seems to stop. In the meantime, almost all manufacturers have begun using this type of radiator. The most recent variant of the RS6 is an absolute 'high flyer', its 5.2 liter V10 produces 580 hp, an impressive performance.

LÖFFLER

In the 90s Audi managed to catch up with BMW and Mercedes initially also thanks to the Avant estates and their sporty variations. In autumn 1998, the Ingolstädt manufacturer presented the TT, a sports coupe which did yet have any equals on the market. The chief designer of this vehicle was Peter Schreyer who, on the eve of the event, stunned the public and experts with two studies, the TT Coupe (International Motor Show 1995) and the TTS Roadster (Tokyo 1995). Because the resonance was so great, both vehicles, based on the A3 (and therefore a Golf IV chassis platform), were produced and sold over three years without major aesthetic changes. This alone should be sufficient to pay tribute to Audi.

TT, according to Audi historians, could also signify 'Tradition and technology' but probably it is reminiscent of the English 'Tourist Trophy', a legendary motorcycle race on the Isle of Man at which DKW once had enormous success. And TTS is also the name of the very fast NSU Prinz, from which the Audi TT borrowed some design features. NSU and DKW both belong to the Audi tradition.

The first TTs were fitted with a 1.8 liter turbo engine developing 180 or 225 bhp, and they were available with front-wheel or four-wheel drive. Over the years, the vehicle range expanded and the most powerful model was eventually a six cylinder, 3.2 liter 250 bhp engines, available exclusively with the 'Quattro' four-wheel drive.

But the TT did give Audi some problems. Soon after it was put on the market, there were some serious accidents because vehicle handling, when going round bends at high speed, was far from problem free. The TTs were improved with the addition of ESP stability control and an automatically retractable rear spoiler. This case was very similar to the famous Mercedes A Class 'Elk Test', but Audi reacted more positively and avoided enormous damage to its image which Mercedes, on the other hand, had suffered.

In the spring of 2006, the second generation of the TT was presented, which fortunately presented only minor differences in terms of design with respect to the previous model. The Roadster, as with the first generation, made its appearance more than a year later and, in the fall of 2008, the sprightly TTS sports car appeared.

Top left and top right. The first Audi TT reached the market in 1998, first as a coupe and a year later as a roadster. These drawings were born during the drafting phase of the second generation TT, presented in 2006.

Bottom right As in the case of the first generation TT, even the new model had its first coupe. The roadster arrived more than a year later. From an aesthetic point of view, the coupe is a nice looking car.

Top left *In 1997, Audi introduced two studies called AI2. They were in anticipation of the A2, which would start production in 1999. Only a few details were changed such as the brand's typical front plate.*

It is surprising that with the A2, a minivan produced from 1999, Audi did not come anywhere near the success of the TT. The designer of the small Audi was once again Peter Schreyer (who today works for Kia, the South Korean car manufacturer). This time, together with Stefan Sielaff and Luc Donckerwolke (subsequently Lamborghini and Sear), the A2 was, after the A8, the second Audi to have the bodywork made completely of aluminum. Probably it was precisely this 'Space Frame' which was the problem with this car. Production of the A2 was very expensive and the high purchase price of this car frightened customers. Furthermore, it was difficult to classify this vehicle. Indeed the A2, because of very similar external dimensions had been conceived as a competitor of the Mercedes A Class, but in so positioning it, the Audi also fell into the Golf category where the car manufacturer was already present with the A3 (based on the Golf).

An interesting variation of the A2 was undoubtedly the 1.2 TDi version. It was powered by a 61 bhp turbo diesel engine and had an average consumption of 2.99 l/100 km (62 mp). But the cost of this three-box vehicle, produced to date only in the five-door version, was considerable. It was not just the bodywork that was made of aluminum but also parts of the chassis and the engine block. There was also an automatic gearbox and various optimizations of aerodynamics and weight; the drag coefficient is 0.25, which together with that of the Honda Insight, is the best of all mass produced automobiles to date. Notwithstanding, the three-box A2 remained stuck in the sale rooms and in five years only 6,555 of them were sold. In total 175,000 units of the A2 were produced and it was a very expensive flop for Audi. It was a hard lesson for the Company to learn, largely due to the high price. The A2 simply came too soon, the market was not ready for a vehicle of this kind.

Bottom center The Audi A3 shares its technical structure with its sisters, the VW Golf, Seat Leon and Skoda Octavia. Of all these models it is definitely the most expensive, and has the best sales margin.

Top right Stefan Sielaff, the current chief designer at Audi, was the man behind the A2 and its preliminary drafts. However, design awards went to Peter Schreyer (currently at Kia) and Gerd Pfefferle.

Top left The Sandwich system and the roomy interiors of the A-Class require a lot of sensibility in its design, although the vehicle is rather heavy, especially when compared to the drawings in the background.

Bottom left The first A-Class (W168) by Mercedes was launched in 1997 and immediately became world-famous for not passing the dynamic stability test. For this reason, it was initially unsuccessful.

Top right In the Mercedes wind tunnel, air flow is analyzed for an A-Class by using aerodynamic probes. Mercedes invested many resources in vehicle safety.

With small cars, Mercedes had more success than Audi. After down-sizing for the first time to the lowly middle sector with the 'Babybenz' (W201 in 1982), in 1997 it took another step towards the small car sector. With the A Class it even took on the compact segment. The Managing Director Jürgen Hubbert saw Mercedes 'on the right track to fall into a trap in relation to positioning'. *"Had we stuck to the S Class we would have ended up in the same range as the Rolls Royce"*.

The A Class (W168) was (and is) a very interesting vehicle from a technological point of view. What really impressed, in particular, was the so-called sandwich structure, in which a part of the component groups could be glued onto the chassis platform. This method of construction guaranteed the small Mercedes (3.57 meters, 12 ft long) a surprisingly large internal space and an improved adaptability. Undoubtedly the Stuttgart company did its best to give the then very small model a young image but thanks to the height of its seats, and its good visibility, the A Class was very popular, above all, with an older public.

The market launch in October 1997 however, did not meet with unanimous support. In a so called 'Elk test', a non- standard maneuver, to change lanes at around 65 km/h (40 mph), which was only done in Sweden, an A-Class overturned only three days after the official presentation of the vehicle. Initially Mercedes took the problem lightly, communication was extremely poor but in a very short time the Stuttgart company was forced to suspend sales and to make adjustments, among other things, with an electronic stability program (ESP). This cost Mercedes around 100 million Euros. The institution of the intermediate warehouse for the A-Class in Kippenheim was just the icing on the cake.

Notwithstanding all this, the A Class was (and is) a particularly successful vehicle. Until September 2004, 1.1 million units of the first series were sold. The second series, the W169 continues to be popular but internally, it has met with competition from the B Class (W245) which is very similar. In future Mercedes intends to produce further models in this sector.

Oh, Smart (officially smart, written in small letters, which supposedly is a combination of Swatch, Mercedes and art) It was an ingenious discovery. Nonetheless, it is considered to be a failure. Nothing needs revolution less than the automobile industry, but today the Smart is simply 'just another' automobile, decisively small and very ingenious indeed, but nothing more. The idea of producing a micro-vehicle has always obsessed the automobile industry. After the oil crises of the 70s efforts were intensified and in the 80s the first projects appeared like the BCC (under the guidance of Professor Tomforde, who was subsequently in charge of designing the Smart) or the Mocar.

But the idea only really became reality when the Swiss Nicolas G. Hayek, watch pioneer (Swatch) began to dedicate himself seriously to the design of an innovative car. He did not simply want to construct a small car but he also wanted to create a concept of traffic circulation. Initially his ideas aroused enthusiasm with VW but the great automobile company of Wolfsburg soon distanced themselves from the initiative; Mercedes became the partner. In 1994 Micro Compact Car AG was founded, a wholly owned subsidiary. But relations between Stuttgart and Biel soon deteriorated because Mercedes insisted on creating a normal car with the Smart whereas Hayek had innovative concepts and technology in mind (such as engines with electrified cores). Finally Hayek withdrew even before the Smart was launched; only his production concept remains closely linked to the supplier's industry.

The first Smart was 2.5 meters (8 ft) long, 1.51 (5 ft) wide and 1.52 meters (5 ft) high and was powered by a three cylinder turbo engine optionally available in 45, 54 or 61 bhp versions. Naturally there was only room for two people. It had a six speed automatic gearbox. This, together with the excessive consumption, was one of the greatest problems of the first generation Smarts. But there was nothing to complain about by way of safety, ESP (in a small version), ABS, airbag. From 2000 onwards it was also available in the diesel Cabrio versions.

In March 2007 the second generation Smart was

launched 19.5 centimeters (8 in.) longer. This eliminated another one of the Smart's advantages, the possibility of transversal parking. Not even the new Smart succeeded in establishing itself as a lifestyle product or as a sales booster. Indeed, unfortunately, the end of the Smart may be near.

A great error for Smart has also been expanding the range of models. There was an absolutely horrendous roadster, one of the ugliest cars for a long time and a four-door version which completely destroyed the original concept of the Smart. These models put the Smart's figures further in the red and their production was rightly ended.

Left The Smart production line is in Hambach, France: the ideal crossroads between history and industry to place an innovative factory, that could revolutionize the way cars are built.

Right A partial view of a Smart by Brabus. Not even the added hp could help this small car – which was brilliant in itself – to beat the crisis.

Opel joined the 'new field' in 1953 and with the American inspired 'Car A Van', had taken an important step for the European automobile industry. These combined vehicles were among the first on the German market. Several years passed before they were truly accepted on the market and were freed from the image of work vehicles.

In the early 80s, there was a further development. The vans which were so popular in the USA became increasingly smaller and increasingly similar to automobiles, having previously been modified vans in the past. In 1984 the Chrysler Voyager and the Renault Espace came onto the market almost at the same time, both the really first big MPV one-box saloons. The Espace was developed starting from 1978 by Matra and was a truly innovative solution. There was an absolute boom of these vehicles and there were few car manufacturers who did not become involved.

But these big mono-space vehicles, as the terms suggests, were big and they had enough space for up to nine passengers. It was only a question of time before smaller vehicles entered this sector and once again it was Renault to set the trend with the Scénic, presented in 1996. The Scénic was an instant best-seller and the market soon demanded other models.

Opel at that time, not really used to success, turned to the development office of Porsche in Weissach, which also took on projects on behalf of third parties (Harley!). Within a relatively short period, from a close co-operation effort with Opel developers, the Zafira was born and launched on the market in 1999. The extraordinary thing about this vehicle was the so-called 'Flex7 System', that made it possible to flatten the second and third rows of seats under a completely flat surface. In other vehicles in this sector it was still necessary to remove the whole third row of seats which could be very difficult, because each seat could weigh more than 20kg (44 lbs.). The Zafira, thanks to its great versatility became an instant success – and thus saved the Opel factory in Bochum which would otherwise have soon had to close down.

The first generation Zafira was produced until 2005, followed by a bigger successor. However, the competition had not been idle, VW in particular in 2003 presented the Touran and the Zafira had left its early success behind.

The Ford Mondeo was officially launched for the first time on 4 March 1993 but its design phase had already been completed in 1986. The long period before its introduction onto the market – and as a result its rather obsolete appearance when it was presented, is due to the fact that Ford designed the Mondeo as a 'world car' which, following the example of the successful Japanese models, should have fulfilled Ford's need to create a car aimed at the middle class worldwide. But this philosophy was not followed through to its small details, indeed in the USA the Mondeo went to the dealers with insignificant modifications, as the Ford Contour or the Mercury Mystique.

The Mondeo meant divorce for Ford from rear-wheel drive after 22 years; for a brief period the vehicle was also available in a four-wheel drive version. Power was guaranteed by modern four cylinder 16 valve engines and a diesel engine; in 1994 a top of the range model was added with a 24 valve, six cylinder 170 bhp engine. Ford had set itself ambitious objectives. Tthe Mondeo should have guaranteed a 15% share of the competitive mid-range segment. It never succeeded, even though Ford constantly expanded the program and just a year after the Mondeo first appeared, it was available in 40 different versions – and the costly chassis (multi-arm rear axle) was put right by the ex Formula 1 champion, Jackie Stewart.

The Mondeo design had already been completely revised in 1997 and in 2001 it was followed by the second generation which, thanks to the 'New Edge Design' now spread by Ford, it had a much more modern appearance but it never reached sales figures expected by the manufacturer. As with its predecessor, it was above all its frame which was appreciated but this was certainly not enough to attract the masses into the dealers. The top of the range model had meanwhile become the ST220 with 226 bhp.

In 2007 the youngest version so far of the Mondeo appeared on the market. Once again the design was completely overhauled and 'kinetic' was the watch word which inspired Martin Smith. The new Mondeo was based on the same modules (comprising the chassis) as the Ford S-Max and the Galaxy and with its sheer size, 4.86 meters (16 ft) long, it created havoc in the medium-high range category. Even the Mk4 (although the Mondeo is still at its third generation) was praised for its excellent chassis. However, the new Mondeo was no longer a 'world car', the American parent company now guides its cart horse, surprisingly, considering that the latest version of the Mondeo was certainly the best Mondeo of all time.

Bottom center Volkswagen came late to the compact van segment, (as late as 2003), but its success confirmed the ability of the manufacturer from Wolfsburg. The Touran obviously draws inspiration from the VW Golf and can carry up to 7 people.

Top right Truth be told, the Opel Zafira (pictured here is the second generation, born 2005) is a rather placid vehicle, suitable for families. But the OPC version offers something for dads in a hurry too: an impressive 240 hp under the hood.

In a completely different category, far from the dreams of young families, Mercedes was in the meantime working away. In only 128 days the then current 'Mercedes engine tuner' AMG (acronym of Hans-Werner Aufrecht and Erhard Melcher di Groassaspach) in the winter of 1996/7 produced a vehicle which Mercedes could find a scope for in the new GT FIA championship when the DTM was phased out. Of course 25 vehicles approved for road use were necessary for certification but the sporting authorities granted Mercedes a special authorization to provide the vehicles at a later stage, because otherwise the starting grid would have been very bare.

The vehicle was known as the CLK GTR, but apart from the name and the shape of the lights it had nothing in common with the standard CLK (W208). The AMG engineers could freely draw from Mercedes, and they did so, creating a racing vehicle with a central V12 engine. The vehicle was so dominant in the GT1 class that it not only won the 1997 and 1998 championship, but also neutralized all competitors. The championship was abolished, but Mercedes/AMG had to provide the 25 standard production vehicles between November 1998 and the summer of 1999 – which was not a good prospect.

Furthermore in 1999, on the occasion of the 24 hours of Le Mans, where Mercedes was represented

On 17 May 1998, Bernd Schneider/Mark Webber won the FIA GT in Silverstone on a CLK GTR. As far as the look of the street version of the CLK GTR, it was barely distinguishable when compared to the race car version. The back spoiler was slightly smaller.

Following pages Much like the CLK GTR by Mercedes, even the Porsche GT1 was originally built as a race car, in 1996. However, for approval, a few street-ready cars were also built. They produced 600 hp.

by an evolution of the CLK GTR, the CLR had a very serious accident. Going over a rise along the track, Peter Dumbreck's car lost contact with the tarmac and suddenly became airborne, somersaulting backwards and ending up in the trees alongside the circuit. Dumbreck survived with a few bruises but after this accident, the then managing director of Mercedes, Jürgen Hubbert declared that his Company would never race at Le Mans again.

Like the racing versions, the bodywork of these road versions was made of carbon fiber. And like the legendary 300 SL, even the CLK GTR had gull-wing doors; in the production versions safety was guaranteed by front and lateral airbags. The engine - in this case behind the driver – was based on the 6 liter 12 cylinder engine that had been used on the S600, enlarged to a capacity of 7 liters developing 631 bhp. Two vehicles were fitted with a 7.3 liter V12 engine from the AMG program which it would seem developed 720 bhp. With a price tag of 2.65 million German Marks, the CLK GTR was (and still is) the most expensive production automobile on the planet, in comparison to which even the 1001 bhp Bugatti Veyron, is a bargain.

In 2002, five units of a second variation of the CLK GTR were produced. These were a roadster version which however, did not have the soft top.

Maintaining the Lead in the Dawn of a New Era

The GT2 was the best of the 911; the 530 Turbo, four-wheel drive, sporty, lightened and full of all that is costly and good. A superior Porsche product.

CHAPTER 9

At the beginning of the 21st century, the German automobile industry had to face new challenges. Traffic congestion, environmental safety, global warming, depletion of oil deposits, and the high price of gas. The automobile was definitely under fire. In 1997, Toyota had launched the Prius, a hybrid car, and the German automobile manufacturers sneered at it and in some cases made nasty comments. But even though it is widely known that the hybrid car is not a permanent solution, the approach of many Japanese companies was successful, and it brought about a change in the way of thinking of even German manufacturers. By 2010, Mercedes and BMW would introduce vehicles with a supplementary electric engine and other manu-

facturers could not afford to simply sit back and observe.

One thing is certain: the near future is sure to be very interesting. The global automobile industry is facing the most massive changes in its entire history and it will never be the same again. It will become a competition between whoever succeeds in satisfying the political and economic requisites of automobiles in the best (rather than fastest) way possible. There will be many more hybrid cars but, in the long term, it's entirely likely that vehicles will be fully electric. What will happen with the much-supported fuel cell technology and hydrogen power is still to be seen, but the chances that this technology, probably one of the most ecologically safe, will succeed in establishing itself in the next 15-20 years, are very slim. More than technical feasibility, it is a question of infrastructure, and a matter of comprehensive energy accounting. At the beginning of the twentieth century, the German automobile industry seemed to be the best equipped to meet the great challenges of the future.

Even though Toyota has succeeded in becoming one of the most successful car manufacturers in the world, high-quality German producers are also at the front of the pack today. Notwithstanding the fact that from a technological and qualitative point of view the Germans are the undisputed leaders, there is no guarantee that things will remain so. In recent years, Korean and Chinese brands in particular have seen exponential growth in both hybrid cars (the former) and electric vehicles (the latter, who have the majority of the raw materials needed to construct batteries and engines). Moreover, it can't be denied that even some mass-market German carmakers have suffered, including Opel, which became part of the Italian-French multinational Stellantis in 2021. Given that, even German automobile manufacturers have shown that they can learn from their mistakes and they will do everything they can to respond blow-by-blow to these attacks. No matter what happens, we can rest assured that German cars will be symbols of quality for decades to come.

By the beginning of the twenty-first century, the heyday of super sports cars had been over for some time. Following the death of the legendary Enzo Ferrari in 1988, there was a spectacular collapse not only in the over rated vintage car market, but also in the market for super sports cars. It suddenly became almost impossible to sell vehicles like the Jaguar XJ220 as well as the Porsche 959.

Top left *With "Efficient Dynamics," the Bavarians had a stroke of genius that went well beyond mere marketing. And they laid solid foundations for the hybrids that arrived in the following years (especially plug-ins.)*

Bottom left and center *The Chevrolet Volt, is a revolution for the auto industry and will be the first electric vehicle slated for serial production.*

Bottom right *General Motors will develop the Volt in the States, but surely even its German branch, Opel, will benefit from this new technology. Fortunately the Volt is also easy on the eye.*

Top left Porsche worked on building the Carrera GT with the most innovative technical means. Using 3D glasses, engineers could create real images of their work on their computers.

Top center In order to maintain the ceramic brakes air brake (incredibly expensive, but very effective) at the optimal working temperature, the Carrera GT is equipped with a special pneumatic system.

Bottom left Before assembling the GT, membranes meant to isolate any noises are inserted. But does a sports car really need those? Ultimately noises and vibrations are part of the game.

Right No conceptual masterpiece, only single components of the Carrera GT. The unitary construction is made completely out of reinforced resin bond with carbon fibers, although the vehicle weighs 1.4 tons.

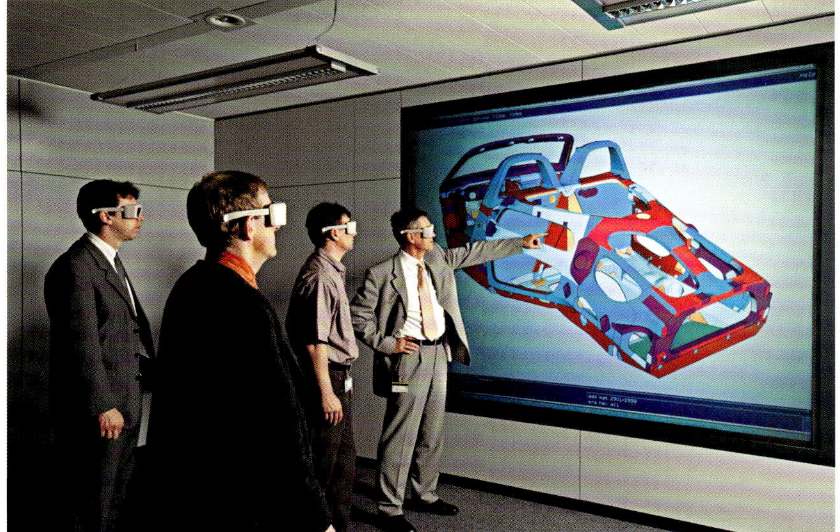

But Porsche had to make the best of a bad job. The Zuffenhausen manufacturer had developed an LMP1 prototype for the 24 hours of Le Mans but it decided not to compete. However, some parts of this racing car, such as the engine and the chassis were used for the Carrera GT which came on to the market in 2003. Even a brand like Porsche, cocooned by success as it had been, had to learn that this was still a difficult field. By April 2006, 1,500 models were supposed to have been produced and sold, but in the end, there were only 1,282 units. Not bad for a vehicle which cost 400,000 euros (excluding sales tax), though the decision-makers over in Zuffenhausen were sure they could sell all 1500 units very easily. Indeed, only Ferrari exceeded its own expectations during that period. It had intended to produce only 349 models of the Enzo but had to add another 50 vehicles due to the huge demand, even before the presentation.

The Carrera GT will go down in history as one of the fastest standard production vehicles of all time. In the test drives at the Nordschleife circuit of the Nürburgring, it completed the circuit in seven minutes and thirty-two seconds, which was sensational at the time. The adjustments to the frame had largely been done by the former rally driver, Walter Röhrl. In the Carrera GT, power was delivered by a central V10, 5.7-liter engine which developed 612 PS. This engine pushed the 1.4-ton vehicle from 0 to 100 km/h (62 mph) in 3.9 seconds (an exceptional performance for a four-wheel drive vehicle) and in 9.9 seconds it reached 200 km/h (124 mph), the maximum speed was 334 km/h (207 mph).

Le Mans '98

Top left Obviously even the outer mirrors were optimized under the aerodynamic aspect: according to the data supplied by the manufacturer the car can reach a max speed of 334 km/h (207 mph), which makes it one of the world's fastest cars.

Bottom left When the Carrera GT was launched in 2003 the technology of the xenon projectors was still rather unusual, but Porsche wanted to equip its sports vehicle with all that was state-of-the art.

Center The first thing to meet the eye was the long rear axis of the sports vehicle with the central engine. According to the manufacturer's information, the Carrera GT went from 0 to 100 km/h (62 mph) in 3.9 seconds, reaching 200 km/h (124 mph) after only 9.9 seconds.

Right The engine compartment of the Carrera GT was created for the first time in the history of automobiles in carbon fiber. The 10 cylinder engine was designed for a Le Mans race car that was never made.

Following pages Initially the Porsche Carrera GT was available in six colors: metallic silver, black, basalt black metallic, Indian red, metallic gray and yellow.

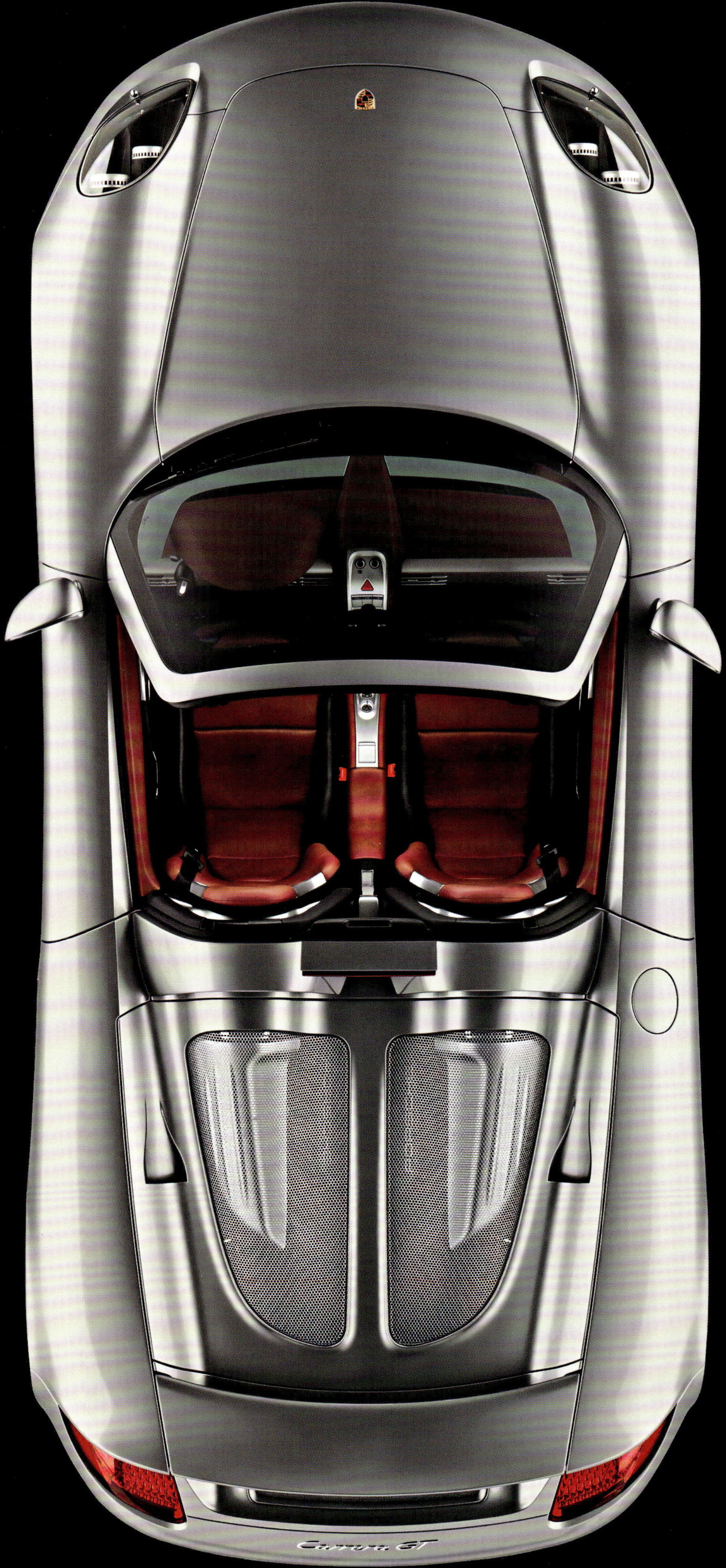

PORSCHE
PORSCHE

PORSCHE

PORSCHE

The engine of the Porsche 997 series was launched in 2006. Its 3.6 liters produces 480 hp, the two turbos have a variable geometry turbine. It reaches 100 km/h (62mph) in 4 seconds.

Following pages The Cayman, presented in 2005, is the fourth Porsche series (in addition to the 911, the Boxsters and the Cayenne). It is built on the Boxster and has the same drive, but is meant for a slightly higher segment.

turbo
RKS 637

The Porsche Boxster has been on the market since 1993; at the time, it was the second series next to the 911. Its design is a modern interpretation of the old Porsche roadsters, the 550 Spider or the 718 RS of the 60s.

Boxster

The rise of the Volkswagen Group, to become the biggest car manufacturer in Europe, truly began in the sixties, more precisely in 1964, when the Wolfsburg company purchased the then Auto Union which later became Audi AG, from Daimler-Benz. In 1986 the Spanish company Seat was added and in 1991 the Czech brand, Skoda. In 1993 Ferdinand Piëch became President of the board of directors – after which there was no stopping Volkswagen. Piëch wanted the Volkswagen Group to be a world leader in car production, not only through acquisitions, but by associating the Volkswagen name with a higher level of quality. And thus, the unfortunate VW Phaeton was born, a truly splendid vehicle but also a huge flop because it never reached its ambitious sales objectives.

In 1998 the Volkswagen Group succeeded in acquiring three prestigious brands; Bentley, Bugatti and Lamborghini. Piëch was just where he wanted to be, very, very high up. But it was not as easy as he had imagined. First, there was a dispute with BMW regarding the rights on Bentley/Rolls Royce from which the

Top left Ferdinand Piëch (born 17 April 1937, here on a chairman's meeting video of the VW Group in April 2008) is one of the most important figures of the German auto industry.

Bottom left VW has recovered very well from the crisis of 2003/2004. In that period, the Golf V sales were on a slope. The situation has improved thanks to new models and renewed products.

Bavarians emerged as victors. Then the long-awaited Bugatti Veyron did not do well and Seat was simply a huge expense. But the hardest blow was certainly the lack of success of the fifth generation of the VW Golf (from 2003). In 2003, the Group was forced to register a decline of 50% in profits, and in 2004, the company was in real trouble. In 2005, added to all this, there was a corruption scandal.

In early 2005, Porsche AG acquired around 21% of the ordinary shares of the Volkswagen Group at a low price, because the VW share price had plummeted alarmingly. By March 2007, Porsche had increased its quota to 30.9% – the major shareholder by a long shot. The policies of the biggest European car manufacturer were therefore now being dictated by a producer of sports cars of significantly smaller dimensions. As of March 2008, Wolfgang Porsche, the grandson of Ferdinand Porsche, was at the head of Porsche Holding, which grouped together Porsche and Volkswagen, taking the place of his cousin Ferdinand Piëch.

Despite the setback caused by Dieselgate in 2015 (which exposed falsified emissions levels produced by turbodiesel engines in the US and Europe), today the Volkswagen Group is stronger than ever, from the Old Continent to the rest of the world. Audi goes from one record to another, Bentley is incredibly successful (if you do not consider the initial investments), as is Lamborghini, Bugatti has finally presented the ultra-fast Tourbillon, Skoda is growing steadily and the youngest in the bunch, Cupra, is already well-affirmed in the market, poised to seamlessly replace SEAT, destined to disappear in the coming years.

Bottom right The Volkswagen group acquired the brand rights to Bugatti back in 1998. However, the Veyron 16.4, 1001 hp (300 existing pieces) only reached the market in September 2005.

MICHELIN
R8

The Audi R8 is a shocking theme. It was presented in September 2006 and its aggressive design was not a complete success. Furthermore, trends had already begun to move away from automobiles whose standard version was powered by an eight-cylinder 420-PS engine: other manufacturers were concentrating on smaller, lighter vehicles that were more economical in terms of consumption. Audi, on the other hand, had created a true rocket on wheels. There was one other problem: the principal shareholder of the Volkswagen Group, to which Audi also has belonged since 2005, was Porsche. And its bestseller, the 911, was in direct competition with the R8.

Apart from this, the R8 was launched at a time when the situation was far from congenial. During the first tests, there were problems which resulted in at least three vehicles catching fire and ending up completely destroyed. Because there had already been problems related to overheating (a few prototypes had caught fire) and the stability of another model, the Audi TT (eventually resolved), serious concerns were raised over the mass production of the R8. It would appear however, that Audi in the meantime succeeded in regaining control of the situation. As such, Audi's super sports car was given the green light. With more than 40,000 units having come off the conveyor belt over two generations, it was finally retired in March 2024. Over the course of its lengthy career, it was fitted with the V10 engine used by Lamborghini (for a total of 620 horses) and it was even offered in a version with rear-wheel drive only (the Rear Wheel Series – RWS).

The Audi R8 is a sports vehicle with a centralized engine and four-wheel drive. The engine comes from Lamborghini; the legendary Italian sports car producer belongs to Audi AG since 1998.

Following pages The R8 had a difficult beginning; from the first trials, thermal problems began and at least 3 vehicles completely burnt up. Today the problem has been resolved and the R8 has had great success.

With an all-aluminum body and a nomenclature inspired by the felicitous Le Mans racecars, production of the Audi R8 began in Ingolstadt before Porsche acquired a controlling stake of Volkswagen. In 17 years of manufacture, over 40,000 of them have been sold.

T. LAMBERTY 4/05

315km
JOY FM
Short-term memory
50%
75%
100%
25%
READY
CHARGE
POWER
P
COMFORT
AUTO
FRONT
REAR
VIEW
RADIO
MEDIA
TELEPHONE
NAVIGATION
PHONE APPS
CAR
FAVOURITES

Center and bottom *The lines and aesthetics of the hyper-sedan from Ingolstadt are futuristic: a quick glance is all it takes to see that it comes from another planet (the electric car planet). It's low, sleek and firmly planted on the ground, imposing even when seen from the side.*

Left *The driver's seat is very close to the ground and amply adjustable: everyone is sure to find their ideal position. Innovation can also be seen in its technical detailing: physical touch buttons, large screens for instrumentation and a multimedia system.*

If on the one hand Audi has abandoned (for now at least) mid-engine sports cars, the engineers up in Ingolstadt certainly haven't been sitting around twiddling their thumbs. Indeed, they've decided to embrace the opportunities presented by the green transition and explore all that electric cars can guarantee in terms of the pleasure and fun of driving. So, alongside the development of the battery-powered SUV range, 2020 saw the launch of the e-tron GT. This sleek, lowered, full-size sedan features cutting-edge hi-tech features and monstrous performance, especially when it comes to the RS version: the two 598-horsepower and 830 Newton-meter (overall) engines let it go from zero to sixty in just 3 seconds, reaching 250 km/h (155 mph) where possible. To be fair, it has to be noted that the technical foundation of the e-tron GT is the same of its cohort, the Porsche Taycan, the electric wonder from Zuffenhausen released just one year earlier. That being said, the Audi model has a personality all of its own, whose silhouette hint at superlative construction methods and technology. In addition to the dual engine, the specs sheet lists an 800-volt on-board network which, among many things, makes lightning-fast recharges possible: at 350 kW charging stations (HPC), the ones often seen near freeways, it takes just half an hour to go from 20% to 80% battery. More recently, it was given an aesthetic overhaul, an opportunity seized by Audi to bring its overall power to an impressive 925 horses (for the RS e-tron Performance) topped with 1,027 Newton-meters of torque, distributed to all four wheels.

When Mercedes presented the CLS (C219 series, based on the E Class, W211 series) in 2003 and launched it as soon as 2004, it was a great surprise. It had been years since such an elegant Mercedes was seen. The coupe, four door shape was well-accepted by the market and copycats (Jaguar XF, VW Passat CC, etc.) soon followed.

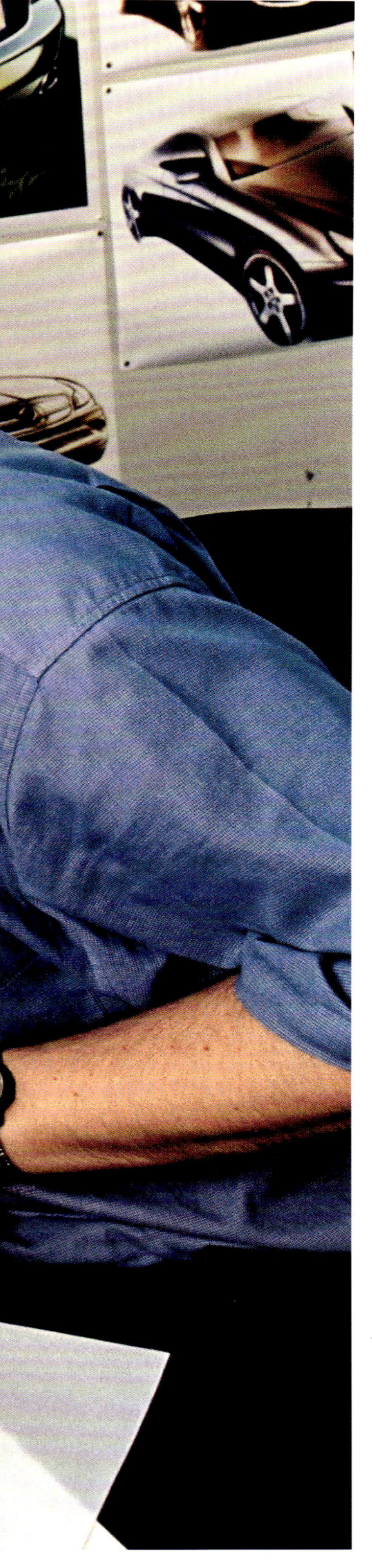

It was a great surprise when Mercedes-Benz presented the future CLS at the Frankfurt International Motor Show in 2003 as the Vision CLS concept car. At the time, Mercedes had a serious design problem and the CLS was a particularly elegant vehicle which brought a much-needed breath of fresh air to the otherwise very conservative line of the time. Fortunately, the aesthetics of the standard production model (C219) had hardly been changed. The four-door coupe (which essentially was a sedan), immediately brought a touch of color into the Mercedes dealerships. After the first CLS, which was based on the E Class (W211), another two series arrived: the C2018 (2010-2018) and the C257 (2018-2023). Obviously, even the engines corresponded with the sporty ambitions and, after minor restyling in 2008, the 224 PS CLS 320 CDI (the basic model was however the 231 PS CLS 280) and the 514 PS AMG version of the CLS 63 hit the market. Before leaving the scene, the more powerful version of the range was the CLS 53 4Matic+ EQ-Boost AMG: with its 435 horses, it had the environment in mind thanks to a mild hybrid system which kept emissions in check.

The sporty 625-PS supercar officially named the Mercedes-Benz SLR McLaren hit the market in 2004. Though 3,500 of them were made, sales never really took off. To do that it took the roadster version, presented in 2007, which was much more successful. In addition to the convertible, there was also the 722, which packed 650 PS and weighed 97 pounds (44 kg) less than the coupé.

The Volkswagen and Porsche Group were even more successful than Mercedes with its CLS with the launch of three "dinosaurs," enormous crossover SUVs, the VW Touareg, the Audi Q7 and the Porsche Cayenne. These three models have the same platform, the same chassis, the same electronics and a few basic components. The Touareg and the Cayenne came onto the market in 2002. Audi, with its Q7 which is much bigger and 5.09 meters (16¾ feet) long (Touareg 4.76 meters, 15⅔ ft; Cayenne 4.8 meters, 15¾ ft), waited until 2006 for its launch. One other thing that all these vehicles had in common was that they sold like hotcakes for years after first appearing at dealerships. The Cayenne, with 39,000 units sold in the first year, is the most successful Porsche; VW has made a fortune with the Touareg; and even Audi certainly cannot complain about the welcome which greeted its Q7 (even if it trailed far behind its sister company).

But the SUVs were not without critics. Coming in at 521 PS and an empty weight of 2.75 tons (2.5 metric tons), the Cayenne Turbo S has long held the last place in vehicles with the highest CO2 emissions. With the restyling of the Cayenne in 2007, the Turbo S was not initially included in the program but it was subsequently re-integrated. In 2019, it was the turn of the coupe with a sloping rear window. Today, at the top of the list is the Turbo e-Hybrid, a plug-in car with 739 PS and a top speed of 189.5 mph (305 km/h). The range of Porsche SUVs has recently been expanded, including downward: in 2013, the small Macan made its debut. The latest version of is entirely electric, but it hasn't lost one bit of its Porsche DNA: the Turbo has two motors, all-wheel drive, and up to 639 PS.

Of course even the Volkswagen Touareg W12, with its W12 6-liter engine (450 PS), was anything but spartan. In today's market, such an engine would be entirely out of place. And indeed, the maxi SUV is still around, though on its third generation, powered by two 3.0 V6s, one diesel (231 and 286 PS) and one gas-electric hybrid (available in 381 and 462 PS variants). Without a doubt, when it comes to SUVs that are relatively basic from a construction point of view though sold at very high prices (and rarely seen off paved roads), there is a great deal of money to be made; the margins are significantly higher than those of other vehicles. Yet these types of vehicles are dwindling in popularity, especially on the Old Continent. Their foothold remains relatively strong in the US and the Middle East, as well as in China and Russia, where they're still popular.

Bottom left In 2002 the VW Touareg, a sister of the Cayenne Porsche and the Q7 Audi. VW is satisfied not only with its sales success but also of the earning margins that this expensive SUV has been giving them.

Right The first Audi Q7 was almost 16¾ feet (5.1 m) long and weighed at least 2.4 tons (2.2 metric tons). Today you'd be hard pressed to find a good reason to make a vehicle that size.

CONCEALED ROOFRAILS

CAYENNE

NEW DETAILS

HIGH-SET SHUTLINE

PORSCHE BADGE ON FRONT CLIP.

911 STYLE AIR INTAKES

PROJECTING LOWER PANEL

• CLASSIC PORSCHE GRAPHICS

Top left Just a few years ago, nobody would have imagined that Porsche could build such an anti-sports model such as the Cayenne, but this SUV has often been the year's best-selling Porsche.

Bottom center The romantic figure of the designer that works with pencil and paper has long disappeared. Drafts are now created on computers, saving time and money.

Top center In designing the Cayenne's instruments, Porsche has kept with the 911's classic design and has managed to follow their intent to elegantly box the surplus of information that a SUV needs.

Top right Today, clay models are no longer hand-made, but are made using extremely precise robots.

Bottom right Of all the SUVs out there, the Cayenne is still the sportiest option. The second generation of the Turbo S (first issued in 2007) churned out 550 PS and could reach a max speed of 175 mph (280 km/h).

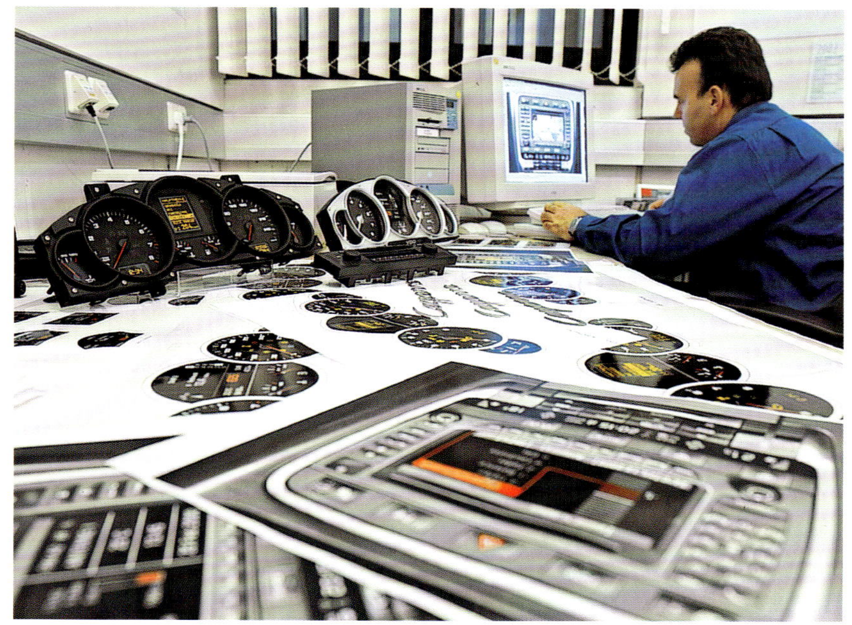

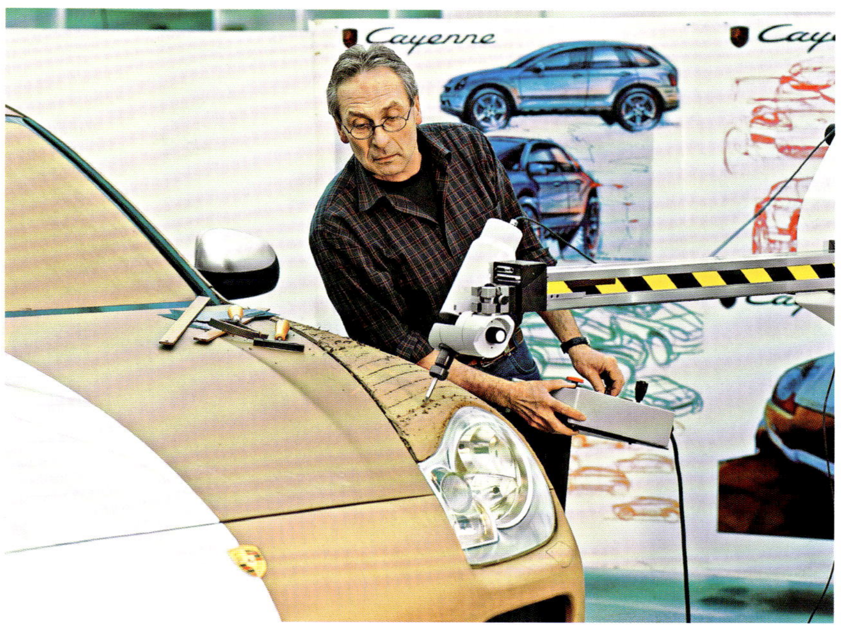

Cayenne

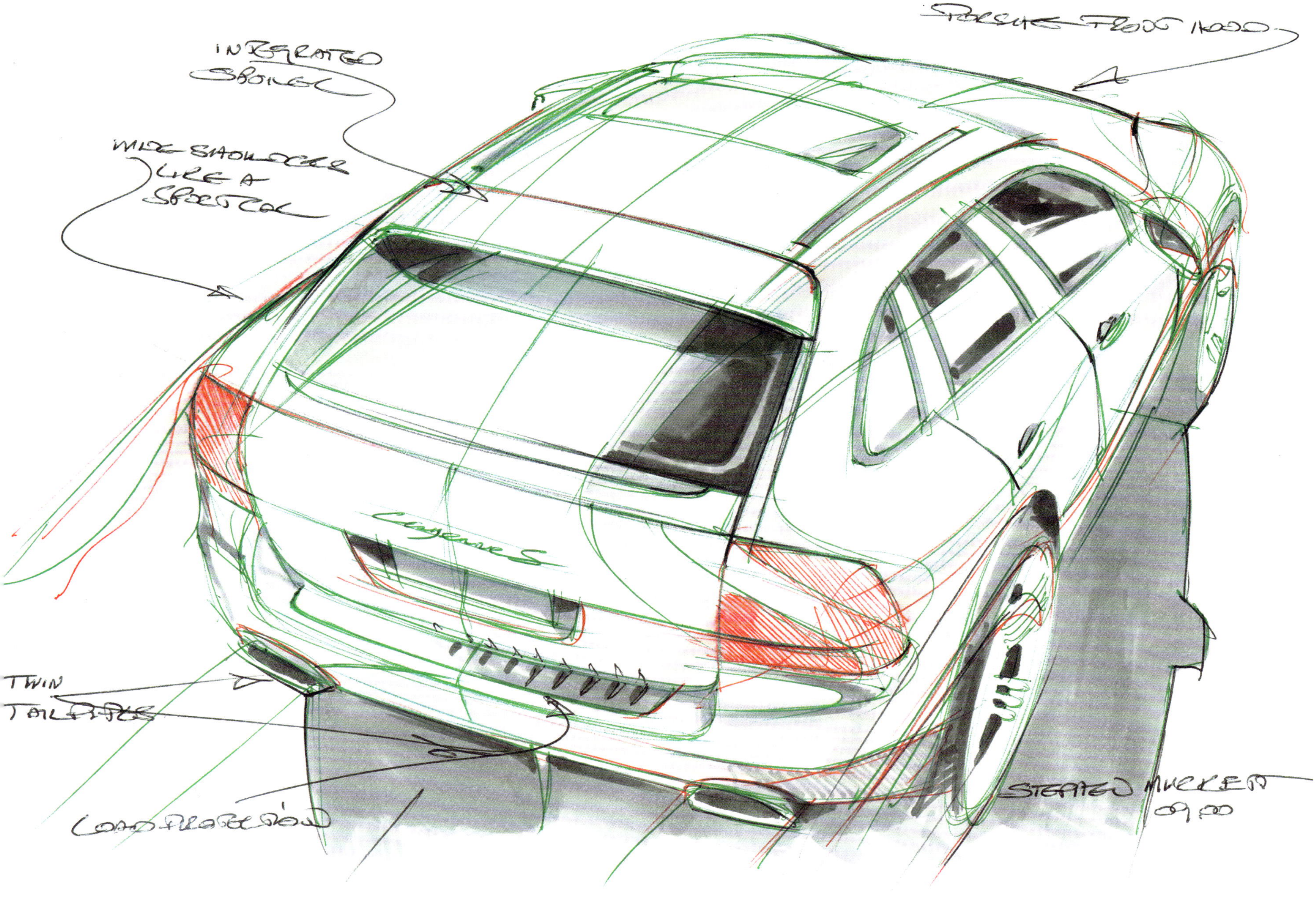
PORSCHE FRONT HOOD
INTEGRATED SPOILER
WIDE SHOULDERS LIKE A SPORTSCAR
TWIN TAILPIPES
LOAD PROTECTION
Cayenne S
09.00

Top left The first generation Porsche Cayenne Turbo S (from 2003) with its imposing front air intakes is very impressive, conjuring up the image of a race car. The success of its design, however, is up for debate.

Bottom left The 'slower' version of the second-generation Cayenne (from 2007), the lower motorization has a six cylinder, 3.6 liter with 'only' 290 hp. It can easily be recognized by the small air intakes on the front.

Right The second generation Cayenne (2007) is available in 5 different drives (here, a 500 hp turbo, 275 km/h, 171 mph). There is also a road version of the GTS.

The exact opposite (or close to it) of the Touareg, Cayenne and Q7 is the Volkswagen ID.3. Just as the Beetle was meant to be "the car of the people" (German people, to be precise), the first all-electric car to come out of Wolfsburg was created as a plug-in for all – one that could provide, in the minds of marketers and designers, a real and viable alternative to the Golf, which had always been the brand's popular flagship. Making its debut in 2019, it was built around the MEB modular car platform, which would then become the basis for almost all of the electric cars manufactured by the group. With the battery embedded in the floor, between the two axes, it maximizes the use of every inch of interior space, which is notable given its length (167.8 in/4.26 m from bumper to bumper), and also to improve its driving dynamics: the lithium-ion battery is very heavy and, placed low to the ground, it helps lower the vehicle's center of gravity. The cockpit is less interesting, much more austere than the Golf of that year, and completely focuses on virtuality, with two screens for instrumentation and the multimedia system, and very few physical knobs and buttons. The motor and thus the drive are rear, just like in the famous Beetle. 204 PS make it jaunty and the 59-kWh battery lets it travel over 400 km with a single charge. It even comes in a version with a larger battery (79 kWh) and over 500 km of autonomy. Despite the makeover in 2023, which improved the interior finishes, and the arrival of the sporty GTX version (with 286 PS), the ID.3 still hasn't managed to make inroads into the hearts of motorists.

As Volkswagen envisioned it, the ID.3 was supposed fill the shoes of the Golf in every way possible. In reality, however, sales never really took off. The reasons can only be sought in its nature as an electric car.

Top right The technical specs include an electric motor on the rear axle (and thus real-wheel drive), a bit like in the old Beetle. That way, its designers managed to carve out ample leg room.

Bottom right Some ID.3s were manufactured in the Transparent Factory in Dresden built by Ferdinand Piëch in 2002 for production of the flagship Phaeton. Volkswagen even organized guided tours here (along the assembly line no less) and summer camps for children.

Germany has no shortage of smaller manufacturers, such as Artega. One of its most famous models is undoubtedly the GT, which was presented at the Geneva International Motor Show in 2007 and immediately aroused great interest in the public. The design was developed by Henrik Fisker (of the Aston Martin DB7, etc.) and the ex-Porsche engineer Hardy Essig was in charge of technology. This two-seater coupe sports car is powered by a rear-mounted 3.6-liter six-cylinder engine produced by VW. The body is based on an Alu-Space-Frame and is made of a composite material reinforced with carbon fiber. The Artega GT had been confirmed to reach a top speed of 270 km/h (168 mph) and go from 0 to 100 km/h (62 mph) in less than 5 seconds. But today Artega as we knew it is no longer: it was absorbed by another company working in electric vehicles, though nothing has come off the construction lines since then.

Even if no longer standing, Gumpert Sportwagenmanufaktur of Altenburg, in Thuringia must have been proud that it went beyond the design phase. Behind this brand was the ex-manager of Audi Motorsport, Roland Gumpert, and his Apollo GT was a racing car approved for road use. The design dates back to 2002 and is the work of Marco Vanetta. The technology was largely of Audi origin, with the famous 4.2-liter V8 engine having been completely customized by Gumpert for the three different power levels (650, 700 and 800 PS). That pushed the Gumpert Apollo to a top speed of 360 km/h (224 mph), and from 0 to 100 km/h (62 mph) in 3 seconds.

Among the current small German car manufacturers is Wiesmann which has already been on the market for a long time. It was founded in 1984 by brothers Friedhelm and Martin Wiesmann and since 1993 the company has been producing its own cars. The first model was the MF, a classic roadster with a steel tubular frame chassis with a three-liter 6-cylinder BMW engine. Later on, more powerful convertibles appeared, fitted with the latest version of the BMW M3 engine (343 PS for a vehicle weighing just 1,200 kg/2,645 lbs.) while in the small range there was also the GT Coupe version, driven by the V10 engine of the BMW M5 (507 PS). Today, the German auto maker has fully embraced the paradigm shift towards electric: the newcomer is called Project Thunderball and is an entirely hand-built two-seater roadster powered by

Bottom left *Lines and proportions don't lie: Project Thunderball is an equally sensual and consistent reminder of what Wiesmann automobiles have always embodied. With a strip of sky overhead, in this case. And without any noise coming from the exhaust.*

Right *From a purely stylistic point of view, the interiors are nothing new. However, they undeniably convey a pleasing sense of quality thanks to the ample use of fine leather. The seven round gauges set into the dashboard are also exquisite*

two electric motors. The total power output is 680 PS, while torque is a remarkable 1,100 Newton-meters. This, together with a curb weight of only 1,775 kg (1.96 tons), allows this out-of-the-ordinary object to go from zero to 60 mph (100 km/h) in less than three seconds. With a shrewd driving style, it is also possible, according to the manufacturer, to cover more than 500 km on one battery charge (92 kWh, in the floorpan). Each Project Thunderball vehicle can be reserved on the Wiesmann website by paying a simple deposit of 3,000 euros, although the price – which varies greatly depending on the materials and finish chosen – is at least 300,000 euros. In any case, if you have fallen in love with it, best hop to it, because production for all of 2025 is already sold out. For now, you can add your name to the list for the cars that will be built in 2026.

There is yet another type of small automobile manufacturer in Germany: (ex) racing engine developers and tuners. The most famous name in this case is AMG (which, as already mentioned, are the initials of Hans-Werner Aufrecht, Erhard Melcher and the town of Grossaspach). This company was founded in 1967 as a workshop for developing and testing engines, in 1999 it was renamed Mercedes-AMG GmbH and in 2005 it was completely bought out by Daimler AG., in the wake of BMW with M GmbH and Audi with Quattro GmbH.

Starting from the C Class (W203), AMG models are the respective top of the range Mercedes models. Over the course of its lucky path, AMG even managed to work on an iconic Mercedes model, though far from the world of performance as it's generally understood: the G Class, a real, true off-roader launched in 1979. Today, although available with pistons and cylinders, (made by AMG no less, with a 585-horsepower mild hybrid system), it has joined the world of e-vehicles with the G580. Housed in the floorpan is a gigantic 116 kWh battery for a range of almost 310 miles (500 km). Powering the car are four electric motors (one per wheel) capable of delivering 587 PS and a whopping 1,164 Nm. As such, the extraordinary off-road capabilities which have been the prerogative of the Geländewagen from the start, with the brilliance of a grand tourer.

Top center In designing the new C class (W204, 2007) Mercedes took advantage of the most innovative technology available, for example, the so-called 'Design Cave', a space that projects three-dimensional computer images.

Bottom center Not only does AMG soup up Mercedes cars with more power, but the beloved SA's (Sonderausstattung, special equipment) also include several parts, which are very expensive–such as on this W203 (2000 to 2007).

Top right Starting in 2003 AMG produced a special edition of the Mercedes DTM, based on the CLK. 100 models were built, that were propelled by a 582 hp V8 engine. An additional convertible series was also launched.

Brabus cannot boast a long history like that of AMG, but the company, founded in 1977 by Klaus Brackmann and Bodo Buschmann, underwent a transformation long ago from a simple development and tuning workshop to a producer of limited series. Brabus, like AMG, works exclusively on Daimler Mercedes products – and is even the official "appointed supplier" of Smart, but without enjoying the same status as AMG.

Brabus isn't exactly known for finesse and moderation both from an aesthetic point of view and a technological point of view. This company's racing cars come with the biturbo V8 made by Mercedes, with 630 to 930 PS, though there is an even beefier 1,000-PS version: the Rocket. Based on the Mercedes-AMG GT 63 S E Performance, this menacing four-door coupé adorned with numerous aerodynamic carbon fiber appendages is a plug-in hybrid with the aforementioned 4.4L biturbo V8 which doles out 796 PS, getting a boost to 1,000 PS thanks to the 204 CV electric motor on the rear axle. That way, the total torque reaches 1,620 Nm (electronically limited). To get there, Brabus engineers tinkered with the drive shaft, the pistons (forged), the turbocharger (pressure was boosted to 1.4 bars), and the exhaust (a special catalytic converter), and they installed a custom control module. All that for performance similar to that of a Formula 1 racecar: thanks in part to the all-wheel drive, goes from zero to sixty (0-100 km/h) in just 2.6 seconds, while the max speed is 196 mph (316 km/h). Of course, the brakes were overhauled too, with carbon-ceramic discs, as were the trim and the tires (21" in the front and 22" in the rear) made by Continental. Taking the interiors into account, almost entirely covered in fine leather, it's no surprise that the price tag well exceeds €500,000 and that only 25 were made.

Top left and bottom right *To house the larger tires and the numerous aerodynamic appendages, the car body grew by almost 2¾ in (7 cm). The four exhaust pipes let out a deep, guttural melody. Just above them is the flap that opens for electric charging..*

Top right *The dashboard picks up on various details from the Mercedes-AMG world, though it was reworked in terms of its finishes. That includes an ample use of carbon fiber, which covers the massive central console over the transmission tunnel, among other things.*

Profile
Navigation
Medien
ROCKET

The German tuner has even tinkered with a few electric cars (like the Mercedes-AMG EQS 53, with 763 PS and 1,020 Nm of torque), and off-roaders aren't safe either, concentrating on the G-Class. Available in a pick-up version, in a 6x6 and a special ops version with lightweight armor. After all, the best Brabus customers do not live in Western Europe but in the Middle and Far East.

From the outside, the electric G Class can be recognized by its unique grill, with pared-back slots so as not to dirty the air flow, and a plastic border along the door posts near the windscreen for acoustic comfort when driving.

D

Ruf is yet another engine development and tuning center, with an excellent reputation. Yet it is not considered an engine tuner and actually has been officially registered as a car producer since 1981. Founded in 1939 in Pfaffenhausen, in Lower Allgäu, the company is specialized in tuning Porsche automobile engines. In addition to the main headquarters in Germany, there is another establishment in Bahrain. It is therefore obvious, as to which geographic area Ruf's main customers are to be found. The flagship model is the CTR3 Evo, a particular evolution with a central flat-six twin turbo engine with power increased to 800 PS at 7100 rpm, able to reach 380 km/h (236 mph). But Ruf's most important business is undoubtedly selling kits and accessories to power up Porsche models, the 911 above all. However, there's also an ample catalog for the Boxster and the Cayman. Unlike AMG and Brabus, not all Ruf-Porsches stand out because of their appearance: the Pfaffenhausen engine tuner maintains a certain degree of sobriety, when necessary.

With the CTR 3, Ruf presented an exceptionally sporty supercar in 2007. The CTR 3 Evo is a worthy heir: thanks to its 3.8L twin turbo boxer engine with 800 PS at 7,800 rpm and numerous aerodynamic extensions, it can get up to 236 mph (380 km/h).

Beyond the slight aesthetic restyling (the project code is 992.2), the latest version of the Porsche 911 hides an important turning point beneath its polished yet everlasting lines: a hybrid powertrain, which is composed of a gas engine (a brand-new six-cylinder boxer, which has been taken up a notch to 3.6 liters, pumping out 485 PS) and two electric ones. The first electric "machine" is mounted within the turbo charger, between the compressor and the turbine wheels: its role is to adjust the rotation speed of the latter (now single and no longer variable-geometry), and guarantee the right boost pressure in the least time possible. However, by harnessing the exhaust gas flow, it also recovers its energy, for an additional 15 PS. The second electric motor is integrated into the dual-clutch eight-speed PDK transmission and pumps out 41 kW for a total of 541 PS and 610 Nm. Both those hearts are assisted by a 1.9 kWh lithium-ion battery weighing 60 pounds (27 kg – in total, the car comes in at 1,595 kg/3,516 lbs), mounted below the hood. The hybrid 911 won't budge if the gas engine is off, but it does promise exceptional performance: 0-100 km/h in 3 seconds for the GTS version. It's an exceptional collection of technology to continue to enjoy the wonders of the 911 series without having to say goodbye to the melodious sounds of the flat-six.

Bottom left and right As per tradition, the 992.2 even also in a cabriolet version with an electronically controlled fabric folding top. In its first release, there is no hybrid drivetrain option for this Carrera: pushing it instead is the classic 3.0L of the pre-facelift GTS, here downsized to 394 PS.

Right In addition to being shorter by 4 1/3 inches (11 cm), the 3.6L 6-cylinder boxer of the GTS offers a hybrid system with 485 PS and 720 Nm, for overall power of 541 PS. The turbocharger is clearly visible on the right side of the engine, hiding one of the two electric units.

Top The idea for the PureSpeed came from the most famous (and winning) race cars with a barchetta-style body. The color was inspired by the Mercedes Rennwagen no. 10 that won the 15th Targa Florio in 1924 in 6 hours and 32 minutes, driven by Christian Werner.

Bottom Revealed at the 2024 Monaco Grand Prix, this tapered-body concept car is actually a preview of the limited series that will be available to 250 lucky clients in 2025. With it, each owner will receive a chronograph clock designed with the brand's partner IWC Schaffhause.

Founded in Affalterbach in 1967 as a pure tuning house, AMG has now officially entered the Mercedes family tree, so much so that, in the sportiest models from the automaker, the three famous letters (an acronym of the founders Aufrecht, Melcher and Grossaspach) appear directly in the name: Mercedes-AMG. The latest, unveiled to the world at the 2024 Monaco Grand Prix, is a decidedly aggressive concept car. Called PureSpeed, it's the first in a long series of limited-edition models (250 units, in this case) dedicated to collectors.

The car is a pure interpretation of the barchetta concept. Modelled after the SL, it has no roof, windscreen or side windows. The only element protecting the driver is a tapered carbon structure inspired by the Halo seen on current Formula 1 cars. The bodywork makes extensive use of carbon, while the colors (red, grey and black) are a tribute to the Mercedes car that won the Targa Florio in 1924.

Concept Mercedes-AMG
PureSpeed

Just like what happened for the Audi RS, the chromosome of family cars found fertile ground even in Munich, in the M series from BMW. Officially, the first to see the light of day was the M5 Touring E34 in 1992, but the M5 E61 shouldn't be ignored either, with its V10 gasoline engine providing 507 PS, able to explore the Olympus of performance (max output reached 7,750 rpm, while the limiter declared game over at 8,250 rpm). However, to see an M3 Touring at a dealership we'll have to wait a few years still: the first prototype, based on the E46, was finished in 2000, but BMW decided to show it to the world only in 2016. And the series production of an M3 wagon began only in 2022, with the G81 series. Beyond its practicality, thanks to a family-proof trunk with a 500-liter capacity), it's still driven by an in-line 6-cylinder engine. In this case, it has two turbos and can unleash between 530 PS and 650 Nm, pushed onto the asphalt by all-wheel drive that, when necessary, can become rear-wheel only.

Top left *The interior has special details, like the seats, sportier compared to those of a classic Touring 3 Series, and carbon fiber inserts here and there. The three-spoke steering wheel is also unique: flattened on the lower part, it's covered in suede-effect fabric.*

Bottom left *The side view highlights the enlarged wheelhouses and oversize proportions, necessary to host abundant mechanics (including four-wheel drive). Regardless, its comfort is similar to that of the other versions. The dashboard is spectacular.*

Top and bottom right *The double kidney with gigantism look certainly is nothing new for more recent BMW models. On the M3, creates an exponentially more menacing aesthetic. Just like the four generous exhaust pipes that peek out from the bumper: the sound is heavenly.*

The M series has even extended into the hyper-SUV category with the XM. Its significance lies, first of all, in the fact that it is the first M model not derived from other mass-made cars, since the historic M1 of 1978. Then of course it's a line that is far from conventional, starting from the front, with the double kidney grill (and LED lights) that's as gigantic as it is threatening. The powertrain is equally daunting: 653 PS and 800 Nm arrive via a plug-in hybrid system in which the spearhead is the twin-turbo V8, which works in symbiosis with a 120-kW electric motor. That way, with the pedal to the metal, it reaches 100 km/h in 4.3 seconds. Because character is a must, even when it comes to SUVs.

Top left *BMW decided to make the XM Label Red a limited-edition of just 500 cars. It can be recognized by the Frozen Carbon Black Metallic exterior combined with Toronto Red details on the double kidney grill surrounds, the alloy wheels and the rear diffusor insert.*

Top right *The Label Red has the same electric motor as the "standard" XM (197 PS and 280 Nm, integrated with an eight-speed Steptronic transmission), but the gas version of the twin-turbo V8 goes from 489 to 585 PS and from 650 to a full 750 Nm of max torque.*

Bottom right *Despite its notable weight of circa 3 tons (2.7 metric tons), this powerful XM manages to go from zero to sixty in 3.8 seconds (compared to the 4.3 seconds of the standard XM), while the self-limiting maximum speed of 155 mph (250 km/h) can be boosted to 180 mph (290 km/h) by choosing a special optional package*

M Power

The Authors

Until late 2007, **PETER RUCH** served as editor-in-chief of the renowned *Swiss Automobil Revue* magazine, and has since been working as a freelance journalist for a wide variety of automobile media. He is a member of the international "Auto of the Year" jury, and is the author of *Panamericana: Mit dem Motorrad von Alaska bis Feuerland* (Panamericana: Motorbiking from Alaska to Tierra del Fuego), the story of his own travel experience through the Americas, and also of *Cadillac: The World Standard*, and *Mini: Die Geschichte einer Legende* (Mini: The Story of a Legend).

Obsessed with cars since he was a child, journalist **ANDREA RAPELLI** has curated the updates found in this new edition. Rapelli began his career writing for *Auto Oggi*, *Panoramauto* and EVO Italia. He's worked at the Italian monthlies *Autotecnica* and *Ruoteclassiche* and with websites such as Motorbox.com, Motor1 Italia and Red Live. Specializing in commercially available vehicles, he loves classic cars and motorcycles. For White Star, he wrote *Motorcycles: the Legendary Models* and *Porsche: the Legendary Models*, and co-wrote *Legendary Convertibles*. He currently works at Quattroruote, where he's responsible for road tests.

Bibliography

Jürgen Barth/Gustav Büsing, Das neue grosse Buch der Porsche-Typen, 3 Bände, Motorbuch-Verlag

Marc Bongers, Audi - Serien-, Sport- und Rennwagen seit 1965, Motorbuch-Verlag

Günter Engelen, Mercedes 190 SL - 280 SL, Vom Barock zur Pagode, Motorbuch-Verlag

Günter Engelen, Mercedes 280 SL - 500 SLC, Der Schritt zur Modellvielfalt, Motorbuch-Verlag

Günter Engelen/Mike Riedner, Mercedes-Benz 300 SL, Vom Rennsport zur Legende, Motorbuch-Verlag

Paul Frère, Die Porsche 911 Story, Motorbuch-Verlag

Thomas Fuths, Golf - Fünf Generationen eines Welterfolgs, Delius Klasing

Thomas Fuths/Jürgen Lewandowski/ Wolfgang Peters, GTI -Drei Dekaden einer Legende, Delius Klasing

Achim Gaier, Personenwagen in der DDR, Motorbuch-Verlag

Hans-Dieter Görg, 80 Jahre Hanomag Komissbrot, Delius Klasing

Giuseppe Guzzardi-Enzo Rizzo, Convertibles, history and evolution of dream cars, 1998

Giuseppe Guzzardi-Enzo Rizzo, Motor Racing, The Drivers and Their Machines, 1999

Peter Kirchberg/Jürgen Pönisch, Horch, Delius Klasing

Peter Kurze, Kleinwagen der Fünfzigerjahre, Delius Klasing

Peter Kurze/Ralf Kiese, Lloyd - der Wagen für Dich, Delius Klasing

Peter Kurze, Borgward Isabella, Delius Klasing

Jürgen Lewandowski, BMW Z1, art & car Verlag

Jürgen Lewandowski, Maybach - Der Weg zur Legende, Delius Klasing

Jürgen Lewandowski, Ford bewegt, Delius Klasing

Jürgen Lewandowski, Opel - Die Automobile, die Menschen, Delius Klasing

Jochen Neerpasch/Jürgen Lewandowski, BMW M1, Delius Klasing

Werner Oswald/HalwartSchrader/Eberhard Kittler, Deutsche Autos, Band 1-6, Motorbuch-Verlag

Matthias Pfannmüler, Mit Tempo durch die Zeit, Delius Klasing

Frank Rönicke, Trabant - Legende auf Rädern, Motorbuch-Verlag

Peter Schneider, Die NSU-Story - Chronik einer Weltmarke, Motorbuch-Verlag

Halwart Schrader, BMW-Automobile, Motorbuch-Verlag

Alexander Franc Storz, Opel seit 1899, Motorbuch-Verlag

Gerd-G. Westermann/Thomas Erdmann, Wanderer-Automobile, Delius Klasing

Bernhard Wiersch, Die Käfer-Chronik, Heel Verlag

Jürgen Zöllter, Smartismus, Motorbuch-Verlag

Aknowledgements

In addition to my precious colleague Jürgen Lewandowski, who established the contact with White Star, my family and my parents, I would like to thank the following people:
Christoph Bleile (Opel), Maria Danner (Opel), Maria Feifel (Daimler), Jolanda Eggenschwiler (Porsche), Dino Graf (AMAG), Donatus Grütter (VW), Georges Keller, Dieter Landenberger (Porsche), Christian Masanz (BMW), Andreas Meyer (Andy's Motorbooks, Zürich), Oliver Peter (Daimler), Erwin Thomann (Ford), Michael Zumbrunn.

Peter Ruch

The Publisher would like to thank:

Matthias Enzinger, Audi Media Services, Audi AG, Ingolstadt, Germany
Maria Feifel, Archives & Collection, Daimler AG, Stuttgart, Germany
Porsche AG Presse, Stuttgart, Germany
Mauro Gentile, (Porsche Italia S.p.A., Italy)
BMW Group Press Fleet Consultant, BMW AG, Woodcliff Lake, New Jersey (USA)
Lorenza Cappello, Italdesign Giugiaro S.p.a., Italy
Olaf Von Dehn-Rotfelser, Loremo AG, Munich, Germany

Photographic Credits

Page 1 Mary Evans Picture Library
Pages 2-3, 6-7, 8-9 Ron Kimball Studios
Pages 10-11 Fotostudio Zumbrunn
Page 13 Ann Ronan Picture Library/Photo12.com
Pages 14-15 Fotostudio Zumbrunn
Pages 16-17 Ron Kimball Studios
Pages 18-19 Fotostudio Zumbrunn
Pages 20-21 Ron Kimball Studios
Page 24 Bettmann/Corbis
Page 25 The Print Collector/Alamy
Page 26 en bas Photo12.com
Pages 26 en haut, 26-27 Science Museum/Science & Society Picture Library
Pages 28-29 Silwen Randebrock/Alamy
Page 29 en haut à gauche Science Museum/Science & Society Picture Library
Page 29 en haut à droite Albert Harlingue/Roger-Viollet/Archivi Alinari
Page 29 en bas The Print Collector/Alamy
Pages 30-31 Science Museum/Science & Society Picture Library
Page 32 en haut Photoservice Electa/Akg Images
Pages 32-33 Hulton Archive/Getty Images
Pages 36-37, 38-39, 40-41, 42-43 General Motors Media Archive
Page 44 Imagno/Contributor/Hulton Archive/Getty Images
Pages 46-47 Mary Evans Picture Library
Page 50 Photoservice Electa/Akg Images
Pages 50-51, 51 au centre Markus Nikot
Page 51 en haut Interfoto Pressebildagentur/Alamy
Page 52 Deutsches Museum
Pages 52-53 Hulton Archive/Getty Images
Page 53 en haut Maurice Branger/Roger- Viollet/Archivi Alinari
Page 56 en haut Deutsches Museum
Pages 56-57 Fotostudio Zumbrunn
Page 57 Deutsches Museum
Pages 58-59 General Motors Media Archive
Pages 60, 61, 62, 63 BMW AG Konzernarchiv
Page 64 en haut Photoservice Electa/Akg Images
Pages 64-65 Fotostudio Zumbrunn
Page 65 Deutsches Museum
Pages 66-67 Ron Kimball Studios
Page 68 Fotostudio Zumbrunn
Page 69 en haut Photoservice Electa/Akg Images
Page 69 en bas Austrian Archives/Corbis
Pages 72-73, 73 Fotostudio Zumbrunn
Page 75 Photoservice Electa/Akg Images
Pages 80-81 Fotostudio Zumbrunn
Pages 84 en haut, 84-85 Ron Kimball Studios
Pages 86, 86-87, 88-89 Fotostudio Zumbrunn
Page 90 en haut Markus Nikot
Pages 90-91 Photoservice Electa/Akg Images
Pages 92, 92-93, 93 en haut à gauche Markus Nikot
Page 93 en haut à droite Photoservice Electa/Akg Images
Pages 94, 94-95 Markus Nikot
Pages 96, 96-97, 97, 98 en haut, 98-99 Fotostudio Zumbrunn
Page 99 en haut, 100 en bas, 102-103 Photoservice Electa/Akg Images
Page 103 Imagno/Contributor/Hulton Archive/Getty Images
Pages 104 en haut et au centre, 106 Photoservice Electa/Akg Images
Pages 106-107 Talking sport/Photoshot
Page 108-109, 109 Charles Best/Alamy
Pages 110-111 Fotostudio Zumbrunn
Pages 112-113 BMW AG Konzernarchiv
Pages 114 en haut, 114-115 Fotostudio Zumbrunn
Page 115 en haut BMW AG Konzernarchiv
Pages 118-119 Ron Kimball Studios
Page 122 Photoservice Electa/Akg Images
Pages 122-123 Fotostudio Zumbrunn
Pages 124-125, 125 Time 6 Life Pictures/Getty Images
Page 126 Photoservice Electa/Akg Images
Pages 126-127 Ron Kimball Studios
Page 127 en haut Photoservice Electa/Akg Images
Pages 128-129 Ron Kimball Studios
Pages 130, 131 General Motors Media Archive
Page 132 en haut à gauche Ford Motor company Archives
Pages 132 en haut à droite et en bas, 133 Photoservice Electa/Akg Images
Page 134 en haut General Motors Media Archive
Pages 134-135 Fotostudio Zumbrunn
Pages 136-137, 138, 139 BMW AG Konzernarchiv
Page 140 en haut à gauche Hulton- Deutsch Collection/Corbis
Page 140 en haut à droite BMW AG Konzernarchiv
Pages 142, 142-143 Ron Kimball Studios
Pages 146-147 Fotostudio Zumbrunn
Page 147 BMW AG Konzernarchiv
Pages 148-149 John Marian/Transtock/Alamy
Page 150-151, 152-153 Ron Kimball Studios
Pages 158-159 Fotostudio Zumbrunn
Page 160 en haut Ron Kimball Studios
Pages 160-161, 162 National Motor Museum
Pages 162-163 Hulton Archive/Getty Images
Page 164 Volkswagen Media
Pages 164-165 Science Museum/Science & Society Picture Library
Pages 166-167, 167 General Motors Media Archive
Pages 168 en haut, 168-169, 169 BMW AG Konzernarchiv
Pages 172, 173 Photoservice Electa/Akg Images
Pages 174, 174-175 Fotostudio Zumbrunn
Pages 176-177 Ron Kimball Studios
Page 181 BMW AG Konzernarchiv
Pages 184-185, 185 Volkswagen Media
Pages 188-189 Fotostudio Zumbrunn
Pages 190-191 National Motor Museum/Alamy
Pages 194-195 Fotostudio Zumbrunn
Pages 198-199, 199 BMW AG Konzernarchiv
Pages 206-207 Fotostudio Zumbrunn
Page 207 en haut Imagebroker/Alamy
Pages 208-209, 210-211, 212-213 Ron Kimball Studios
Page 214 BMW AG Konzernarchiv
Pages 214-215 Fotostudio Zumbrunn
Pages 216, 217 BMW AG Konzernarchiv
Pages 218, 218-219 Ron Kimball Studios
Pages 220-221 Getty Images
Pages 222, 222-223 Ron Kimball Studios
Page 225 en bas General Motors Media Archive
Page 238 Martin Goddard/Corbis
Pages 238-239 Car Photo Library
Pages 240-241 National Motor Museum
Page 241 en haut General Motors Media Archive
Pages 244-245 Fotostudio Zumbrunn
Pages 246-247 Ron Kimball Studios
Pages 248-249, 249 General Motors Media Archive
Pages 254-255, 256-257, 257, 258-259, 260, 260-261 Ron Kimball Studios
Page 262 en haut Krafft Angerer/Getty Images
Page 262 en bas Sean Gallup/Getty Images
Pages 262-263 National Motor Museum
Pages 274, 274-275 Ron Kimball Studios
Pages 276 Drive Images/Alamy
Pages 287, 288 Car Photo Library
Pages 288-289 Ron Kimball Studios
Pages 292-293 Car Photo Library
Page 300: Mariusz Burcz / Alamy Foto Stock
Page 301 en haut: Gabo_Arts/Shutterstock
Pages 300-301: Mariusz Burcz / Alamy Foto Stock

Avec l'aimable autorisation de :
Pages 4-5 Audi AG/Audi Media Services
Pages 22-23 Daimler AG
Pages 34-35 Porsche AG Presse
Pages 44-45, 48, 49, 54, 55, 70, 71 Daimler AG
Pages 74 en haut, 74-75 Audi AG/Audi Media Services
Pages 76, 76-77, 78, 78-79, 82, 83, 100 en haut, 101, 102 en bas, 104-105, 105 en haut Daimler AG
Page 110 en haut BMW AG
Pages 116-117 Audi AG/Audi Media Services
Pages 120-121 Daimler AG
Page 141 BMW AG
Pages 144, 144-145 Daimler AG
Pages 148, 149 en haut, 151 Porsche AG Presse
Pages 154, 155, 156-157, 157 Daimler AG
Pages 159 en haut, 161 en haut Porsche AG Presse
Pages 170, 171 Daimler AG
Pages 178-179 Italdesign Giugiaro S.p.a.
Pages 180-181 Porsche AG Presse
Pages 182, 182-183 Italdesign Giugiaro S.p.a.
Pages 186-187, 187 Audi AG/Audi Media Services
Page 189 Italdesign Giugiaro S.p.a.
Page 191 en haut Porsche AG Presse
Pages 192, 192-193, 196, 197, 200, 200-201, 201, 202, 203, 204, 204-205, 205 Daimler AG
Page 208 Porsche AG Presse
Pages 220, 221 BMW AG
Pages 224, 224-225 Italdesign Giugiaro S.p.a.
Pages 226, 227, 228-229, 229, 230, 230-231, 231, 232, 232-233, 233, 234, 234-235, 235 Audi AG/Audi Media Services
Pages 236, 236-237, 237, 242-243 Daimler AG
Page 248 en haut BMW AG
Pages 250, 251, 252, 253 Porsche AG Presse
Pages 264-265, 266, 267, 268-269 Audi AG/Audi Media Services
Pages 272-273, 273 Daimler AG
Pages 276-277 Audi AG/Audi Media Services
Pages 278, 279, 280, 280-281 Porsche AG Presse
Pages 282-283 Loremo AG
Pages 284-285, 285: Wiesmann Sports Cars GmbH
Pages 286, 286-287 Daimler AG
Pages 288, 289 en haut, 289 en bas: Brabus GmbH
Pages 290-291, 291: Mercedes-Benz Group AG
Page 293 en haut RUF Automobile GmbH
Pages 294-295, 295 en haut: Dr. Ing. h.c. F. Porsche AG
Pages 296-297, 297: Mercedes-Benz Group AG
Pages 298, 298-299, 299 en haut, 299 en bas: BMW AG
Pag. 308 Audi Media Services

Cover: BMW 507 (1957)
Tom Wood/Alamy Foto Stock

Updates to the introduction and chapters 6 and 9 by Andrea Rapelli

Piazzale Luigi Cadorna, 6
20123 Milan, Italy
www.whitestar.it

Updated edition

ISBN 978-88-544-2153-0
1 2 3 4 5 6 29 28 27 26 25

Printed in China

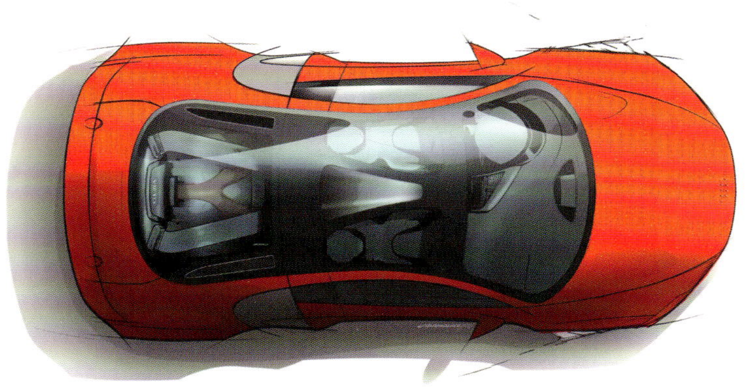

The R8 Le Mans means a new era for Audi: Ingolstadt today also produces super sports cars.